27104 ✓

189.5 T629 1986
Tobin, Frank.
Meister Eckhart : thought and
language

COLUMBIA BIBLE COLLEGE

4444 00000 5900

D0488153

MEISTER ECKHART

The Middle Ages

a series edited by

EDWARD PETERS

Henry Charles Lea Professor

of Medieval History

University of Pennsylvania

MEISTER ECKHART:

Thought and Language

F R A N K   T O B I N

upp

University of Pennsylvania Press · Philadelphia · 1986

Designed by Adrianne Onderdonk Dudden

Copyright © 1986 by the University of Pennsylvania Press
All rights reserved

Library of Congress Cataloging-in-Publication Data

Tobin, Frank J.
Meister Eckhart, thought and language.

(The Middle Ages)
Bibliography: p.
Includes index.
1. Eckhart, Meister, d. 1327. I. Title. II. Series.
BV5095.E3T63   1986   189'.5   85-24034
ISBN 0-8122-8009-1 (alk. paper)

Printed in the United States of America

CONTENTS

PREFACE

This study was written with three audiences in mind. It is meant to profit, first of all, the educated reader who has no particular background for understanding Meister Eckhart but who is serious enough to want to understand him on his own terms. Second, it is written for Germanists, scholars who are trained to appreciate and explore his virtuosity in using a fresh but immature medium—Middle High German—to express thoughts seldom expressed as successfully in any medium. But, alas, such scholars are often unfamiliar with the air of scholasticism which the preacher and professor breathed and which provides the academic context for understanding his originality. This unfamiliarity has been the cause of numerous pitfalls and not infrequently has rendered scholars' work superficial or given it an air of incompleteness. At any rate, it is striking how small their share of the really important studies on Eckhart has been in recent years, compared with that of historians of medieval thought. And this need not be so. Third, this study is directed to those engaged in studying medieval thought in general and Meister Eckhart in particular. These people will find much that is not new and some things with which they beg to differ. Where I have not been original, my intent has been to glean the fruits of what I considered the best scholarship and present them clearly. There are, however, even for this audience insights laying claim to originality. My main message for these historians of thought is that to study Eckhart's language is not to concentrate on something incidental. How he casts his thoughts in words is not the relish which adds a certain piquancy to the feast but is of no real substance or nutritional value. Rather, his use of language follows with remarkable consistency from his view of language, and to study what he does in practice is, when done rightly, not to study accidental form emptied of essential content, but to achieve insights into content by an appreciation of what he accomplished through linguistic form.

Some readers might object to the emphasis given to the professional concerns of the schoolman and especially to the space given to his conception of being (*esse*) and related matters. Such topics were given detailed treatment in the conviction that it is the best and surest way of gaining entrance into his world. The man has been called a mystic. Certainly he was an interesting and unusual thinker. In any case, he used the traditions that surrounded him to express his concerns. Comparing his ideas with non-Christian religious traditions can be valuable. Finding his place in the Western philosophical tradition is a stimulating pursuit. Basic to accomplishing such goals, however, is a solid grasp of the man himself. To achieve this, one must explore the terms most central to his thought in the contexts of his own work and his own time. This I have tried to do. The brief explanations of the thought of Thomas Aquinas and of terms common to Eckhart and most of his contemporaries are meant to serve this goal. Introducing such material is in no way an attempt to pursue seriously the question of which thinkers influenced him. Eckhart's command of his source material, even for one living in an age where prodigious memories were not uncommon and were a necessary part of academic life, was truly remarkable, as the notes in the critical edition attest. More worthy of our attention, however, is the manner in which he took this material and fashioned it into something really his own.

I was able to write a significant portion of this book while on sabbatical leave granted by the Regents of the University of Nevada. For this leave I wish to express my gratitude. I also wish to acknowledge that in Chapters 1 and 5, and in the Epilogue, I have included material reworked from articles published previously. These are in chronological order: "Eckhart's Mystical Use of Language: The Contexts of *eigenschaft*," *Seminar* 8 (1972), 160–168; "The Mystic as Poet: Meister Eckhart's German Sermon 69," *Studia Mystica* 2 (1979), 61–75; "Meister Eckhart: Scholasticism, Mysticism and Poetic Style," *Amsterdamer Beiträge zur älteren Germanistik* 16 (1981), 110–133; "Creativity and Interpreting Scripture: Meister Eckhart in Practice," *Monatshefte* 74 (1982), 410–418; "Mysticism and Meister Eckhart," *Mystics Quarterly* 10 (1984), 17–24.

I would like to express my sincere thanks to Professor Bernard McGinn, who read most of the manuscript, for many helpful suggestions. And if this study is found to have some degree of intelligibility, this is in large measure due to the efforts of Robert Reardon, whose many hours of toil often brought clarity to intractible or half-digested material. I am grateful for his help, and even more so for his friendship. Finally, I feel a debt of gratitude to the subject of this study, Meister Eckhart. Having been allowed a glimpse into his world has been exhilarating. Though many times in the course of my efforts to understand him and to share this understanding with others I have felt unequal to the task, I never doubted its value. To become acquainted with the man through his works is to get to know one of those few truly extraordinary people whose presence on our planet enhances our species' often debatable dignity. The author will consider his labors to have been well directed if he has with some measure of success transmitted to the reader a spark of the force and vitality of Eckhart's spirit.

ABBREVIATIONS

German and Latin Works of Meister Eckhart

Unless otherwise noted, all Meister Eckhart's works are cited according to the edition of the Deutsche Forschungsgemeinschaft under the general editorship of Josef Quint for the German works and Josef Koch for the Latin works: *Meister Eckhart. Die deutschen und lateinischen Werke* (Stuttgart and Berlin: Kohlhammer, 1936–).

Hereafter the German and Latin works will be abbreviated as follows:

German works: DW, followed by volume number, page(s), and line numbers

Latin works: LW, followed by volume number, page(s). They are also cited by their numbered sections (n. and nn.)

Abbreviations for Individual Works by Meister Eckhart

German Works

BgT	*Daz buoch der götlichen troestunge* (*Liber "Benedictus"* I) (*The Book of Divine Consolation*). DW V.
Pr. 1, 2, etc.	German Sermons. DW I–III.
RdU	*Die rede der underscheidunge* (*Counsels on Discernment*). DW V.
Va	*Von abegescheidenheit* (*On Detachment*). DW V.
VeM	*Von dem edeln menschen* (*Liber "Benedictus"* II) (*Of the Nobleman*). DW V.

Latin Works

In Eccli.	*Sermones et Lectiones super Ecclesiastici cap. 24* (*Sermons and Lectures on Ecclesiasticus, chapter 24*). LW II.
In Exod.	*Expositio libri Exodi* (*Commentary on Exodus*). LW II.
In Gen. I	*Expositio libri Genesis* (*Commentary on Genesis*). LW I.
In Gen. II	*Liber parabolarum Genesis* (*Book of the Parables of Genesis*). LW I.
In Joh.	*Expositio sancti Evangelii secundum Johannem* (*Commentary on John*). LW III.
In Sap.	*Expositio libri Sapientiae* (*Commentary on Wisdom*). LW II.
Prol. expos.	*Prologus in opus expositionum, I et II* (*Prologue to the Work of Commentaries, I and II*). LW I.
Prol. gener.	*Prologus generalis in opus tripartitum* (*General Prologue to the Tripartite Work*). LW I.
Prol. prop.	*Prologus in opus propositionum* (*Prologue to the Work of Propositions*). LW I.
Q. Par.	*Quaestiones Parisienses* (*Parisian Questions*). LW V.
Serm.	*Sermones* (*Sermons*). LW IV.

Abbreviations for Other Documents

Laurent	M.-H. Laurent, "Autour du procès de Maître Eckhart. Les documents des Archives Vaticanes." *Divus Thomas* (Piacenza), Ser. III, 13 (1936), 331–348, 430–447.
Pelster	Franz Pelster, "Ein Gutachten aus dem Eckehart-Prozess in Avignon," *Aus der Geisteswelt des Mittelalters. Festgabe Martin Grabmann*, Beiträge Supplement III (Münster, 1935), 1099–1124.
RS, Théry	Gabriel Théry, "Édition critique des pièces relatives au procès d'Eckhart contenues dans le manuscrit 33[b] de la Bibliothèque de Soest," *Archives d'histoire littéraire et doctrinale du moyen âge* 1 (1926), 129–268. This is the *Rechtfertigungsschrift*, or *Defense*, offered by Eckhart to his investigators in Cologne.

Abbreviations for Translations

The majority of the translations are my own. However, I have made frequent use of the excellent translations from the Latin and Middle High German in *Meister Eckhart: The Essential Sermons, Commentaries, Treatises and Defense*, translation and introduction by Edmund Colledge and Bernard McGinn (New York: Paulist Press, 1981).

In the case of translations from the Latin, this volume will be cited thus:

McGinn, followed by the page number.

For translations from Middle High German it will be cited thus:

Colledge, followed by the page number.

References to the introductions will be cited thus:

Colledge, "Historical Data"
McGinn, "Theological Summary"

MEISTER ECKHART

I
BACKGROUND

The life of Meister Eckhart has all the markings of a medieval success story, yet it is capped by what his contemporaries and he himself must have considered a tragic ending. He was highly successful at all the important tasks his order asked him to undertake. As an academic, he received his profession's most prestigious honor: a chair of theology at the most distinguished university in the medieval West. He was entrusted repeatedly with positions of great administrative and spiritual responsibility within the Dominican order. Yet he was perhaps most widely known in his own time for the vernacular sermons that form the basis of his posthumous reputation and current popularity. At the end of his life, however, his energies had to be directed to defending himself, ultimately with little success, against what must have been for him the most repugnant of accusations, that of preaching and teaching heresy.

Because much of the material in circulation on Eckhart's life contains factual errors or does not represent the present state of our knowledge, it is appropriate to devote a few pages to what biographical facts we have and to the conclusions we can prudently draw from them.[1] Whatever claims can be made for the timeless quality of Eckhart's thought, our understanding of it can be improved by a brief look at its historical setting. It is also well for us to realize that the impact he made on later centuries through the works that have survived consumed only a part of his energies. Many of the tasks to which he devoted his talents for long periods of time are without resonance today. The man was more than what we have of him.

3

Early Life, Education, and Career

The date of Eckhart's birth is uncertain, but the supposition that he was born about 1260 has never been seriously questioned. A village named Hochheim, either one near Gotha or one near Erfurt, both within Thuringia in central Germany, is referred to in one document as his place of origin. The claim that he was of noble birth is not based on convincing evidence,[2] nor does there seem to be any reason for giving him the name John, as several studies in English do. He entered the Order of Preachers, becoming a novice at the Dominican house in Erfurt. Exactly when is difficult to say. There is some evidence that he was in Paris as a student of the arts faculty before 1277.[3] If we keep in mind that students often came to the university much younger than they do today, and that one could normally enter the Dominican order at age fifteen, dispensations to enter earlier being possible, then a birth date of "about 1260" is still a reasonable guess. If he studied arts in Paris in the mid-1270s, it would mean that while still very young he came to know the exhilarating intellectual climate of the university and experienced firsthand the bitter controversy between the proponents of Aristotle and those who considered this new doctrine irreconcilable with the Christian faith, preferring traditional thought based largely on Augustine. The Dominicans were directly affected when, in 1277, the archbishop of Paris condemned 219 propositions and threatened with excommunication anyone defending them. The main targets of this condemnation were Aristotelians of an Averroist bent like Siger of Brabant, an influential teacher in the faculty of arts, whose teachings seemed to contradict Christian doctrine on several points. However, several of the condemned propositions clearly reflected teachings of Eckhart's illustrious fellow Dominican, Thomas Aquinas, who had died three years earlier. Whether present in Paris at the time or not, Eckhart was very much aware of the affair. Fifty years later, when defending the orthodoxy of his own teachings before his accusers, he would compare his fate to that of Thomas, who had been finally vindicated and who had been canonized a few years earlier.[4]

After one year of novitiate, a time of learning by practice the Dominican way of life, the candidate was accepted into the order and then spent two years studying the divine office and the constitutions of the order before beginning the study of philosophy and theology. This usually took eight years, with five years devoted to philosophy and three to theology. In theology, one year was spent studying and attending lectures on the Bible, followed by two years of study and lectures on the *Sentences* of Peter Lombard. Lombard's *Sentences* was a collection in four "books" of the topics of theology: God, creatures, the incarnation and redemption, the virtues, the sacraments, and the last things. Consisting mainly of quotations taken from Augustine and, to a lesser extent, from other primarily Latin theologians, it was for centuries the principal nonbiblical text which theology professors used as the point of departure in their lectures. Some of the most important medieval works on theology and philosophy are commentaries on the *Sentences*.[5]

Following these years of study, Dominicans of special talent were sent for further study in theology to one of the *studia generalia* established by the Dominican order for this purpose. There is little doubt that Eckhart studied at the *studium generale* in Cologne, which had been founded in 1248 by Albert the Great, one of the most astounding and universally curious minds of medieval times. Until 1252, Albert's most famous pupil in Cologne was Thomas Aquinas. A more illustrious beginning for a house of studies is hardly imaginable. There is some evidence that the young Eckhart came under the direct influence of the aging Albert. This would put him in Cologne about 1280, the year of Albert's death. In an Easter sermon years later, he quotes Albert as often qualifying his comments on some learned matter by saying, "This I know in the way we know (generally), for we all know very little."[6] Whether this reference to a frequent saying establishes direct contact between the two or not, it is an indication of Eckhart's roots in perhaps the most thriving and productive intellectual tradition of the times. Also, it appears significant that Albert, who devoted his long life to the increase of knowledge in several areas, was quite aware of the limitations of human knowledge and that Eckhart, who would attempt daring formulations about the nature of God and man's union with him, found the phrase worth repeating.

If we can say that Eckhart probably studied theology in Cologne around 1280, the years following are completely a matter of conjecture. It would not be unusual for one destined for Paris to spend some time teaching younger fellow Dominicans, so it is possible that Eckhart spent some years thus engaged at the house in Erfurt where he had entered the order. At any rate, we find him in Paris in the school year 1293–1294 listed as lecturer on the *Sentences*. Lecturing on this text was one of the requirements a bachelor of theology had to fulfill on his way to attaining the doctorate, or *magister*, as the highest degree awarded was called. Other requirements were lecturing on two books of the Bible, participation in disputations on various philosophical and theological propositions, and in general engaging in several years of further study.

Eckhart's stay in Paris came to an end a short time later, and we find him entrusted with two important posts for some of the time between 1294 and 1298. He was prior of the Dominican house in Erfurt and was also vicar of the Dominican houses in Thuringia. As superior of a religious house, his duties would have required administrative and financial skills, but more important, a keen appreciation for the aspirations of those under his care as well as great sympathy for their personal problems. His most serious obligation would have been the spiritual welfare of the community, especially that of the younger members still in their formative years. How seriously and in what spirit he fulfilled this responsibility is evident from the treatise *Counsels on Discernment* (*Die rede der underscheidunge*), which was written during this period. His duties as vicar no doubt involved traveling to the various houses in Thuringia and acting as the representative of the provincial who, in these years just prior to the division of Germany into two provinces, must have required such assistance. That Eckhart held these offices simultaneously testifies to the esteem he enjoyed. In 1298, however, a general chapter of the order prohibited anyone from continuing to be both prior and vicar because of the conflicting demands the offices imposed. Eckhart may have remained prior in Erfurt until 1300.

In 1302 he was called to the Dominican chair of theology in Paris, which was reserved for a non-Frenchman, and thus achieved the highest recognition attainable in contemporary academic circles. For the school year 1302–1303 he was *magister actu regens* (actively teaching). The degree of *magister* must have been conferred at the beginning of his tenure, since all the requirements had been met by then. When later ages refer to him as *Meister* Eckhart, they are consciously or unconsciously calling to mind this scholastic achievement. *Meister* is a Middle High German corruption of the Latin *magister* (teacher), and within the mystical tradition of northern Europe, Eckhart's vernacular works bear the imprint of the thought of the schools to a much higher degree than those of other authors.

At the end of this school year, Eckhart assumed new administrative duties. The original German Dominican province, Teutonia, was to be split, with northern Germany becoming a separate unit. Eckhart was appointed first provincial (1303–1311) of the new province, Saxonia, which included forty-seven houses of male Dominicans as well as a number of convents. As its first provincial, the former university professor had the additional responsibility of setting up the organizational machinery by which he would govern. His chief concern would be the spiritual and material well-being of those under his care. This would involve preserving or improving spirit and religious discipline, making the best use of the talents of those under him, both for the various external ministries and for the internal functioning of the religious communities, and seeing to it that each house was economically secure and integrated into its civic environment. That there was occasionally friction between the city fathers and the Dominicans, who in contrast to orders founded earlier sought living quarters within the towns, is evident from one of the few documents we have which bears the seal of Eckhart as provincial. In a letter to the town council of Göttingen, he gives assurances that the Dominican house there will not increase its property within the town without the council's approval.[7]

The new provincial not only mastered such daily minutiae but could by the end of his time in office point with satisfaction to the establishment of three new Dominican communities. It is clear that Eckhart was also respected for his abilities in the difficult area of governing religious communities, furthering idealism and improving spirit even when reprimanding proved necessary. In 1307, while still provincial, he was entrusted with the task of reforming Dominican houses in Bohemia, and he did so as the vicar of the Dominican general. One can hardly imagine a more difficult task—as an outsider representing power from above—than that of attempting to secure the one prerequisite for any substantial reform: the good will of people already disaffected. In an age of instant communication, it is easy for us to overlook a very important aspect of Eckhart's duties as provincial and vicar general: constant travel on foot often under arduous conditions. The provincial was required to make regular visits to all houses under his jurisdiction. For Eckhart this would have meant journeys to towns like Groningen (Holland), Hamburg, Rostock, Stralsund, Erfurt, Halberstadt, Göttingen, Braunschweig, Minden, and Dortmund. When one adds to this journeys to general chapters of the order in Toulouse, Strasbourg, and Piacenza, and travel as vicar general in Bohemia, one can understand why Koch concludes that, with the possible exception of two Latin sermons with appended short lectures given, perhaps, at provincial chapters, little from Eckhart's works dates from this period.[8]

Another indication of Eckhart's success as a religious superior is the attempt by the electors of the province of Teutonia to secure him as their provincial in 1310. The general chapter at Naples in 1311 refused to confirm this appointment, however, and relieved him of his administrative duties in order to send him again to Paris as professor of theology. A second such appointment was an unusual occurrence and has to be considered a great honor, one which Eckhart shared with his predecessor Thomas. Some of his Latin scriptural commentaries, or at least what were to become sections of them, were probably composed during this two-year stay in Paris.

His professorial duties ended in 1313 and his activities and title in the years following are uncertain. Documents dating from 1314 and 1316 point to activities in Strasbourg. In 1322 he acts as vicar general in visiting a convent of Dominican nuns south of Strasbourg in Unterlinden. What scant evidence there is leads us to believe that Eckhart had been charged with the spiritual direction of Dominican nuns in the province of Teutonia. Because of a heavy concentration of convents in and near Strasbourg, this city was a likely location for one engaged in such work. Here he would also find large numbers of laity seeking spiritual direction. At any rate, it is generally assumed that many of the vernacular sermons which have come down to us were preached here, although there is not a single reference to Strasbourg in any of them.

The few sermons whose place of origin has been identified were given in Cologne, where Eckhart went not earlier than 1323. Again the evidence is meager, but, in addition to preaching in the vernacular to both Dominican and Cistercian nuns as well as to lay audiences, he seems to have been professor of theology at the *studium generale* where he had once been a student. In this post he would, with the help of one assistant, direct the studies of those thirty to forty students from the Dominican provinces of Germany and eastern Europe chosen for advanced work in theology. If this was actually his main task in Cologne, it was his preaching that attracted not only eager listeners but also the disapproving attention of church authorities.

Trial and Condemnation

If Eckhart's life up to this point had been filled with success and approving recognition of his talents, the two or three years left to him were to be taken up with the dismal business of defending himself before ecclesiastical courts against charges of heresy and of leading simpler minds astray in matters of faith and morals.[9] It was the first time a member of his order had to face such charges. Part of the tragedy of these years lies in the very nature of legal proceedings. To be accused is to live under a cloud until the matter is settled. Eckhart was not to live to see the end of the affair—which in any case went against him. We can only hope that he met the challenge to his peace of mind with the conviction found in the words he had composed years before as prior in Erfurt for the spiritual instruction of young religious:

> God is not moved to perform any deed by anything else than his own goodness. Our deeds do not move him to give us anything or to do anything for us. Our Lord wants his friends to forget such false notions, and this only out of his generous goodness; and he should be their support and comfort, and they should see and consider themselves as a mere nothing among all God's great gifts. For the more man's spirit, naked and empty, depends upon God and is preserved by him, the deeper is the man established in God, and the more receptive is he to God's finest gifts. For man should build upon God alone.[10]

Although we have some documents giving us essential information about the proceedings, we do not know nearly enough to make a judicious appraisal. Besides the gaps in our knowledge, the documents we have present many puzzles. Nevertheless, they do allow us to reconstruct the course of events in some detail. How, why, and by whom Eckhart's preaching was first called to the attention of the archbishop of Cologne, Henry of Virneburg, is not known. Information offered on these points in secondary literature will be found on close scrutiny to be surmisals resting on insufficient evidence.

Sometime in 1325 or early 1326, Eckhart's teachings were first examined by Nicholas of Strasbourg, a member of his own order, who found nothing in them to censure. Nicholas was functioning as papal visitor at the time and had the task of restoring discipline in the province of Teutonia. We have no records of this examination, but it is referred to by Eckhart in a letter of appeal to the pope dated January 24, 1327, in which he protests against the trial initiated by Henry of Virneburg on the grounds that he had previously been found innocent of the same charges by a higher (papal) authority and may not therefore be retried.[11] This line of reasoning seems to have had little effect. It is probable that, at the time, Nicholas was Eckhart's *lector* or assistant at the *studium generale* in Cologne, and it is hardly surprising that Nicholas's judgment on his academic superior's orthodoxy would not carry much weight. The question is, rather, why did Nicholas undertake the investigation in the first place? Koch sees it as an attempt to head off an investigation by the archbishop.[12]

If this was the reason for Nicholas's investigation, it did not have the desired effect.[13] Henry of Virneburg instituted an inquisitorial process, setting up a commission to check Eckhart's orthodoxy. On September 26, 1326, Eckhart offered his first defense before the commission by responding to a list of forty-nine articles taken from the Latin and German works, both treatises and sermons, which seemed to be erroneous and to smack of heresy. The provoked *magister* showed spirit in his opening statement. He questioned the commission's jurisdiction over a member of an exempt order, especially over one whose whole life and teaching had the approval of his entire order as well as of men and women of all lands. He was certain that such measures would not have been taken against him if his reputation and zeal for justice had been less, but he recalled that those who suffer for justice are blessed. He expressed ironic surprise that only twelve articles from his *First Commentary on Genesis* were found objectionable, for there and in other books he had written a hundred things and more that their uncultivated minds (*ruditas ipsorum*) had not grasped. However, if errors were found in his works, he said, he would always be willing to yield to the better opinion. He admitted that he was capable of making an error in doctrine, but stated that he could never be a heretic, because that was a matter of the will, and he never willingly taught anything that church authorities considered erroneous.[14] After laying down a few basic principles of his thought, he took up the incriminated articles one by one.

A short time later we find Eckhart responding to a list of fifty-nine other articles taken exclusively from vernacular sermons. There followed a third list taken from his *Commentary on the Gospel of John*, and subsequently a fourth and possibly a fifth. The latter two or three lists have been lost. Nicholas of Cusa was familiar with the third list, and at least one more list is needed to explain articles that are not contained in the first two lists or in the *Commentary on John* but that appeared in the final condemnation by the pope.

On January 24, 1327, three months after his response to the first list, Eckhart appealed to the pope, alleging delays in his trial in Cologne which were leading to public scandal for clergy and laity alike. He noted that the charges against him reflected on the whole order, and submitted in advance to any correction by papal authority.[15] Since the only documents we have upon which to form a judgment about the trial in Cologne are the two lists containing a total of 108 objectionable articles and Eckhart's responses, we can say nothing about the legitimacy of his complaints. From the two lists we can conclude that the commission generally exercised care and fairness in collecting and translating the articles. We have no other evidence concerning the progress of the trial.

Shortly after his appeal, Eckhart again took the initiative. On February 13, 1327, he ascended the pulpit in the Dominican church in Cologne and preached to the congregation. After the sermon, he called upon a fellow Dominican to read a notarized Latin document, which he then translated into German for the congregation. In it he declared his detestation of heresy and his readiness to recant anything he wrote or preached which might be inconsistent with sound church doctrine. He then offered a clarification of three points that seemed to have been misunderstood.[16] Nine days later the archbishop's commission informed him that it had denied his appeal to the pope.[17] This denial, however, was a mere formality, since the appellant had the right to pursue the matter despite such a denial. In effect, the commission was merely giving its opinion that the appeal had no merit. We have no further information about the workings of the commission. Undoubtedly it sent the results of the investigation to Avignon.

Soon thereafter Eckhart traveled to Avignon himself in the company of the provincial and three lectors of the province of Teutonia. Obviously, he could still count on the support of his order. These men accompanied him to neutralize the testimony and to seek the punishment of two renegade Dominicans who apparently had been active against Eckhart during the trial in Cologne. Also at the papal court awaiting the disposition of his case was the famous Franciscan philosopher William of Ockham. In two passages William testified to Eckhart's presence in Avignon but dismissed what he had heard of the Dominican's teachings as absurd.[18] While this may be symbolic of the divergent paths late scholasticism was taking, the polemical intent and clear irony in William's remarks limit their value as his considered professional opinion of Eckhart's thought.

In Avignon the papal commission examined a shorter list of articles. In the surviving document in which the commission reported its deliberations and expressed its verdict, we find that the approximately 150 articles from the various lists in Cologne have been reduced to a more manageable 28. Because every major Latin Bible commentary, a German treatise, and several German sermons are represented in the remaining twenty-eight articles, one principle used in selecting them might well have been to see that judgment was passed on Eckhart's work in general and not just on his German sermons. The document lists each offending article, followed by Eckhart's explanation and defense of it. The commission then states its reasons for considering the defense insufficient. Ultimately the commission decided that all twenty-eight articles were heretical as stated (*prout verba sonant*).[19] It appears from the document that Eckhart gave his defense in person before the commission, but whether he lived to hear its verdict is uncertain.[20] On April 30, 1328, in a reply to an inquiry from Henry of Virneburg regarding the proceedings against Eckhart, Pope John XXII referred to Eckhart as dead and assured the archbishop that he could count on an expeditious disposition of the case.

This was accomplished a year later through the bull *In agro dominico* dated March 27, 1329,[21] in which Eckhart is described as one who, wanting to know more than he should, had planted thistles and thorns in the field of the church. The judgment of the bull differed from the verdict of the theological commission in that seventeen articles were condemned outright as heretical, but eleven were judged less harshly and were described as evil-sounding, dangerous, and suspect of heresy but capable of an orthodox sense with many explanations and additions. Two of the articles judged heretical were placed at the end of the list with the explanation that Eckhart never admitted teaching them but was merely reputed to have taught them. The bull stated further that at the end of his life Eckhart recanted and rejected the twenty-six articles and any other erroneous doctrines he may have taught, insofar as they might create error in the minds of the faithful, submitting himself and what he had written and spoken to the judgment of the Apostolic See. Finally, in a letter dated April 15, 1329, to Archbishop Henry of Virneburg, the pope instructed the archbishop to publish the bull in all areas under the jurisdiction of the archbishop of Cologne, but restricted its publication to just these areas.[22] Apparently the pope, while making every effort to satisfy the archbishop, saw no reason to increase unnecessarily the damage that the condemnation surely caused.

These sad events at the close of Eckhart's life have been the subject of many diverging interpretations. Leaving aside for the moment his replies in defense of individual articles and their cogency, we can make some general observations about the trial and its circumstances. First, although Eckhart clearly felt wrongly accused, there is no indication of a revolutionary consciousness in him. He had no intention of challenging the authority of the church as such. Both before the commission in Cologne and in his appeal to the pope, he declared his readiness to retract anything that could be shown to be wrong. There is as little reason to doubt his loyalty to the church as there is to doubt his conviction that he was misunderstood. That he questioned the jurisdiction of the archbishop of Cologne over him is a matter of church law. It is interesting that in his correspondence with the archbishop the pope clearly indicated that Henry was acting within his authority.[23]

Did Eckhart receive a fair trial? Certainly it is difficult for many of us today to have sympathy with a bureaucracy which passes judgment on the orthodoxy of someone's professional convictions. It seems pointless as well as ahistorical for us to approach the question philosophically. The concepts "academic freedom" and "religious freedom," as well as "pluralistic society," would probably be as difficult for Eckhart to grasp as for his judges. If we leave the question of the justice of the "system" aside and answer in the historical context, we can note the care taken by the commission in Cologne to quote Eckhart correctly. Since we have no record of how the commission replied to Eckhart's responses, we cannot evaluate his complaint that they lacked theological sophistication. The replies of the commission in Avignon show no such lack. They counter Eckhart's arguments with acumen and dexterity.[24] Two aspects of the trial, however, do seem questionable. First, articles were taken from Eckhart's vernacular sermons, and any written versions of these were very likely not under his editorial control but were probably jotted down by a member of the audience. Only with regard to one issue, however, namely, that there is something uncreated in the soul, does Eckhart deny having said something contained in an article.[25] Nevertheless, such material seems to be a shaky basis for charges of heresy. Second, the articles were judged without any reference to their original context. Scholastic theological terminology of the period was reasonably well standardized, which mitigates the seriousness of this failing. Still, this practice seems to have bothered at least one member of the commission, Cardinal Fournier, the future Pope Benedict XII. In a similar trial a few years later, Fournier refused to give his opinion because he did not know the articles in their original contexts.[26] Perhaps the memory of Eckhart's trial troubled him.

If we can point to faults in the trial itself, we must also admit that Eckhart's handling of his defense left much to be desired.[27] Certainly those acquainted with the literature will agree that, in the case of several articles, authors of our own century, and not just those wishing to defend Eckhart's orthodoxy at all costs, have delivered a more competent defense. Even a sympathetic observer who finds the quality of parts of the *Defense* equal to anything we have from

Eckhart admits that the embattled theologian's responses were un-even.[28] Not infrequently Eckhart admitted to being in error but de-fended the article anyway. In many such cases, and in others where he conceded no error, he cited in his defense an old saw of scholastic thought which seems to have at best only a slight connection to the besieged article. The theologians at Avignon often commented that his response was not to the point. An important conclusion for any-one investigating Eckhart's thought is that the *Defense* should not necessarily be considered either the best explanation or his final opinion on difficult points. Eckhart's explanations in the *Defense* are often less clear and less helpful than passages in his works treating the same questions.

The central issue which separated the defendant from his judges and made a meeting of the minds impossible was Eckhart's frequent appeal to his *intention* in having preached or written something and the opposition's constant juridical insistence that the articles be examined as to their *literal meaning (prout verba sonant)*. Just as Eckhart denied from the outset that he could be a heretic because he did not *will* to be a heretic, so he also often insisted that his words did not have a heretical sense because his intention was not heretical and because they were capable of being understood in a theologically sound or morally uplifting manner. This was repeatedly his defense tactic, even when he admitted that an article was or sounded errone-ous. Often he pointed to a theological underpinning which he felt should clear up any misconception when properly understood. Or he countered that he was speaking in the manner of a preacher, attempt-ing to convince and arouse in the audience moral sensibilities.

This appeal to intention is interesting because it may contain clues to understanding Eckhart's conception of how language func-tions. However, his judges would have none of it, and the papal bull of condemnation is the embodiment of the *prout verba sonant* prin-ciple. Or so it would seem. And yet in a sense, Eckhart was not to be denied having the last word. If one reads carefully the section of the bull containing Eckhart's recantation, one sees that he recants and de-plores the twenty-six condemned articles and anything else he may have taught which could cause error or heresy in the minds of the faithful *according to that sense (quoad illum sensum)*.[29] In other words, Eckhart took back only an interpretation of his words that would lead to heresy or error. He did not take back the words them-selves, which, he had insisted, allow for an orthodox and morally up-lifting interpretation.

Reputation

There is no evidence of anyone carrying on the tradition of Eckhart's thought and teaching after his death. This is probably due at least in part to the troubles of Eckhart's final years. But in the works of the two most prominent Dominican mystics coming after him, John Tauler and Henry Suso, the influence of Eckhart is obvious and runs deep. Tauler spoke often of the birth of God in the soul and of the ground (*grunt*) of the soul, but the context is less speculative and the orthodoxy of such terms is never in doubt. Suso, who was probably a student under Eckhart at the *studium generale* in Cologne in the mid-1320s and who tells us that Eckhart freed him from a serious scruple, defended the orthodoxy of his former teacher's thought in his earlier writings, carefully distinguishing the true legacy of the *magister* from the errors of certain religious movements which were then running afoul of ecclesiastical authorities. Suso would be made to suffer for this loyalty, and in his later writings he stayed away from controversial topics. Despite such influence and signs of esteem, both Tauler and Suso avoided attempting to combine scholastic speculation with mystical concerns, an endeavor which touched the heart of Eckhart's strivings. Several pseudo-Eckhartian texts bear witness to the strong influence Eckhart continued to exert in popular spirituality, and he frequently appears as the main character in spiritual anecdotes current among the common people. Still, one searches in vain for a tradition carrying forth in a substantial manner the rich thought of the professor and preacher.

The extent of influence Eckhart's thought had on various late medieval religious movements originating among laypeople in the Rhineland and the Low Countries is a matter of dispute. That several guardians of orthodoxy found him worth attacking is some indication of his influence. Eckhart's fortune through the centuries, the contrasting images of the man that emerge, his rediscovery and fate at the hands of his interpreters in the nineteenth and early decades of the twentieth century, and the problems accompanying the efforts to initiate a critical edition make fascinating reading.[30]

Because Eckhart has been viewed as a champion of so many different causes, several of them revolutionary in nature, it seems important to insist on just how medieval he was. Conscious though he was of his stature as a professor at the university in Paris, he probably would have been amused to hear himself described in all seriousness as a *German* thinker. Moreover, in view of his frequent references to and obvious respect for the Jewish thinker Maimonides, he would not deserve the fashionable popularity he enjoyed among those for whom *German* was (and is) essentially a racial term. In the best medieval tradition, he considered the search for knowledge and the community of scholars as something universal. One considered the cogency of the argument, not its origin.

If Eckhart's activities had any effect on political or social change or on the structure of organized religion, it happened without his knowledge, intent, or consent. His only complaint against church officials was that they misunderstood his thought. Heresy was definitely an evil for him, and he occasionally made a point of distancing his views from those of heretics.[31] In an age when even loyal Christians found much to criticize in the church, he offered no commentary on either abuses or reform, nor did he express any opinion on political problems, such as the ongoing feud between pope and emperor or the social unrest in Cologne and Strasbourg. Instead, it is the degree to which he excluded merely "temporal" considerations from his preaching and writing that is worth mentioning. From the few passages in which he addressed the concept "order," one must assume that he considered the medieval sociopolitical order a given that he never found occasion to question and that, as order, was good.[32] Whatever groups may have later claimed him for their own, Eckhart, at least in his works as we have them, was too exclusively taken up with his professional concerns—exploring the metaphysical and theological dimensions of God and his universe and sharing these with others—to give attention to problems that were "merely" social or political. One may find such an attitude deplorable, but it is more honest to admit the limitations his focus imposed upon his efforts than to make him into something he was not.

Although the vernacular sermons were preached to nuns and probably also to lay audiences that included Beguines (women belonging to no religious order but living a life resembling that of nuns), one must be careful in making him a proponent of feminist spirituality to explain what this might mean in a medieval context.[33] The quality and intensity of these sermons certainly bear eloquent witness to how important he, the professor and former provincial, considered such work and such audiences. And their content leaves little doubt, although he realized that not everyone understood him, that he did not equate lack of education with lack of intelligence. To the criticism that he should not preach on such elevated topics to unlearned audiences he had a ready answer: "If we are not to teach people who have not been taught, no one will ever be taught, and no one will ever be able to teach or write. For that is why we teach the untaught, so that they may be changed from uninstructed into instructed." But we should not be too ready to see in this statement a desire to change social boundaries, for, he continued, clearly with himself in mind as the physician, "Our Lord says, 'Those who are healthy do not need medicine' (Luke 5:31). That is what the physician is there for, to make the sick healthy."[34] Despite his obvious commitment to the spiritual guidance of women, we find Eckhart using women in the typical medieval fashion to symbolize that which is of less value, for example, as the sensitive as opposed to the intellectual or spiritual part (man) of the soul, or mere matter as opposed to form, the higher principle of corporeal reality.[35] Such uses are incidental and, as is the case with clichés, are employed without much thought. However, they hardly reveal a man set apart from his contemporaries by a special feminist awareness. His very real feminism remains a medieval feminism. His unstinting efforts on behalf of female audiences show an appreciation for women's intellectual and spiritual equality with men and were motivated by his conviction that every human soul is, in a sense to be more closely defined, divine.

These and other similarly distorted interpretations of the man distract our attention from that in which his greatness and his value to us consist. He explored the vastness of spiritual reality as only few have. Conscious of the paradox involved, he boldly investigated the dimensions of metaphysical infinity, an infinity which he found also in man. What he has left us is his attempt to describe the results of these explorations, an attempt that tested both the man and language itself. It is for this that we owe him gratitude.

Eckhart's Works

The term "works" seems to be the only appropriate term, since even the usually inoffensive term "writings" covers neither all the genres that Eckhart employed nor the manner in which they came down to us. It is his sermons, particularly those in the vernacular, which cannot be called writings. First, sermons are meant to be spoken, and the style of Eckhart's sermons shows his awareness of this. Second, since the written forms of the sermons that we have are most likely derived from members of the audience who jotted down his words, the preacher exercised little or no control over them—and yet they are usually judged to be the most valuable part of his works. Anyone acquainted with the goals and spirit of the Dominican order will not be surprised at Eckhart's emphasis on preaching. In the sermon, he was able to combine his learning and intense spiritual awareness with an unusual talent for expression. In his Latin works, because they were written for theologians in the language of the profession, he lacked the freedom of expression granted by the sermon. Yet even in these professional writings there are passages one does not hesitate to call beautiful. The history of the texts that have come down to us is interesting, and some knowledge of it is important for anyone wishing to read them intelligently.

As interest in Meister Eckhart grew in the nineteenth century, a good edition of his vernacular works was the highest priority. Franz Pfeiffer published an edition in 1857, but never published the critical apparatus which he had promised would soon follow. A new generation of Germanists questioned the reliability of the edition as a basis for serious work. Because of Eckhart's condemnation, copies of his vernacular sermons and treatises often circulated anonymously and became part of a corpus of anonymous mystical literature. On the other hand, because of his fame, his name often became attached to mystical writings that were not his. Also, excerpts from various sermons were collected into "treatises" which listed him as author. In addition, he played a main role in several religious legends. The main criticism leveled against Pfeiffer's edition was that it in no way distinguished between what was really Eckhart's and the large body of additional texts merely attributed to him. The question was, How could one develop criteria to distinguish the genuine works from the others? It was suddenly realized that the trial documents—Eckhart's *Defense* in Cologne, the verdict of the commission in Avignon, and the papal bull—contained many quotations, albeit translated into Latin, which Eckhart had admitted preaching. With the aid of sixteen *incipits* (the initial phrase or sentence of a sermon) included in the *Defense*, scholars began searching for sermons containing these quotations. It was found that such quotations provided a solid base from which to start. In the 1930s the critical edition of the German works began to appear under the superb editorship of Josef Quint. Before his death in 1976, Quint was able to see through to completion four volumes (I, II, III, and V) of the five planned. The quality of this edition cannot be emphasized enough. The four completed volumes contain eighty-six sermons and three treatises. The sermons are grouped according to degree of authenticity.[36]

One should not imagine that Quint's edition is able to give us the exact words of the preacher in every case. In his critical introduction to a sermon, Quint will occasionally point out that a section of the text is hopelessly corrupt. On the other hand, concerning the *Book of Divine Consolation*, a treatise which authorities agree was actually written and edited by Eckhart, Quint stated that its manuscript tradition contains variants about equal in degree and number to variants in the majority of sermons (DW V, 3). It should also be remembered that at his trial, with a few exceptions, Eckhart accepted the articles under attack as genuine excerpts from his sermons.

One important consequence of the condition of the texts is that one should not draw conclusions about the preacher's thought based on a single passage. However, Eckhart repeated his favorite and most characteristic themes often enough that an individual passage is not obliged to bear such weight. Stylistic investigations must also be able to point to multiple occurrences to prove a point. But here again the problem is not as serious as it seems. The sheer bulk of the available texts and the frequent repetition of stylistic elements enables us to have a high degree of confidence in the results of studies based on a wide sampling of texts. This repetition of favorite themes and stylistic elements is so characteristic of Eckhart that Quint rightfully considered them strong secondary criteria for establishing the reliability of a text. In a broader sense, it is the quality and independence of thought and expression that distinguish Eckhart's sermons from those of his contemporaries. In his study of the *Paradisus anime*, a collection of sermons by Eckhart as well as by several other preachers of the time who attempted to make scholastic thought available to the unschooled, Lauri Seppänen demonstrated the differences between Eckhart and his closer contemporaries. While the others were content to explain basic scholastic concepts and concerns, Eckhart used scholasticism creatively to enthuse his hearers for union with God.[37]

The vernacular sermons in the critical edition are, by and large, most likely from the period of Eckhart's activities in Strasbourg and Cologne. They reflect the thought and expression of his mature years, coming after the professorial duties in Paris. Besides these sermons we possess three other vernacular works. Probably the earliest is his *Counsels of Discernment* (*Die rede der underscheidunge*), written between 1294 and 1298, when Eckhart was prior in Erfurt. It consists of twenty-three sections that were probably meant to be read during meals to the Dominican community entrusted to him. Each section considers a different spiritual topic, but the underlying theme and final thought of the collection is that man's goal and happiness is achieved when he has united his will totally to God's will. As a spiritual guide it is sane and full of human warmth and understanding. Although its style gives us some indication of what is to come, it lacks the intellectuality of the sermons, coming as they do after his university years. Nor is the formulation of his thought as intense, although there are some characteristic rhetorical formulations and an abundance of paradox. The *Counsels* are eminently suitable for young religious who are yet without formal training in philosophy and theology.

The treatise *The Book of Divine Consolation* (*Das buoch der götlichen troestunge*), mentioned above, and the attached sermon, *Of the Nobleman* (*Von dem edeln menschen*), which taken together are known as the *Liber "Benedictus,"* were dedicated to Agnes, queen of Hungary, to console her for the loss of either her father, King Albert (murdered in 1308), or her mother, Queen Elizabeth (died in 1313). Whether the rarefied thought had the desired effect we do not know. The treatise and sermon are replete with Eckhartian themes. A third work, the short treatise *On Detachment* (*Von abegescheidenheit*), is difficult to date, and not everyone is convinced of its authenticity. However, in describing how this mystical virtue prepares the soul to receive God, and in maintaining the preeminence of detachment over other virtues, it reveals many affinities with the German sermons both in thought and in expression.

Eckhart's Latin works, rediscovered toward the end of the nineteenth century, do not present the problems the German works do for establishing the original text. They represent what Eckhart might have called his professional output and, with some exceptions, are part of what he titled his *Tripartite Work* (*Opus tripartitum*). He undertook this work, he informs us in the General Prologue, to satisfy the wishes of certain brethren who *long ago* urged him to write down what they had heard from him in lectures, sermons, discussions, and the like. This probably means that the General Prologue was written relatively late, at Strasbourg or Cologne, and also possibly that the plan for the *Tripartite Work* was not conceived until then. However, it also seems probable that at least earlier versions of writings finally subsumed into it existed before this time and owe their origin to Eckhart's activities in Paris. As with the German works, the critical edition of the Latin works numbers five volumes. Although several scholars contributed substantially to the editing, the efforts of Josef Koch (1885–1967) stand out most prominently.

The plan of the *Tripartite Work* is grand indeed. No one seriously believes that Eckhart brought it to completion. Yet because he refers to several sections that have not been found, a sizable portion of it may have been lost. Unfortunately, lack of information allows us to say no more. The first part, the *Work of Propositions* (*Opus proposi-*

tionum), was to contain over a thousand philosophical theses or statements with their demonstrations. Nothing of it survives except the Prologue, in which we are given a preliminary example of how the author intended to treat the first proposition: being is God (*esse est deus*). The author considered this proposition to express the sum of all knowledge. The lack of this first part of the *Tripartite Work* is particularly regrettable because in the author's own mind the second and third parts were dependent upon it and of little use without it (*Prol. Gener.* n. 11; LW I, 156). The second part, the *Work of Questions* (*Opus quaestionum*), was to be much less ambitious and was to contain *quaestiones*, that is, the results of problems treated in disputations, public lectures, and discussions insofar as the author had had occasion to participate in such. We have five *quaestiones* from Eckhart's two periods of teaching at Paris, but we have no indication whether he intended these to be included. Otherwise, nothing of it survives.

What do survive are several sections of the third part, the *Work of Commentaries* (*Opus expositionum*), which was to contain commentaries on selected books of the Old and New Testaments as well as Latin sermons. Volume IV of the critical edition is devoted entirely to sermons, but only a handful can be considered complete sermons. The rest are detailed notes or dispositions for sermons. In view of their inchoate form, we cannot be certain that Eckhart intended to include them, as we have them, in the *Tripartite Work*. The bulk of what survives, then, are biblical commentaries: two on Genesis and one each on Exodus, Ecclesiasticus, Wisdom, and the Gospel of John. They, together with the surviving prologues, comprise Volumes I–III of the critical edition. Volume V, when completed, will contain the *Parisian Questions*, a lecture on Peter Lombard's *Sentences*, some short miscellaneous pieces and fragments, and all documents relating to the trial.

In these commentaries, the author tells us, he intends to give interpretations that are not generally found elsewhere. He does not treat each verse of scripture equally, but devotes long pages of comment to passages of special interest to him, while passing over entire chapters. As one might expect, it is more often the passages that offer opportunities for his speculative interests, such as the first chapter of John, that receive extended treatment.

Because many investigators have approached Eckhart with very specific goals or with insufficient preparation, distorted statements have been made about the relationships between the German and Latin works and about their relative value. Those whose background is medieval German literature, for example, emphasize the vigorous expression and creative flights of thought of the works in his native tongue, where he was free of the inhibiting rigidity of Latin and the confining terminology of the schools. Historians of thought, on the other hand, can point to the preeminence of the more precise Latin of Eckhart, the professional philosopher and theologian, for determining what he really thought.

Much of this provincialism is now disappearing, and the opinion is beginning to prevail that the most valuable studies have been those that emphasize the basic unity of the German and Latin works and make full use of both to elucidate his overall cultural impact. This basic unity, incidentally, was a guiding principle of Eckhart's judges, and one the defendant objected to only insofar as he thought they were confusing the differing demands of strict theology and devotional works.[38] It is true that certain themes or important terms in the German works, such as "breakthrough" (*durchbruch*) and "ground of the soul" (*grunt der sêle*), are at best peripheral concerns in the Latin works. Also, few would deny that the language of the German works is more interesting and gives us better indications of the man's poetic talents. However, with equal emphasis it must be maintained that the Latin works often provide clearer and more elaborate presentations of Eckhart's philosophical thought, as well as more precise formulations of basic characteristic doctrines, and are thus important in their own right and indispensable for understanding the German works. Differences do arise, of course, because of the potentialities and limitations of both Latin and medieval German. Yet other more important reasons for the differences can be found in the disparity of the audiences addressed in each language and in the genres employed. One of Eckhart's most remarkable talents was his ability to transmit highly speculative thought to unlearned audiences, and the success of a popular sermon will be the result of principles of form different from those used for a successful scholastic commentary on scripture. Part of Eckhart's genius was to recognize this. To judge one genre better than the other is to misunderstand both. Both the Latin works and the German works eminently reward serious study and are necessary for understanding Eckhart.

At the same time, it must be admitted that not every German sermon is a masterpiece of linguistic and mystical intensity. The preacher was capable of unspectacular sermons, just as the professor was capable of including interpretations in his commentaries that differ little from those of his rightfully forgotten contemporaries. The occasional mediocrity of a sermon or the unevenness of the Latin works should not be held against Eckhart, especially because he lacked editorial control over the sermons and because the *Tripartite Work* remained incomplete.

Eckhart as Interpreter of Scripture

Because almost everything we have from Eckhart is in some sense a commentary on the Bible, it seems appropriate to consider at the outset his approach to interpreting scripture, especially since what he does in practice is often unconventional. The most obvious examples of biblical exegesis are his commentaries (*expositiones*), which make up the bulk of his Latin works, but the sermons are hardly less exegetical, since they almost exclusively take a scriptural text as their point of departure and are often detailed explanations of the meaning of each word of the biblical text. Even in the generically philosophical *First Parisian Question* we find Eckhart demonstrating his point that God is more properly understanding and not being (*esse*) by referring to John 1:1: "In the beginning was the word" (*Q. Par.* I, n. 4; LW V, 40). Thus it is important to understand how he draws meaning from scripture if we are to understand him at all. This is no simple task for a modern reader accustomed to more scholarly and plausible methods. Even within the context of his times, his interpretations have a character all their own. They cannot simply be grouped together with other allegorical interpretations. Although he occasionally uses terms familiar to practitioners of allegorical interpretation, such as *moraliter, theologice, corporaliter, historice, spiritualiter, allegorice,* and even the adjective *mysticus* to describe manners of interpretations, such terms do not provide him with a clearly defined method or structure. Nor does he make use of the widespread practice of dividing interpretations into the four categories: literal, allegorical, moral or tropological, and anagogical. On the other hand, the distinctiveness of his interpretations does not arise from any attempt to make them academically more acceptable, as in the case of Thomas. Eckhart shows little concern for what we might call the literal sense, often neglecting it entirely and passing on immediately to his own original free interpretation. The relationship of the literal meaning to the meaning he draws from a passage, and the relationship of the interpreted verse to its own scriptural context, usually receive little or no attention. At times, like other patristic and medieval exegetes, his interpretation will depend on combining texts that are quite separate, even coming from different books of the Bible. What distinguishes Eckhart's efforts from that of others is his originality, his ability to uncover unexpected and intellectually stimulating, at times breathtaking, meanings of a speculative or mystical nature in what is often, to all appearances, a straightforward and even drab biblical passage.

Although he does discuss his principles of exegesis in some detail, his remarks cannot be taken as a full-blown theory of biblical interpretation. One learns just as much, if not more, by observing his actual practice of the art. It thus seems advisable to speak of his attitude toward, rather than his theory of, interpretation.[39] This term also seems more suitable because it is not so much intrinsic principles of exegesis as extrinsic factors that most evidently determine what happens in practice. One can point to three such factors which are clearly at work when he approaches a biblical text.

First, and perhaps most important of all, the preacher is animated by the desire to amaze and startle his audience. This desire is coupled with a basic intellectual urge to find a deeper meaning in a text. In the General Prologue to the *Opus tripartitum*, he warns us that some of what is to follow will seem at first glance strange (*monstrosa*), questionable (*dubia*), or wrong (*falsa*), but that if it is considered carefully and intently, its agreement with other accepted authorities will clearly shine forth (*luculenter*) (n. 7; LW I, 152). Since the author applies these statements to the *Opus tripartitum* as a whole and not just to meanings he uncovers in scripture, we can see that the urge to startle is based on his conviction that in spiritual matters the truth is often startling, that the shocking, the unheard of, is true. This conviction reveals itself again and again in his descriptions of God and the union of the soul with God. His attempt to startle through scriptural interpretations can be illustrated by a few examples of how he sees scripture describing the nature of created beings. His often repeated contention that creatures are pure nothing finds corroboration in John 1:3, "sine ipso factum est nihil" (usual translation: "without him nothing was made"), which by taking *factum* as a participial noun he construes to mean "without him [the Word] that which has come about is nothing." To demonstrate the dependence of creatures on God for their being, he takes the first half of the same verse, "omnia per ipsum facta sunt" (usual translation: "through him all things were made"), changes the word order to "omnia facta per ipsum sunt," and interprets it to mean "all things that were made are or have their being through him" (*In Joh.* n. 53; LW III, 44). In treating Genesis 1:2, "Terra autem erat inanis et vacua" (usual translation: "Now the earth was a formless void"), he sees a reference to the scholastic doctrine concerning matter. *Inanis* (empty) is an apt word for describing the earth or matter in itself, because by fantasizing on its etymology one can render it *sine an est*, or without being or existence, which is the usual scholastic conception of matter separate from form (*In Gen.* II, n. 41; LW I, 507–508).

In the prologue to the *Book of the Parables of Genesis*, Eckhart states clearly his wish to search out the profundities of scripture. This second commentary on Genesis owes its origin to his intention to go beyond the more obvious meanings of the text and, as an example for the more learned to follow, to coax out (*elicere*) certain things under the shell or skin of the letter (*sub cortice litterae*). Scripture is seen to contain a wealth of meaning hiding under the images and surfaces of the literal sense (*latentia sub figura et superficie sensus litteralis*). He then refers to Maimonides's description of the truth of scripture as a golden apple covered with filigree work in silver. When seen from afar without intellectual insight, only the beautiful silver is perceived. A closer, sharper look reveals the yet more valuable gold beneath. If one is able to scoop out (*exsculpere*) a hidden meaning, it is like taking honey from the comb. He quotes Augustine as admiring scripture because, while it is accessible to all, it reserves the dignity of its innermost mystery for a more profound understanding (*In Gen.* II, n. 1; LW I, 447–449).

Although these thoughts are offered by way of introduction to a specific commentary, they reflect an attitude which Eckhart puts into practice repeatedly in contexts where the words of scripture are to be explained. Before preaching a sermon in German on the text of Wisdom 5:16, "The just shall live forever," he urges his listeners to pay close attention to the meaning because "though it may sound simple and commonplace, it is really noteworthy and good."[40] He then proceeds to deliver a sermon of astonishing richness by uncovering what he finds contained in the words "just," "live," and "forever." The attitude is hardly original; the profound meanings hidden beneath the surface often are. So, for example, he distinguishes four meanings of the nothing which the stricken Saul saw when he rose from the ground (Acts 9:8). First, this nothing is God, who is the nothing beyond being; second, he saw nothing but God; third, in all things he saw nothing but God; and fourth, when Saul saw God, he saw all things as nothing (Pr. 71; DW III, 211–231). He translates "he was found just" (Eccles. 44:17, *inventus est iustus*) as "er ist inne vunden gereht" (he was found inwardly just), making the *in* in *inventus* do double duty, and immediately thereafter translates it as "gerehticheit hât er vunden von innen" (justice he found from within;

Pr. 10; DW I, 161, 4–5). When Martha receives Jesus into her home (Luke 10:38), the Latin for receive (*excipere*) is rendered by the Middle High German *enpfâhen*. Eckhart is thus able to take advantage of the receive-conceive ambiguity of the word to elaborate on the conception of Jesus by the virginal soul that frees itself from all *eigenschaft*, or self-seeking (Pr. 2; DW I, 24–45). That this ambiguity occurs only in his Middle High German translation does not seem to concern him. It is still part of the wealth of scripture.

A second factor governing Eckhart's approach to scripture is his tendency to erase the borders between philosophy and theology. This leads to an unusual conception of the connection between reason and revelation. While he does not deny that revelation gives access to truths unattainable for unaided human reason, his chief concern in examining scripture is to show how much philosophy it contains when interpreted in a wider sense. At the beginning of his *Commentary on John*, he states that it is his intention here as in all his works to explain the text by means of the natural arguments of philosophers (*per rationes naturales philosophorum*). By this he does not mean that he wishes to shore up the truths of revelation by philosophical arguments. Rather, just as Augustine found much of the first chapter of John contained in the writings of Plato, he wishes to show, conversely, how the truths of philosophy (*veritates principiorum et conclusionum et proprietatum naturalium*) are clearly contained in sacred scripture for those who have ears to hear (*In Joh.* nn. 2–3; LW III, 4). Later in the same commentary, when treating the relationship between John the Baptist and Christ (John 1:6ff.), he writes that the things happened historically (*historica veritate*) but that he wishes to pursue in them truths of natural things and their properties (*veritates rerum naturalium et earum proprietates*). What is said of John teaches us about change, both as to natural forms and as to moral dispositions. What is said of Christ clarifies the question of the properties of substantial forms in matter and of moral dispositions in the soul (*In Joh.* n. 142; LW III, 119–120). In other words, the truths he discovers beneath the surface are the often highly technical doctrines of scholastic philosophy. In the prologue to the *Book of the Parables of Genesis*, he divides these truths into *divina*, *naturalia*, and *moralia*, and these are indeed the three classes into which the interpretations are usually grouped: the nature of God, the nature of creatures and physical laws, and finally ethical and morally uplifting interpretations (*In Gen.* II, n. 1; LW I, 447).

Our surprise that Eckhart is able to uncover so much philosophy in biblical texts should not lead us to assume that he was trying to prove in his commentaries the validity of philosophical doctrines arrived at by natural reason. As mentioned, he emphasizes instead the dependence of the commentaries on the philosophical parts of the *Tripartite Work*, especially on the *Book of Propositions* (*Prol. gener.* n. 11; LW I, 156). He wishes to show that the truths of philosophy are in agreement with sacred scripture (*consonant*) and that scripture hints at them, as it were, darkly (*innuit quasi latenter*) in a parabolic manner (*parabolice*) (*In Gen.* II, n. 4; LW I, 454). He thus maintains the presence of these doctrines in scripture while at the same time diminishing their visibility there and the necessity of finding them. He wishes to make no exclusive claims for his methods, but he does see value in their being different. His fellow Dominicans who urged him to write the commentaries wished to have in written form what they could not recall hearing elsewhere. Eckhart comments that the new and unusual stimulates the mind more pleasantly than what one has grown accustomed to, even though the latter might be better and more important (*Prol. gener.* n. 2; LW I, 148–149).

Some of the puzzles and paradoxes that Eckhart's position generates can be at least partially dissipated by calling to mind a third factor guiding his commentaries. The commentaries were to be not just a product of and for the schools. They were also intended to help fellow Dominicans in their own lives as religious and in their work as preachers. This more practical goal for his writings is implied in Eckhart's expressed intention of writing to oblige the wishes of his brethren. It is also reflected frequently in what he does in practice. Often the truth derived from a passage will be one bearing principally on ascetical or religious practices or attitudes. In the Second Prologue to the *Work of Commentaries*, this matter of interpreting for personal spiritual gain is given more explicit mention. Eckhart states that he has often interpreted verses without reference to their literal sense, but that, as Augustine teaches, such interpretations are useful and productive (*utiliter et fructuose*). He adds that important verses are given several interpretations so that the reader can choose now this one, now that one, as seems useful (*prout indicaverit expedire*; *Prol. expos.* II, nn. 3–5; LW II, 321–322). In the *Commentary on John* he again urges the reader to choose from among the interpretations offered on the basis of usefulness (*prout ipsi videbitur expedire*) and explains that this is his usual manner of proceeding (n. 39; LW III, 33).

It is therefore not exclusively some academic notion of truth which determines his interpretations in practice, but rather a mixture of truth and usefulness. The problems that might arise in trying to combine both goals or in trying to distinguish a true sense from a false sense are not seriously addressed. Also, nowhere does he work out the relationship of the literal sense of a passage to parabolical meanings. He is acquainted with and uses the distinction between literal and other interpretations, but in the Prologue to the *Book of the Parables of Genesis*, he offers an explanation of *literal sense* that makes any such distinction impossible. With heavy borrowing from Augustine, he states that since God, who is truth, is the author of sacred scripture, every true sense is a literal sense, for everything that is true is from the truth (God) who intends all truth. And thus God made scripture fertile and sowed into it and sealed onto it the imprint of everything that anyone's mind can coax out of (*elicere*) it (*In Gen.* II, n. 2; LW I, 449–450). Such a theory provides the perfect justification for what the preacher and scripture commentator practiced with great success.

Besides these important factors, we can note a few other considerations which influenced Eckhart's attitude toward biblical interpretation. From Maimonides he adopts the idea that there are two kinds of parables. In the first kind, each word or almost every word by itself points to something parabolically. In the second kind, the parable as a whole is the expression of that other sense which it represents. In this second type, many words are merely decorative and do not directly contribute to the understanding of the truth parabolically expressed. At times such words serve to hide the parabolical sense (*In Gen.* II, n. 5; LW I, 454–455, and *In Joh.* n. 174; LW III, 143). In practice, both in sermons and in commentaries, Eckhart seems to have considered most of the texts he treats as examples of the first type of parable. The biblical text is examined word for word, and almost every word is forced to yield one if not several unsuspected parabolical senses. It must also be mentioned that this practice is by no means limited to what one usually thinks of as the parables of the Bible. Every conceivable category of biblical text is analyzed in this fashion.

In the *Commentary on Wisdom* he offers another insight into how meaning is contained in scripture. After giving nine senses in which one can understand how wisdom is "quicker to move than any motion" (*omnibus mobilibus mobilior*, Wisd. 7:24) and explaining that in the ninth sense the text indicates that the wisdom of God is immovable, he remarks that scripture often teaches us about divine things by hinting at them (*innuendo*) rather than by stating them directly (*exprimendo*). This, he assures us, is proper because of their incomprehensibility and sublimity and our imperfection and unworthiness. Thus the wise man is able to achieve more by acuity and indirection (*subtiliter et occulte*) than by direct statements, as in this passage, where he teaches God's immobility by saying that wisdom moves more quickly than moving things (*In Sap.* nn. 132–133; LW II, 469–471). This is an apophatic way of describing God as well as an example of Eckhart's love of paradox, which reveals itself everywhere in his works. It should not surprise us to come upon contradictory interpretations of a single text, especially a text about God, which he does not attempt to harmonize.

In his thoughts on interpretation of scripture, Eckhart might best be described as an eclectic within the broad tradition of Christian Platonism. The more scholarly but confining views of Thomas are rejected, at least in practice. As elsewhere, Eckhart reveals himself as an adherent of older, pre-Thomistic teachings, although loyalty to his fellow Dominican makes him reluctant to stress the point. His remarks concerning exegesis are incomplete and in certain areas inconsistent. Certainly the quality of his interpretations and their ability to stimulate are what distinguish him from others using the same tradition. From a modern point of view, we are tempted to consider the only limits on his interpretations to be those of his own mind. And yet, although he can enumerate such a variety of riches hidden under the surface—the properties belonging to God alone which point to his nature, the virtues, the principles of the sciences, the keys to metaphysics, ethics, and physics and their general laws, the workings of the Trinity, and the production of creatures—there is nonetheless a center of scripture which gives orientation. No one can be thought to understand the scripture, he assures us, who cannot find hidden there its core or marrow: Christ, the truth (*In Gen.* II, n. 3; LW I, 453–454). Again, this is not a principle of interpretation capable of satisfying minds concerned primarily with the objective validity of his method, but it is one that certainly guided his attempts. He gave no further explanation of how one should use this principle. Against the background of his works the possibilities are many. One wonders what one could call such a principle—except, possibly, mystical.

II
GOD AND CREATURES

Those who investigate Meister Eckhart's thought against the background of mysticism characterize his type of mysticism as *speculative*. Those who emphasize his philosophy and theology generally admit that his speculative thought transcends the usual borders of these fields into areas often darkly described as *mystical*. Thus, to call the preacher-professor a speculative mystic seems clearly justified, and the best approach for trying to grasp the mystical aspects would seem to be to begin by examining some basic concepts of the speculative tradition of scholasticism in which Eckhart stood and which he used in all his works to explain ideas that bear his personal stamp. In describing these concepts, we shall use thoughts taken from Thomas Aquinas for purposes of clarification. Contrasting the two on key issues is appropriate because there is much evidence that Eckhart frequently had his fellow Dominican's thought in mind when formulating his own position. The reader should keep in mind that this approach may have the unfortunate effect of making the philosophies of the two thinkers appear further apart than they actually were. The fact is that examining Eckhart's thought in this way is productive precisely because he and Thomas belonged to the same philosophical tradition and used the same basic terminology. One should also realize at the outset that no full-blown presentation of Thomistic thought is being attempted, and hence must excuse the flatness the thinking of Thomas assumes when thus used.

Esse: The Crucial Point of Departure

The basic notion around which scholastic metaphysical thought revolved was that of *being*. Since metaphysics is that branch of study which considers reality taken as a whole, "being," a term that appears capable of being applied to all individual things making up reality, was chosen as a pivotal concept. Everything is a being. The Latin terms clarify some of the ambiguity of the English. These are *ens*, *esse*, and *essentia*. *Ens* (plural: *entia*), a present participial noun, is used to signify a being (or beings) in the concrete. What all beings have in common is that they exist, they are. For this act of existing the infinitive *esse* (to be) was used. Yet beings do not exist as such. Men, horses, and trees exist: beings do not. The principle which accounts for the differences in beings is that of *essentia*, or essence. Essence limits the *esse* an individual concrete being has. One should not imagine that medieval philosophers thought that the principles of *esse* and *essentia* were in any sense physical constituents that could be physically separated or for which empirical scientific evidence could be adduced. Nor do such principles explain how a concrete being, such as a tree, physically comes to be. They are metaphysical principles necessary to explain the existences of things that are and that are different from each other.

Essence is often described as *that which* exists (*in quod est*) and *esse* as that *by which* (*id quo est*) something (the *id quod est*) has being or existence. One can consider the essence of a thing without necessarily thinking of it as existing. Hence the necessity of a second principle: *esse* (*quo est*). And in *esse* by itself it is impossible to find the reason why concrete beings are this or that kind. Hence the necessity of a principle (*essentia*) which limits the *esse* of a being (*ens*) to a definite kind. Both principles are necessary to explain the beings one encounters empirically. However, a being is conceivable in which, because its act of existence or *esse* is not limited in any way, the essence or what it is (*id quod est*) is identical with its *esse*. A being of infinite essence is simply pure *esse*, pure infinite act of existing. To describe a being in which *esse* and *essentia* are completely one and cannot be distinguished is to describe God. God has no essence insofar as this is considered as a limiting principle. One can say simply that God is *esse* (*Deus est esse*) or *esse subsistens* or *esse absolutum*, since he is in no way restricted or dependent, or *esse necessarium*, since God cannot not be. One must admit, however, that *ens*, *esse*, and *essentia* are not always used, in scholastic thought or by Eckhart, in exactly the senses given here. Moreover, *ens* may be qualified by adjectives that give it more precise meanings. For Eckhart, *ens* usually means a created being, but occasionally it can also refer to God.[1]

Being (*esse* or *ens*) is, then, a term through which the philospher is able to embrace all reality. Are there other such terms? Are there terms that say something about all of reality, about God as well as creatures, the material world as well as the nonmaterial? Some terms are obviously limited. For example, "green" can only be predicated of a material object, such as a plant or a wall. "Ubiquitous," on the other hand, can only be applied in a literal sense to beings having a different relationship to time and space than corporeal beings have. Most medieval thinkers would answer that there are terms coextensive in their applicability with *ens*. These terms (called "transcendental") are *unum* (one), *verum* (true), and *bonum* (good). A being must have a degree of unity to exist. Division is an imperfection. The more unity a being possesses, the higher it is on the scale of existence. Living beings are one in a higher sense or have more unity than inanimate beings. The soul, which has no physical extension in itself, is more one than the body but is not perfectly one because it has the faculties of intellect and will that are separate from each other and are not the same as the essence of the soul. God, of course, has no division of any kind and is perfectly one. However, all beings must have some degree of unity to exist.

Likewise, all beings can be said to be true in the sense that they are intelligible. They have a definite connection to intellect or the power of understanding. They are intelligible to the degree that they are. A higher being, such as man, is more intelligible than, say, a rock because there is more being to know. God is infinitely true or intelligible. That we might find lesser beings more intelligible than God is due to the limits of our ability to understand. God, whose understanding is not limited, understands himself perfectly, infinitely. Also, beings are intelligible because they proceed from absolute truth, which is God. Creatures bear the mark of intelligibility because they were called into existence by a creator possessing infinite intellect. This intellect was involved in their creation.

Similarly, all beings are good in the sense that they are desirable. In addition to their connection to intellect, they also have a connection to will. Again the degree of being they possess determines their degree of desirability. Evil is not a being and does not properly exist. It is rather a lack of being that should exist, a disorder or privation. Just as division does not exist as such, but is only the negative side of unity and measures the degree of imperfection in a being that is in some sense unified, so evil can exist only in a being that is in itself good. Sickness is a lack of health, sin a lack of the proper moral order. If a human being is at times less desirable than a lesser being, it is because it lacks some degree of being that it should have. God, who is infinitely good and the source of all goodness, is the ultimate object of all willing, the only being that can satisfy completely all desire, human or divine.

Therefore, "being," "one," "true," and "good" are words that can be applied universally to all that exists. But among these terms, "being" is generally given a certain preeminence. It is the foundation upon which the other terms rest. Since only being exists, it is the cause of unity, intelligibility, and desirability in things. Things are one, true, and good because they are and to the extent that they are. Just as they depend on God for their being, they have these qualities in dependence on him.

One now has to ask, however, whether employment of these general terms really puts one in the position to say something that applies to all reality. If one says that God and man are beings, has one really said the same thing about both of them? Or is it not rather blasphemy to unite God and man in the same term? How can one possibly join the infinite with the finite in the same concept? The differences between infinite and finite can only be infinite. Thus it would seem to be an illegitimate use of language to apply the same word to God and creature. And if our words are drawn from our experience of the world of creatures, is it not fair to conclude that our knowledge is limited to this sphere and that we have no knowledge of God?

In order to come to grips with such problems, scholastic philosophy developed the doctrine of analogy. In broad outline the doctrine is as follows: concepts are either equivocal, univocal, or analogous. The concept "cheerful" is equivocal when applied to weather and to a man because it applies properly only to the man. The concept "plant" is univocal when applied to ivy and to a rose bush because it refers to each of these in exactly the same way. However, if we use the concept "healthy" to refer to a man and to certain foods, we are using it analogously. Most properly, "healthy" refers to a man because he possesses the quality of health, but it can also legitimately be applied to foods, since they are the cause of health or, to use a medieval example, to urine, since its color can be a sign of health. This example we can call an analogy of attribution, because although foods and urine have a real connection to health as a cause and a sign of it, only a man has health in the completely proper sense (*formaliter*).

This, however, does not exhaust the meaning of analogy, nor does it explain completely the sense in which Thomas Aquinas, who never developed his doctrine of analogy in a complete and orderly fashion, thought concepts like being, goodness, justice, and similar perfections, which in themselves imply no limitations, could be used to refer both to God and to creatures, for God and creature are both beings in a very real and proper sense (*formaliter*) even though not in exactly the same sense. God is *esse* infinitely and necessarily; man has *esse* finitely and in dependence on God as the cause of his *esse*. Nevertheless, *esse*, or being, can be properly (*formaliter*) attributed to both. This type of analogy is often called analogy of proportion.

The doctrine of analogy must fulfill two important functions. First, it is invoked to safeguard the enormous differences between God and creatures. One should not think that in saying, for example, that God is good one has attributed goodness to God in the same way as when one says that a man is good. Analogy of attribution saves God's otherness from the dangers of anthropomorphizing him through human language. However, this type of analogy does nothing toward solving the problem of showing that human language is in some way capable of expressing something about God's nature that is properly true. Analogy of proportion, which maintains that goodness can really (*formaliter*) be attributed to God as well as to creatures, even though the meaning is not exactly the same in the case of each, is the medieval attempt to save metaphysics, or at least large areas of natural theology, the science which examines the nature of God through natural reason.

The Personal Contours of Eckhart's Ontology

God as Intellect, as Nonbeing   On the basis of this brief summary of general Thomistic thought, we can now turn to Eckhart's particular use of these metaphysical concepts, which for him too provide a structure for talking about God and his creatures. It should not surprise us to find Eckhart using them in unsettling ways that seem to contradict traditional scholastic thought. In order to enhance the idea of God he declares in the *First Parisian Question* that being or existence (*esse*) cannot be predicated of God.[2]

The problem to be discussed in this university exercise is whether existence and understanding are the same in God (*Utrum in deo sit idem esse et intelligere*). Eckhart begins by giving reasons, known to his audience from Thomas, why these are identical in God and probably in our thinking as well when we apply them to God. He then repeats an argument of his own to show that, although *esse* and *intelligere* are convertible terms in God, *esse* in its all-embracing fullness in God is the basis for knowing: God knows because he is. Such familiar lines of thought hardly prepare his hearers for what follows: he is now convinced, he continues, that this order is reversed. God *is* because he *knows* (*quia intelligit, ideo est; Q. Par.* I, n. 4; LW V, 40). Knowing is the foundation of being.

His first arguments for his position are scriptural. In the beginning was the Word, not being (John 1:1). Christ describes himself as truth (John 14:6). "Word" and "truth" refer to knowing, not to existing. On the other hand, it is creatures that *are.* This Eckhart shows by his interpretation of John 1:3 to mean that all things made (*facta*) exist, or are, through God. This leads him to his first argument from reason, an argument which also has the authority of the *Book of Causes* behind it: being is a term restricted to creatures.[3] This is why one must refer to God as understanding or knowing, and not as being or existence. Eckhart's main reason for limiting *esse* to creatures is his affirmation of the principle that something cannot be formally (*formaliter*) both in a cause and in the effect which the cause brings about. Thus if creatures are beings, we cannot call God being.

He adduces other reasons for denying that being and knowing are coextensive. For example, knowing is higher because it directs the activity of being. We perhaps have a false conception of knowing because our knowing is dependent on beings that cause it. God's knowledge, however, is the cause of beings. Knowing also has broader application than being, since beings in the mind cannot really be said to be. Indeed, it seems to be the condition of things in the mind as not really existing, but only as intelligible images of existing things, which makes them knowable. The point of all these arguments is to show clearly that it is not legitimate to use the term *esse* to describe God in any real sense. *Esse* is limited to creatures and thus is too confining to be applied to God. Knowing, on the other hand, leaving aside for the moment other implications, is of a higher and more inclusive order and thus more adequately describes God.

It is obviously not Eckhart's intention to deny God's existence. Certain concessions he makes in the course of the question further clarify his intent. First, while insisting that *esse* is not in God formally, he says he will not object if one wishes to call knowing (*intelligere*) being (*esse*) in God as long as it is clear that being in God derives from understanding. Second, while denying being of God, he allows the attribution to God of the purity of being (*puritas essendi; Q. Par.* I, n. 9; LW V, 45). Third, although God is not being, all things are contained in his knowing *virtually* (*in virtute; Q. Par.* I, n. 10; LW V, 46), that is to say, in a higher manner but not formally. Because these concessions imply some basis for comparing God and creature, however shaky, and because he admits that God can in some sense be correctly perceived as pure knowing, we would not be justified in pushing the Dominican thinker into the camp of those for whom God is simply an unknowable completely Other. Eckhart's purpose might well have been to unsettle the complacent conviction of his colleagues that in calling God being they had somehow captured the reality of God in their philosophical system. The key words from scripture which had been used at least since the time of Augustine to establish the doctrine of God as being were those of God to Moses: "I am who [I] am" (*Ego sum qui sum*; Exod. 3:14). Twice Eckhart quotes this passage to support his own differing position. God had spoken these words as one who, when asked on a dark night his identity and wishing to remain unknown, uses them instead of giving his name.[4] Here and in the concluding lines Eckhart construes this quotation, because of the reduplication of the verb "to be," to indicate not that God is that which without qualification *is*, but rather that he is the hidden being of being, the purity of being and superabundance, the root and cause of all things. This is what God wished to express in saying "ego sum qui sum."[5]

Since the *Tripartite Work* stands under the motto "Being is God" (*esse est Deus*), one could pose the question whether, at some point, a radical change occurred in Eckhart's thinking. As we shall see, there are several reasons why this is unlikely. One reason we can offer immediately is that there are echoes of the *First Parisian Question* in other works, including at least one passage of the *Tripartite Work*. In the *Book of the Parables of Genesis*, Eckhart notes that there are two aspects that must be considered in God: first, as he is true, real, primordial *esse*; second, as he is intellect. Less apodictically but unmistakably, he states that considering God as intellect seems to be a higher way of viewing God because all really existing beings are directed to goals from a higher principle, namely, the intellect.[6] Here *esse* and *intelligere* are considered less as opposites than in the *First Parisian Question*, but knowing is again considered superior.

This point of view that does not allow God to be called *esse* can also be found in the vernacular sermons, where the thought of the university professor often makes an abrupt appearance. Sudden changes of theme or point of view disrupt the logic of argumentation. Academic concerns are subordinated to a religious message. What such passages gain in eloquence and force is often bought at the price of clarity. Neither the audience nor the preacher are interested in fine distinctions, but rather in vital spiritual truths. The preacher captures well the force of these truths in a language unaccustomed to expressing them.

Often he must create the context himself. In Latin the level of educa-tion of his audience and the vocabulary of the schools provided the necessary background, but in his vernacular preaching Eckhart can count on nothing of the kind. A classic passage for denying being to God can be found in Sermon 9, where he comments on the saying "God is something that is of necessity above being."

> Everything works in being; nothing can work above its being. Fire can only work in wood. God works above being in the open where he can move. He works in nonbeing. Before being was, God was work-ing. He worked being when being did not exist. Unsophisticated theologians say God is a pure being. He is as high above being as the highest angel is above a gnat. I would be speaking as incorrectly in calling god a being as if I were to call the sun pale or black. . . . One teacher says: whoever thinks that he knows God, if he knows any-thing, he does not know God. In saying that God is not a being and is above being, I have not denied being to him, rather I have raised it up in him.[7]

Here again we see that being is restricted to creatures while God moves in regions beyond being. Yet being is not denied to God, but is ennobled or purified in him. Nevertheless, by his reference to calling the sun black, the preacher stresses the same impotence of concepts which the professor had emphasized: to call God being is to utter a statement containing more falsity than truth. In this sermon we also find the claim repeated that the *puritas essendi* of God can better be described as knowing. To perceive God as being, he tells us, is to see God in his antechamber. Intellect is the temple where God actually dwells.[8]

God as Being: *Esse est Deus*   If there are passages where Eckhart insists that we refrain from thinking of God as being, these are few compared to those where *esse* becomes the central term he uses to express his thought about God. Characteristically, but not merely for reasons of rhetorical emphasis or style, he does not choose the more traditional formula, God is *esse*, in which the predicate may have a wider area of application than the subject and which, in the present instance, would allow things other than God to be in some sense a suitable subject. Rather, the first thesis of the *Tripartite Work* and the cornerstone of Eckhart's thinking is the uncompromising: *esse* is God. If the first position, that of denying *esse* to God, has left us with many unanswered questions, this more pervasive statement of what seems to be the opposite position adds to our puzzlement. The first step in attempting to solve some of these puzzles will be to look at a few of the ways in which Eckhart uses being to describe God and his relationship to creatures.

Several formulations reproduce this basic thesis, that being is God, with the same lapidary single-mindedness of the original phrase. In commenting on Deuteronomy 6:4, "our God is the one God" (*deus noster deus unus est*), Eckhart adds by way of explanation "solus est," that is, God alone *is* (*In Exod.* n. 22; LW II, 29). He is the fullest and purest being (*plenissimum et purissimum esse; In Exod.* n. 21; LW II, 27). *Esse* is his very own characteristic and personal possession: "Gotes eigenschaft ist wesen."[9] If *wesen*, or being, was described as merely God's antechamber in contrast to the temple of knowing in German Sermon 9, in another context his house is "the unity of his being" (*diu einicheit sînes wesens;* Pr. 19; DW I, 314, 1–2).

If being is God, what is everything else? With incontrovertible logic Eckhart answers: nothing. Outside of God is nothing: "Whatever is outside of God, inasmuch as it is outside of being is not something else or something at all. For whatever is outside of being is nothing and does not exist."[10] What are creatures? In their own right, at least, they are nothing.[11] Or, in the formulation which caught the eyes of the judges in Cologne, "All creatures are a pure nothing. I do not say that they are only of little value or are anything at all; they are a pure nothing. Whatever does not have being *is* not. All creatures do not have being."[12]

These examples show how absolutely the gap between God and creatures can be formulated by the preacher and professor. Such statements must be taken very seriously as true expressions of Eckhart's philosophical positions and possibly of mystical insight. Nonetheless, these quotations have been taken from contexts which qualify them; and Eckhart, while firmly maintaining their truth, does not simply stop there as though there were nothing more to say. Being is not only a means of separating God and creatures. It also serves to show how they are one. This union is more than physical. However, given the nature of language, concepts arising from physical reality must serve to describe it. That such descriptions involve physical contradictions only enhances their power to provide insight into a metaphysical union. Thus, for example, Eckhart stresses not only the presence of God in creatures but also their presence in him.

A favorite expression for this union is calling God *esse omnium* (the being of all things). Eckhart's frequent use of this phrase is uninhibited by doctrinal implications since it rested upon the almost

apostolic authority of pseudo-Dionysius and since, in at least one instance, he quotes it as coming from Bernard of Clairvaux (*In Sap.*
n. 90; LW II, 423). Similarly, he refers to God as *anima mundi* (soul of
the world), once attributing this way of speaking to the ancients (*In
Gen.* I, n. 112; LW I, 266) and once using the phrase as his own to emphasize that it is precisely as intellect that God is able to create beings and being out of nothing (*In Sap.* n. 299; LW II, 632). The phrase
esse omnium is expanded and intensified in a Latin sermon: "omne
ens et omne omnium esse ipse est" (God himself is every single being
and every bit of the being of all things, *Serm.* VI, 1, n. 53; LW IV, 51).
He repeatedly calls our attention to the fact that *esse* comes immediately from God. As a consequence, God is closer to creatures than
they are to themselves. Paraphrasing Augustine, he writes: "The creature is outside, God is within and in the innermost parts of the
creature." God as *esse* is "intimus omnium et in intimis omnium"
(inside of all things and in the innermost of all things). He sinks himself into the essence of all things.[13]

If God as *esse* is at the center of creatures, creatures can only be
thought of as existing in God. The theologian considers this point
important enough to include in the General Prologue to the *Tripartite Work*. This is one of the meanings of Genesis 1:1, "creavit in
principio." Here, as in his interpretation of the first chapter of the
Gospel of John, Eckhart takes advantage of the ambiguity of *principium* (beginning/principle) to extract metaphysical content. That
God created *in principio* means that he created all things in himself.
To create is to give *esse*. But God is *esse*, and nothing is outside *esse*.
Therefore, he created them in himself, *in principio, in esse*. We
should not imagine creatures as somehow outside. Genesis explicitly
states that things were not just created *by* a principle but *in principio*
(*Prol. gener.* n. 17; LW I, 160–162). Similarly, Eckhart insists that all
life exists only in God because John (1:4) states: "All that came to be
had life in him" (*In Joh.* n. 62; LW III, 51). Eckhart can even tell us
"where" in God creatures exist: in the Son. But we must postpone for
the moment further exploration of this subject.

One way of understanding Eckhart's frequent statements that all
esse comes *immediate* (immediately, with no intervening means or
cause) from God is to consider God as the cause of being in creatures.
Without assuming that this interpretation exhausts his meaning, we
can readily agree that for him God alone is the cause of *esse*. In a not
isolated statement that seems to contradict his earlier mentioned
wish to reserve *esse* for God alone, he pointedly interprets Wisdom
1:14, "creavit enim, ut essent omnia," to mean that as cause of *esse*

God created all things that they might *be*: "The whole perfection of all things is their *esse*" (*In Sap.* nn. 19–20; LW II, 339–340). Secondary causes, causes that we observe empirically in the world, only bring about change (*fieri*) in being. In the schools, a frequently used division of the kinds of causes was the Aristotelian division into material, formal, efficient, and final causes. Thus, for example, the material cause of a chest is the wood it is made of; its form is the shape or structure given to the chest. These two causes are the internal causes that remain operative even after the chest has come to be. The maker of the chest who actually fashions the matter into its form is the efficient cause, and the purpose of the chest—that someone has something to store things in—is the *finis*, or final cause. The efficient cause, the cabinetmaker, builds the chest according to an idea he has of it in his mind. In a sense, then, the chest had a kind of existence in the mind of the cabinetmaker before it was produced as a real chest. The idea, the form of the object in the mind before it is wedded to matter to become an empirical object, is the exemplary cause. The exemplary cause is the Platonic element in medieval thinking on causality. The terms in the example given, a standard example and one used by Eckhart chiefly to illustrate the Platonic side of causality, must, of course, be rethought and refined if one wishes to transfer them from the level of secondary causes, those bringing about change in already existing things, to the primary cause, God, who alone is responsible for the being of all things. Nonetheless, Eckhart interprets Romans 11:36, "Ex ipso, per ipsum et in ipso sunt omnia" (All that exists comes from him; all is by him and in him) according to these causes. Since God is spirit, there is no mention of him as material cause; but *ex ipso* signifies his efficient causality by which things gain existence or attain "that they are." *Ex ipso* also seems to imply that as efficient cause God brings about the separateness of creatures from himself. *Per ipsum* indicates that God is the form of all things or the cause of forming them (forma omnium sive formans omnia). Thus they receive their "what they are" from God as well. Finally, *in ipso* signifies that God is the *finis*, or goal, of all things. God is their ultimate and exclusive goal (*Serm.* IV, 2, n. 29; LW IV, 29). While each of these causes plays a role in Eckhart's thought, it is God's formal causality that he most frequently stresses.

Turning again to *esse* and related terms as they express something about God, we find Eckhart agreeing with the conventional notion that in God essence, or *what* he is, in no way functions as a limiting principle but is identical with his infinite *esse*. The scriptural text providing the springboard for his detailed remarks is Exo-

dus 3:14, "Ego sum qui sum," the same text he quoted in the *First
Parisian Question* to bolster his contention that *esse* was not a
proper word to use in referring to God. In his *Commentary on Exodus* he devotes several pages to this verse, which is regarded as revealing several things about God, especially because of the repetition of
sum. It indicates that *esse* can be affirmed of God with a purity that
does not allow *esse* to be denied him in any sense. He possesses *esse*
in its purity and fullness. The reduplication points both to the solid-
ity of *esse* in God resting on itself as its own foundation and to the
immanent dynamism of God's *esse*, which is described as giving
birth to itself, bubbling up in itself (*in se fervens*), liquefying and
boiling up in itself and into itself (*in se ipso et in se ipsum liquescens
et bulliens*), or penetrating itself with itself, like light. Regarding God
alone can one answer the question *who* he is by saying *that* he is, and
regarding God alone can *sum* be both subject and predicate of a statement. Also, the fact that *esse* is what God is implies that he is necessary being, that is, he cannot not be and is thus eternal being (*In
Exod.* nn. 14–21; LW II, 20–28).

Wesen, the word almost always used for *esse* in the vernacular
works, is also the word with which the preacher usually translates
essentia.[14] Hence one must rely on context to determine more precisely the meaning of *wesen*. This is usually not difficult, however,
and parallels to the ideas of the Latin works are frequent. God is the
cause of being: "The noblest thing that God works in all creatures is
being."[15] "All creatures receive their being immediately (*âne mitel*)
from God" (Pr. 10; DW I, 170, 6). God himself is *wesen*. The Father,
in begetting the Son, begets "the abyss of divine being and divine
nature" (*die abgründicheit götlîches wesens und götlîcher natûre*;
Pr. 29; DW II, 84, 7). God, as he is in himself, is pure being (*lûter
wesen*; Pr. 37; DW II, 216, 5–6). At times the ambiguity of *wesen* as
both *esse* and *essentia* leads to compact, poetic formulations whose
clarity is sacrificed to richness of meaning: "God is such a being/
essence which carries within itself all beings/essences" (*Got ist ein
solch wesen, daz in im treget alliu wesen*; Pr. 71; DW III, 230, 4). In
the same sermon the preacher seems to attempt to approximate the
scholastic doctrine that being and essence are one in God, and does so
by relying on *wesen* alone, but at the same time he provides a context
that points his hearers in the right direction. He states, "One must
comprehend God as manner [of being] without manner and as being
without a limited essence (*wesen âne wesen*), for he has no limited
manner [of being]." To clarify further he adds a quotation attributed
to Bernard, to the effect that to take the measure of God one must

measure him beyond measure.[16] Instead of making the usually limiting term *essence* infinite by identifying it and filling it, as it were,
with God's boundless *esse*, Eckhart takes the reverse approach, first
predicating the term *wesen* of God and then paradoxically denying
it to him (*wesen âne wesen*). What was achieved in Latin through
reduplication (*sum qui sum*) is approximated here by affirming of
God a term with negative implications and then denying this term
to God.[17]

   If these instances have shown how Eckhart exploits the verb *esse*
in its various forms to explore the richness that is God and that creatures have from, in, and through him, they have done little to help us
understand how all these examples can be brought into a harmony
that does justice to the man as a theologian respected by his contemporaries. How, for example, can one explain his insisting in one context that God is *intelligere* and not properly *esse*, and in another that
only God is *esse*? If he alone is *esse*, what are creatures? How can
esse both express the gap between God and creatures and yet be a uni-
fying force as well? Or, if God alone is *esse* and causes *esse* in creatures, in what sense are they nothing and how are we to understand
the act of creation?

   Analogy   There are good reasons for beginning our search for answers to such questions by investigating Eckhart's concept of analogy.
First of all, Eckhart himself felt that his doctrine of analogy was misunderstood and that this led some to misunderstanding other aspects
of his thought. In his *Second Lecture on Ecclesiasticus, Chapter 24*,
he makes one of his infrequent negative comments about his contemporaries, saying that certain of them poorly understand the nature of analogy and thus rejecting it find themselves in error up to
that very day, whereas that he himself has a true understanding of
analogy, as is made clear in his (not extant) *First Book of Propositions*
(*In Eccli.* n. 53; LW II, 282). Even more striking is his repeated appeal to
the doctrine of analogy in defending himself in Cologne. He charges
that his accusers either have forgotten or have never seen how Saint
Thomas Aquinas used the distinction between univocal, equivocal,
and analogous and are objecting to this same line of thought in suggesting that his (Eckhart's) doctrines are heretical.[18] A second reason for
looking carefully at this concept is that some of the most enlightened
scholarship has centered on his notion of analogy and has confirmed
the accused Dominican's appraisal of how important it is for understanding his thought. What these scholars have clearly disagreed with
is Eckhart's claim of solidarity with Thomas on this point.[19] Al-

though analogy is not explicitly mentioned in the vernacular works, as far as I can see, its implications are everywhere. The frequent references to it in the Latin works assume that one understands the doctrine. When it is explained, the treatment is brief, so that we can well wish we were in possession of the lost or never completed section treating it in the *Book of Propositions.*

The clearest explanation of analogy is found in the *Second Lecture on Ecclesiasticus, Chapter 24,* where, as we have just mentioned, Eckhart complains that the doctrine is misunderstood. *Esse,* as that for which everything hungers, is the topic under discussion. To explain analogy, he makes use of the standard example of the term "health" and how it applies to a healthy person, to food, and to urine. He then adds, for further clarification, the example of the wreath hung outside taverns to indicate that they have wine to sell (a practice still found in parts of Europe today):

> The one and same health which is in the living creature is the very same health, not a different health, in food and in urine; thus, there is absolutely nothing of health as health [in its formal or proper sense] in food and in urine, no more so than in a stone; rather, urine is called healthy for the sole reason that it signifies that numerically same health which is [really] in the living creature, just as a wreath, which has nothing of wine in it, signifies wine. Being or existence, however, and every perfection, especially general perfections such as being, one, true, light, justice, and the like are attributed to God and creatures analogically. Thus it follows that goodness and justice and the like [in creatures] have their goodness completely from something outside them to which they are related by analogy, namely, God.[20]

This, as one can see, is what we have called analogy of attribution, which limits the real presence of the quality being attributed to only one of the objects being compared. Eckhart is here maintaining that being, goodness, and the like are only really in God and are no more in creatures than health is in a stone. In the *First Parisian Question,* where *esse* is denied to God, Eckhart's line of reasoning is really the same (even though he concludes there that one cannot call God being): "In those things which are said to be related by analogy, what is in one of the things in a real and proper sense (*formaliter*) is not so in the other." He then gives the example of health, as above, and concludes: "Since things that are caused (i.e., creatures) are beings in a proper sense, God will not be a being in this sense."[21]

This gives us at least part of the answer concerning Eckhart's seemingly contradictory statements about *esse.* If we attribute *esse* to creatures, then we must use some other term for God, such as *intel-*

ligere or *puritas essendi*. If, on the other hand, we call God *esse*, then creatures cannot in any real sense also be included in the term. They are rather in themselves pure nothing. Nowhere does Eckhart mention any kind of analogy in which both objects have an attribute *formaliter*. When he speaks of analogy, he means analogy of attribution.

One could object that food is much more than something merely external to health. It causes health. Similarly, urine is not just some arbitrary sign for health. Its composition or color is an effect of the healthy organism. It is probably to anticipate such an interpretation, one that would see more than an external relationship of food or urine to the health of a person, that Eckhart, while retaining the traditional example of health, adds comments that make his meaning clear: the wreath must certainly be considered an arbitrary sign for wine with no real connection of any sort existing between them, and health cannot properly be attributed to a stone.

Thus, in the *Tripartite Work* with its basic thesis that *esse* is God, and in other contexts with this perspective, creatures are—in a much more radical sense than is usual in scholastic thought—nothing in themselves. All medieval thinkers stress the complete dependence of creatures on God, both for their coming to be and for their being sustained in existence. For them too it would mean the annihilation of the creature if God were to withdraw his sustaining hand for only an instant. Nevertheless, creatures are usually considered to have a being which, though given them, is really their own. This does not seem to be true for Eckhart: "The things which are analogous to something (i.e., creatures) have nothing in themselves by which they are in a positive way rooted to the form which is the basis of the analogy. . . . Therefore, every created being has positively from God and firmly rooted in God, (and) not in its own created self, being, living, and knowing."[22] In this vein he interprets John 1:11, "He came unto his own" (*in propria venit*): "Through his coming and presence God immediately and with no other agent brings about in all things being, unity, truth, and goodness; but, of course, in the manner of analogy."[23] In other words, creatures have no being, unity, truth, or goodness in themselves as creatures. God is their being, unity, truth, and goodness.

Images of *Esse*   This unusual conception is certainly not simple to grasp stated in this abstract manner, and it leaves many questions unanswered. Fortunately for minds less gifted in metaphysical thinking, Eckhart expresses the same ideas through images, not only in sermons for the unlearned but also in his professional Bible commentaries. These images give added definition to his ideas and serve to strengthen one's hold on them.

The passage from Ecclesiasticus which occasioned Eckhart's explanation of analogy was "They who eat me will hunger for more, they who drink me will thirst for more" (24:29). Many of his extensive comments on the passage are couched in the language of the schools, but beneath them all is the Augustinian thought of the infinite desire of creation for its infinite goal. Those things whose goal is infinite continually eat and drink, and their appetite grows the more they consume (*In Eccli.* n. 42; LW II, 271). God is infinite truth, goodness, and being; and all things that are true and good and are eat and drink of him because they are and are true and are good. They continue to hunger and thirst because he is infinite (*In Eccli.* n. 43; LW II, 272). Eckhart introduces Avicenna's statement that everything desires *esse* and its own perfection as *esse*, adding, "From beings there is no *esse* nor is the root of being in them." Then, to clarify further, he says that every concrete being (creature) "does not have from itself but from something else, which is higher, the *esse* for which it hungers and thirsts and which it desires. Wherefore, in the creature itself *esse* does not attach itself nor adhere nor take its origin."[24] This image of the creature's consuming yet continuing to hunger after *esse* captures well the dynamism of the creature's utter dependence on *esse*, an *esse* which is within it yet, coming from above, refuses to join itself to the creature as such in any firm or lasting way.

Another frequently used comparison, one which has the idea of *root* in common with the one just mentioned, is that of the sun's illuminating force. In the first chapter of the Gospel of John, light and darkness provide the setting for the manner in which *esse* comes to creatures: "The light shines in the darkness, and the darkness did not take hold of it" (John 1:5). Light is *esse*, and for a creature not to be illuminated is not to be (*In Joh.* n. 151; LW III, 125). Light is God, and the darkness is everything created. The light of *esse* illumines creatures, but it functions as an analogical cause and not as heat—a univocal cause—functions. Heat takes root in the medium being heated so that the medium remains warm after the cause is removed. Heat causes the medium to become warm little by little, part by part. Heat inheres in the medium and enables it to be a cause of heat. Not so light. Light illuminates the medium all at once, and its effect is immediately gone when the source of light is removed. Nor can the medium become a source or cause of light. More particularly, light in no way inheres in the illumined medium or takes root in it.[25] Just as air is permeated and illumined by light that remains utterly separate from it, so the creature has no hold of any kind on *esse*. And not to be illuminated is not to be.

A third metaphor, and perhaps the most effective, is that of the image in a mirror. Its application extends to explaining the relationship of Son to Father as well as that of creature to *esse*. Eckhart explains what makes the image apt for such purposes: "An image receives its being completely and immediately from that whose image it is, and it has one being with it and is the same being."[26] On the basis of this definition of image we can understand the preacher's question in another sermon: "One can ask where the being of the image most properly is: in the mirror or in that from which it originates? It is more properly in that from which it originates. The image [of me] is in me, from me, to me. As long as the mirror stands exactly opposite my face, my image is in it; if the mirror were to fall, the image would cease to exist."[27] Eckhart's actual application here is to the dependence of spiritual beings, angels, on God as understanding. However, it does not seem illegitimate to extend it to all creation. Creatures are like mirrors, empty in themselves but capable of reflecting the image of something real as long as this reality is opposite them. Creatures, like mirrors, are fragile and receive passively an image of being which is really in the object outside them, projecting itself onto them. In themselves they are empty of content, capable only of capturing a mere image of *esse*. In like manner, the just man receives justice totally from justice itself: "Virtues, justice and the like, are certain fleeting shapes rather than something molded in a permanent medium that remains fixed within or takes root in the virtuous person, and they are in continual flux, like brilliant light in a medium or an image in a mirror."[28]

In the *Book of Divine Consolation* there is a passage that can justifiably be taken as a description of the *esse* of creatures even though no equivalent for the word *esse* is mentioned. While in other contexts Eckhart speaks of God's gifts to man, here he wishes to be more specific:

> Everything that is good and goodness God has loaned him, not given him. Anyone who sees the truth knows that God, the heavenly Father, gives everything that is good to the Son and to the Holy Spirit; but to his creatures he gives nothing good, he lets them have it as a loan. The sun gives heat to the air, but makes a loan of light; and that is why, as soon as the sun goes down, the air loses the light, but the heat remains there, because the heat is given to the air to possess as its own.[29]

Because he mentions the difference between the effects of the sun in causing light analogically and heat univocally, we can legitimately assume that being also is not bestowed upon creatures as a gift but only as a loan (*ze borge*). While this image confers a bit more stability on the being of creatures, it indicates that their being does not really belong to them at all. In addition, "loan" implies a temporary condition that is brought to an end through a return of the object loaned.

Other images are used incidentally: that of the creature, which is nothing in itself, as a worthless copper coin that has been covered with the silver or gold of *esse* which it has from without, from God, and hence has the appearance of value (*In Joh.* n. 308; LW III, 256); and that of creatures being a mere shadow of being (*umbra quaedam ipsius esse*), so that once the object casting the shadow is removed, the shadow disappears as well (*Serm.* XXXIV, 3, n. 352; LW IV, 305). In a German sermon Eckhart effectively depicts the dependence of creatures by saying that they have no being because their being hangs suspended (*swebet*) from God's presence.[30] *Sweben* is difficult to translate, but it conjures up the image of something floating or fluttering aimlessly this way and that. In Middle High German literature it is often used to indicate human indecisiveness.

What is constantly emphasized in all these images is the fleeting, ephemeral nature of being in creatures. One can well understand why students of mysticism have often stressed a similarity between the medieval Dominican and Eastern mystics. Such comparisons are not without foundation. However, because these images, before all else, have the function in Eckhart's thought of illustrating his conception of *esse*, a conception truly his own yet expressed in the terminology and within the context of medieval scholasticism, they are most valuable and most precisely understood within this context and easily lose exactness and focus in comparative studies.

Further Clarification of *Esse* We have seen that Eckhart conceives of analogy in such a way that only God is truly *esse* and that creatures no more have *esse* than a stone has health. We must conclude that his calling creatures *pure nothing* is not just rhetorical exuberance but an important facet of his outlook. However, analogy so conceived is not Eckhart's sole approach to investigating *esse*, and we must not think that he denied the existence of what we might call empirical reality. His biblical commentaries are filled with long discussions of the nature of the physical universe and show his obvious interest in it for its own sake. Nor is there any reason to push him into the camp of pure pantheism. Despite the *esse est Deus* thesis, there are several indications that he considers creatures truly distinct from God. The being-nothing relationship of God and creatures is true, but it expresses only one side of his thought. It is now necessary to explore other formulations which provide the proper perspective for this daring thesis.

Besides the strict *esse est Deus* thesis, we find milder formulations. For example, in explaining how the second *sum* in *ego sum qui sum* excludes any kind of negation of *esse* to God, he states: "Everything this side of God, insofar as it is this side of *esse*, is being (*ens*) and nonbeing (*non ens*), and some *esse* can be denied it since it is below *esse* and this side of *esse* and thus negation is possible regarding it" (*In Exod.* n. 74; LW II, 77). There is nothing outside of (*extra*) God or *esse*, but one can speak of creatures as beings which are below (*sub*) or this side of (*citra*) God.

Also, although he prefers his categorical formulation (*potest dici subtilius*) in interpreting Wisdom 7:8 ("Compared with her [Wisdom], I held riches as nothing"), he cites with favor a passage from the *Book of 24 Philosophers*: "God is the opposite of nothing through the mediation of being" (*deus est oppositio nihil mediatione entis*) and interprets it to mean that just as created being exceeds nothing, so God exceeds or surpasses created being (*In Sap.* nn. 90–91; LW II, 424). This would seem to yield the proportion nothing is to creature as creature is to God, allowing us to see created being as a middle point between nothing and God. The irony of the thought, however, is immediately apparent. There is no middle point between nothing and infinity. Created being is still infinitely removed from God. Nevertheless, in such a proportion it is conceived as different from nothing. While preferring his own more extreme phrasing, Eckhart at least indulgently approves of this way of expressing it. And he himself had had no objection to attributing "being" to creatures as long as one did not also apply this term to God.

Another important point that has an extremely wide application across several areas of his thought, as he tried without much success at his trial to convince his judges, is what we might call the *in quantum* principle. In his Latin works, which often manifest a more careful mode of expression than the vernacular sermons, the qualifying phrase introduced by *in quantum* or *utpote* (insofar as) is everywhere. In the trial documents he explains it thus: "The words 'insofar as,' that is, a reduplication, exclude from the term in question everything that is other or foreign to it even according to reason" (McGinn, p. 72; *RS*, Théry, p. 186). As an example of what he means, he notes that, although being and understanding are the same in God, God is not evil because he knows evil. Similarly, since evil is not being but rather a lack of being, the devil, *insofar as he is evil*, does not exist (*In Sap.* n. 55; LW II, 382). This principle has bearing on Eckhart's claim that creatures are pure nothing because in claiming this he is speaking of the creature *insofar as it is creature*. This reduplication of the word "creature," as he says, excludes every other aspect of the object signified by the word "creature" and concentrates totally on the object precisely as creature and as nothing else. Thus the same creature that will be called the only-begotten Son of God, or the just man, or be referred to as being one with God, is being considered purely as creature when the claim is made that it is pure nothing. The concrete and, except for purely spiritual creatures, empirically perceived, created object is not what Eckhart is calling pure nothing. By repetition of the term "creature," he removes everything from the object except its "creatureliness." The predicate "pure nothing" applies only to this aspect of the object. This is true even if the method of concentrating on or separating out this one aspect of the object from everything else can be accomplished only in the mind. If one calls this mental operation abstraction, one must be careful to remember that for Eckhart this was not just a mental exercise. Although the abstracted aspect is not in any physical sense separate from the other aspects in the object, it corresponds to something real in the object. To say that a created object, insofar as it is created, is pure nothing expresses a real truth about the object and not just about our thinking about the object. However, this does not exclude the possibility of making quite different statements about the object, *insofar as* it is considered under a different aspect. Just how far Eckhart pushes this principle is made strikingly clear in a passage where he employs the phrase "Man . . . insofar as he is God" (*homo . . . in quantum deus*; *In Joh.* n. 107; LW III, 92).

Another method Eckhart uses in attempting to describe what *esse* means when predicated of God and creature is drawing comparisons from the realm of scholastic thought, more particularly as it had incorporated notions used by Aristotle primarily to explain the metaphysical composition and operation of physical being. As we shall see, the *in quantum* principle is much in evidence as a necessary qualification when Eckhart approaches the *esse* of creatures by means of such comparisons.

The distinction between *potency* and *act* provides him with one such comparison. Aristotle had introduced these principles to explain how something could undergo a change and yet remain basically the same thing. A young man standing beneath the window of his beloved suddenly bursts into song. The man remains a man, and the change is from a silent man to one singing. Some principle had to be present in the man even before he began to sing to account for the sudden change in him. Such changes are not without a preparatory basis which precedes them. The change was one from a condition of merely possessing the ability or potential to sing to a condition of actual singing, in other words, a change from potency to act. Eckhart uses the principles of potency and act to explain creatures' *esse* in conjunction with the image of hunger and thirst that are never stilled. The creature is, "insofar as it is in itself, bare and just potency for *esse*. The potency is appetite and thirst for *esse* itself."[31] In itself the creature is related to *esse* as potency to act. The paradoxical nature of potency, however, is that as such it does not exist. The potential to sing is precisely not singing. Only when fulfilled by or reduced to act does potency really exist. Thus creatures, which Eckhart here calls beings (*entia*), in themselves exist only potentially and not actually. This fits in well with his frequent assertion that creatures are "a pure nothing." And yet, in another sense, potency differs from nothing. A man could never perform the act of singing if he did not have the potential to sing. If we consider the *lack* of potency as more truly pure nothing, the creature as potency is somehow a contributing factor to its real existence.

A second comparison is that of creature and *esse* to *matter* and *form*. If the principle of form is necessary to explain classes of objects differing from each other, like trees and horses, there must be another principle to explain the existence of several individuals within a class. This second principle is matter. Of course, neither matter nor form exists separately. They are principles necessary to explain material things. Matter is in itself pure potentiality and is "activated" by its form. Change is really a change of forms. Matter as potentiality is capable of assuming all forms. As a material object changes, the new form is educed out of matter's potentiality. It can never be without a form. Eckhart noted two characteristics of the metaphysical union of matter and form which seem to make it apt for such a comparison. First, it illustrates well the total and immediate union of God and creature: "The form of fire with nothing mediating envelops all at once with its whole self the whole essence of its matter and forms by penetrating it not part by part but [by penetrating] individual parts through the whole."[32] Second, because of its infinite potentiality for forms, it "hungers and thirsts" continually after other forms, never resting satisfied with the form it has and never finding the form of all forms (*In Eccli.* n. 42; LW II, 271). The potentiality of matter/

creatures, their nothingness, their emptiness, is their capacity for form, for *esse*. Because of change, however, the composition of matter and form is unstable, precarious. Only a composition with the form of all forms would provide permanence and stability. One matter-form composition is especially singled out for comparison with creature and *esse*: the body-soul unity. As in the case of the form of fire, it is the total immediate oneness of the soul with the body as a whole and with its parts that is emphasized (*Prol. prop.* n. 14; LW I, 174).

Two remarks are appropriate before leaving these comparisons. First, Eckhart speaks of two types of union: those that are and those that should or shall come about. In exploring the union of *esse* and creatures, we have restricted the investigation to descriptions of the creature as it is constituted in its nature. However, especially in the German sermons, the preacher speaks of a unity between God and creature which is not simply a metaphysical fact but rather something one must strive to achieve. This kind of union will occupy us later. Second, the comparisons noted here have in common that they are taken from the realm of the metaphysical principles constituting creatures. The implication is that *esse* and creature can well be understood as principles through which (*entia quibus*) a thing is constituted. To consider *esse* part of the makeup of the created being is not an unusual position. However, the *esse* that is meant is not the same *esse* of creatures that Thomas Aquinas posited. Thomas considered the *esse* of a creature to be a "con-created" principle which, together with *essentia*, comes about at the moment of creation, raising the creature and its *essentia* from possibly existing to really existing. He emphasized, of course, that God as *esse subsistens* or pure *esse* was *esse* in the full sense, whereas the *esse* of a creature only participated in the perfection of *esse*. Nonetheless, the *esse* by which creatures pass from merely possible to really existing retains, in the thought of Thomas, a degree of independence from God as *esse subsistens* which makes the complete identification of God and creature impossible. For Eckhart, however, *esse* is simply God.

The Implications of God's Oneness   The preceding comments do not in themselves give a very satisfying explanation of how Eckhart's conception of analogy fits together with other ideas characteristic of him, but it is a beginning. The most immediate problems remaining have to do with the following. Eckhart's remarks on *esse* and creatures lead us to conceive of the union of God and creature as that existing in one being. At the same time, the difference between them is stated as being the difference between infinite existence and pure nothing. Both themes exist side by side in the writings of many Christian mystics, but no one tries, to the extent that Eckhart does, to provide an academically acceptable philosophical basis for these themes. In the case of most mystics such themes are founded on personal experience alone, and no attempt is made to claim academic validity for writings based on such experiences. This difference between Eckhart and others in the mystical tradition was a major source of his difficulties once he stood before the ecclesiastical tribunal. By and large, he defended the incriminated doctrines philosophically and theologically. One accusation lodged against him both then and later was that he went beyond the boundaries of orthodoxy in his extreme formulations, on the one hand making God and creature one while at the same time throwing up an insuperable barrier between them. The union, described as similar to that of potency and act, matter and form, body and soul, would seem to destroy the difference necessary to protect God's independence from and transcendence over creatures. At the same time, the barrier remains too great to allow any grounds for likeness. Eckhart's doctrine of analogy demands that we call creatures nothing if we call God *esse*, or that if we attribute *esse* to creatures we must call God something else. The essential feature of this doctrine of analogy is that it is not legitimate to join God and creature in any single concept. Two questions must be pursued if we are to dispel some of the uneasiness engendered by this paradox of union and separation. First, does Eckhart anywhere employ a vocabulary that deals more successfully with this paradox? Can one find in his works an approach to the problem which more successfully reconciles the uncompromising character of separation, which is a consequence of his teaching on analogy, with his equally resolute insistence on union? Second, what is it in the metaphysical composition of creatures that allows them to be one with God, to have God in them and them in God, pure nothing though they are?

To begin with the first question, God is often described as the purity and fullness of being (*puritas et plentitudo essendi*). God is the "purity of being," as we have seen, because nothing else is being (*esse*); and he is "the fullness of being" because his *esse* includes everything that is, all *esse*. Both these aspects are intended when Eckhart says that God is one. More frequently among his contemporaries, the term "one" (*unum*) stressed just the purity of oneness. God as one was utterly without division or duality in his being and was totally separate from all other things (*indivisum in se, divisum a quolibet alio*). For Eckhart, however, for whom *esse* is God and God is *esse omnium*, calling God one also states something about his relationship to creatures. Because the *esse* of creatures is, in a sense to be more precisely determined, God, they are not in every sense excluded when one says that God is one. In a sermon on the text *Deus est unus* (Gal. 3:20), he states this second aspect of oneness explicitly: "One is indistinct from all things. All things and the fullness of *esse* are in him [God] by reason of indistinction or unity."[33] That God's oneness implies both separateness from and union with creatures is treated at length twice in the Latin commentaries, once by contrasting the concepts "distinct" and "indistinct" (*In Sap.* nn. 144–157; LW II, 481–494) and once through the opposition of the terms "similar" and "dissimilar" (*In Exod.* nn. 110–126; LW II, 109–117). His line of argument is very abstract, but because it represents an important complement to his thinking on analogy, it is necessary to view at least its essential points.

In the *Commentary on Wisdom*, arguments are offered for the contradictory statements that nothing is so distinct as God and creature (n. 154; pp. 489–490) and that nothing is so one and indistinct as God and creature (n. 155; pp. 490–491). His reasons for the first thesis are: (1) Things that are indistinct from each other are more distinct than two things that are distinct. His example: something having no color is more distinct from a colored object than this is from another differently colored object. Creatures are by nature distinct from each other. God as one is indistinct from everything. (2) "One" is not a number but is the opposite of number and beyond number. God as one cannot be numbered. Creatures fall into the category of things that can be numbered. Number and one, and thus creature and God, are opposites and completely distinct. (3) Things that are distinguished by indistinction are the more distinct, the more indistinct they are. Conversely, because they are distinguished by their distinction, the more distinct they are, the more indistinct they are. Therefore, the more distinct God and creatures are, the more indistinct they are; and the more indistinct they are, the more distinct they are.

His reasons for the second thesis (that God and creatures are indistinct) are: (1) No things are so one or indistinct as creature (*ens*) and *esse*, potency and act, matter and form. This is the relationship of creature to God. (2) Nothing is so indistinct or one as God's oneness and the plurality of creatures which his oneness constitutes. (3) That which distinguishes creature from God, like plurality as opposed to oneness, or createdness as opposed to *esse*, is precisely what makes them indistinct.

The point of these mental gymnastics is to show that contradictory terms can be used to describe the relationship of God and creature, and that both terms express a philosophical truth. What is more, the contradictory terms "distinct" and "indistinct" are not just opposed. Each term becomes the necessary condition for correctly understanding the other. Because these intertwining arguments are difficult to follow, it might be well to inspect similar lines of thought where "similar" and "dissimilar" are opposed.

Eckhart's argument has the same structure as in the previous case: Nothing is so dissimilar as creator and creature, and nothing is so similar. He then immediately gives an indication of the tension and interaction in this opposition by adding: Nothing is so dissimilar and similar *to an equal degree at the same time (pariter)* than God and creature (*In Exod.* n. 112; LW II, 110). The arguments for dissimilarity are: (1) Nothing is so dissimilar as that which is indistinct is to that which is distinct. For example, man and non-man are more dissimilar than two human beings. God is indistinct from all creatures. Creatures are distinct from each other by the fact of their being created. (2) No greater dissimilarity is possible than between the infinite (God) and the finite (creature). (3) The greatest dissimilarity exists between things that have no genus in common, and God is completely beyond any genus. The arguments for similarity are: (1) Creatures receive and have *esse* totally through relationship and dependence on God (*esse*), and their *esse* is completely derived or copied (*exemplatum*) from God. (2) *Esse*, truth, goodness, and the like, which are in the innermost of creatures, are God. (3) Creatures live and are in God. The addition of *pariter*, the simultaneity and proportionality of similarity and dissimilarity, is based on the argument that the dissimilarity is the similarity just as the indistinction is the distinction. And yet he adds that no similarity may be posited between God and creatures because the more one posits it, the less one posits it, and the more dissimilar the similarity becomes.[34]

One has to admit that the strength of these arguments does not lie in their conceptual clarity. An Abelard or a modern logician would find much to object to in them. Certainly the term "indistinct" is in need of much further precision than it receives through the examples used to explain it. Yet, rather than dwell on possible deficiencies, we should ask what the force of the argument is and what function it fulfills. Eckhart insisted, as few have, on the insuperable distance separating God and creature, but at the same time maintained a unity between them that disturbed orthodox sensibilities. This paradox was as much a problem he found himself confronted with as it was his own invention. The biblical point of departure for his thought on dissimilarity and similarity is the prohibition in Exodus (20:4) of making any likeness of the divinity, with its theological implication that God cannot be grasped by the human mind. He then juxtaposes this text to two others: one that speaks of the creation of man in God's image and likeness (Gen. 1:26) and one in which John avows that we shall be similar to God and see him as he is (1 John 3:2). His explanations of dissimilar and similar are an ingenious attempt to reconcile these conflicting scriptural passages. God and creature are infinitely dissimilar, as Exodus maintains. This infinite dissimilarity in which God is everything and the creature is nothing is the basis for the similarity between them. Everything that creatures have and are is from God and is God. Hence the great similarity and oneness of God and creature. And this similarity or oneness is, in turn, the basis for the infinite dissimilarity.

This type of thought process in which opposites are reconciled is usually called dialectic, and we are certainly justified in saying that Meister Eckhart practices it in the examples above.[35] One can discover many related types of expression when he attempts to describe God or God-creature relationships, so that one can rightfully claim that it was for him an important mode of expression. However, care must be taken to avoid misunderstanding what is meant in this case by dialectic. Most important, the basis for dialectic here is the limited capacity of the human intellect. Man cannot grasp God (and consequently the divine aspects of creatures) as he really is by capturing him within a system of concepts and logic. Hence, in his attempt to approximate the truth concerning God, man must have recourse to placing opposing concepts in dialectical relationships. Eckhart is not describing a process occurring in God or in reality. God's nature is perfect and cannot change or become in any way. The process involved is one of human thought and exists in the human mind and because of the human condition. Only creatures are capable of becoming, and the process through which they divest themselves of their nothingness and become one with God is almost exclusively the theme of the vernacular sermons.

Ens Creatum: **The Composition of Creatures**   Still to be examined is how Eckhart conceived creatures to be constituted. Which concepts does he employ, and what distinctions does he make? The difficulty in responding to this lies largely in the fact that his abundant remarks on the subject are couched in a variety of terms. One is easily overwhelmed with the wealth of material to draw on. The unanimity of the most knowledgeable critics regarding the more general issues and their divergent opinions concerning particulars bear witness to this. The area is still in need of much detailed study. We shall attempt to describe the main features of Eckhart's thought, especially those features that furnish the basis for understanding the major topics in his vernacular sermons.

To understand Eckhart's conception of creatures it is, first of all, important to realize just how much he owes to the Platonic tradition. While it is an oversimplification to categorize him simply as a Platonist, it is generally admitted that in key areas of his thought his views are Platonic. Certainly, he also makes use of the Aristotelian system, whose acceptance in the schools had been pioneered by Thomas; and much of the misunderstanding surrounding Eckhart has arisen from the assumption by many that, because he frequently availed himself of their terms, he stood closest to Thomas and Aristotle. But he quotes no one as often as he does the great Christian Platonist of the West, Augustine. And his Platonic tendencies are certainly part of the reason for wishing to call God understanding rather than being. For a Platonist, ideas and their counterpart, the intellect, represent a higher form of reality than mere being. Also, Eckhart's thought, in contrast to that of Aristotle and Thomas, does not start with an examination and explanation of the physical world and from there ascend to universal principles. In his view, the center from which all considerations set forth and to which they return is not things; rather, it is the ideas of things, from which the things themselves derive. For a Christian Platonist these ideas are in God and are God.

One clearly Platonic feature of Eckhart's doctrine on creatures is the emphasis on their formal cause. He does not, of course, deny that God is the efficient and final cause of creatures as well, as his repeated interpretation of the Pauline phrase *ex ipso* (efficient cause), *per ipsum* (formal cause), and *in ipso* (final cause) attests. Nevertheless, it is the formal causality of God as *esse* that receives a preeminent position. His frequent comparison of creatures (*entia*) and being (*esse*) to the relationship of white in an object to whiteness, when speaking of causality without specifying what kind of causality, indicates that formal causality was primary in his mind. Thus, for example, "Being itself is the cause of all things which are beings, just as whiteness itself is the cause of all things that are white. But God is being itself . . . and will be the cause of all things which are beings."[36] *Esse* is the form that confers existence on creatures, just as *unum*, *verum*, and *bonum* confer unity, truth, and goodness on them. Such general terms as these are not to be confused with accidents in things. Accidents depend on the substantial beings or objects themselves. They are characteristics of an existing thing and are limited to it. For example, size and location are accidents dependent on a physical being like man. The general terms are quite the opposite. They are beforehand. They are not qualities deriving from things. Things derive from them. Thus a concrete being (*ens*) is much less real than its formal cause *esse*. *Esse* is the formal cause par excellence. It is the "act and perfection, the actualization of all things, even of forms" (*Prol. gener.* n. 8; LW I, 152–153).

What does the individual being contribute to its composition? Nothing. Concerning *hoc ens* Eckhart says: "When I say *this* being or this or that one (thing) or this or that true (thing), the words *this* and *that* add absolutely nothing to the content of being, unity, truth, or goodness to this being that is one, true, and good" (*Prol. prop.* n. 4; LW I, 168). Since it is derived totally from these "forms" existing prior to it, the individual as such adds nothing to its own being. Especially in the Prologue to the *Work of Propositions*, which is devoted to the nature of *esse* and those terms that are convertible with it, Eckhart strives to clarify his position. And it is the Christian-Platonic relationship of things to their forms which is most in evidence.

When we compare these thoughts with those of Thomas on the nature of creatures composed of *esse* and *essentia*, striking differences become apparent. For Thomas, *esse* and *essentia* are metaphysical principles that account for the existence and nature of a being. *Esse* is the principle actualizing the *essentia* and causing it to exist. But it is a created *esse* limited by the *essentia* in each case. God's causality is necessary to explain both how this *esse* came to be and how it is sustained. However, this *esse* is not identical with God's *esse*, though it participates in the perfection of *esse* which is God's *esse*. Despite their mutability and contingency, creatures possess an *esse* which is really a creature's own and which *in itself* is the basis for real similarity with God's *esse* because it shares in the perfection of the divine being.[37] Although the notion of participation in Thomas narrows the distance of his thought from that of Eckhart, it nevertheless remains true that Thomas attributes a certain independence to creatures which is totally lacking in his fellow Dominican's thought. For Eckhart, God alone is and really has *esse*. While *esse* is separate from and untouched by creatures, at the same time it sinks itself into the essences of things so that they might be. No distance can be greater than that between the nothingness of creatures and the infinite *esse* which is God. Yet nothing can be closer than the air and the light which illumines it, than the mirror and the image in it, than the body and the soul which "animates" it; and these images express the closeness of creature and God.

At his trial in Cologne the defendant gave an explanation which, at first glance, seems to contradict this and give creatures an *esse* which is really their own. In defending his thesis *esse est Deus*, Eckhart states that this is true "concerning absolute being" (*de esse absoluto*) but not true "concerning being formally inhering" in a created being (*de esse formaliter inherente*; RS, Théry, p. 193). However, this distinction must be viewed in the light of his teaching as a whole and of his frequent references to analogy in his *Defense*. This *esse formaliter inherens* seems to be reminiscent of Thomas's *esse* of creatures, but it is not the same. Eckhart is very insistent, as we have seen in his doctrine of analogy, that a term like *esse* can be applied in a proper sense only to one of the objects being compared, that, for example, health is only in a living being and no more in urine than in a stone. Thus *esse* is only properly in the *esse absolutum*, which is God. The *esse formaliter inherens* is not really *esse* and has no real basis within itself for being similar to *esse absolutum*. It is at best a sign of *esse*, as the wreath hung outside the tavern is a sign of the wine within.

It is especially the adjective *inherens* which forces one to interpret Eckhart's distinction in his *Defense* as we have done. When describing the *esse* through which creatures are, he points out, as we have seen, that it in no way inheres in or takes root in creatures, no more than the light of the sun takes root in the air. When in his *Defense* he speaks of an *esse* that formally inheres in the creature, he is not talking about the same *esse* that throughout his works is that by which, through which, and in which creatures exist. *Esse* cannot be formally in both God and creature. The *First Parisian Question* makes clear that if we call this *esse* in creatures formal *esse*, then we can only talk of a purity of being in God. And it is this purity of being, this *esse* which is God, that, while not inhering, animates the nothingness of creatures that they might be.

Esse Formale and Esse Virtuale   The *esse formale* of creatures, this nothingness of theirs that points to God's purity and plentitude of being, is only part of Eckhart's explanation of how creatures are constituted. The *esse formale* of creatures is a sign pointing to their own origin as well, where their being is one with the being of God. Just as one cannot limit one's consideration to his discussion of the distinctness and dissimilarity between God and creation to the neglect of his statements on their indistinctness and similarity, so it would be wrong to emphasize the *esse formale* of creatures without mentioning their *esse virtuale*. This latter *esse* actually plays a much larger role in Eckhart's thought than the nothingness of creatures because it is both a metaphysical fact and a mystical goal for man. Especially as the latter it receives prominent attention in some of his vernacular sermons.

To understand *esse virtuale* as part of the metaphysical makeup of creatures, we can return to the example of the chest and the artisan who makes it. The artisan, before he actually begins constructing the chest, has an idea or a mental conception according to which he directs his efforts in making the chest. Thus it exists as an idea before it exists as a thing. This holds true for anything owing its origin to a cause acting according to its intellect and, although the strictly human features of the example must be removed, will therefore hold true for God in creating the world. Since at least the time of Augustine the preexistence of creatures in God as ideas or *rationes* had been a part of Christian thought. Few thinkers, however, were as consistently Platonic as Eckhart in the value they gave to the *ratio* or *esse virtuale* of creatures. Others considered the *esse formale* to be what bestows real existence on creatures. Traditional Christian thought concentrates more on the real and independent character of the *esse formale* of creatures than on their existence in the mind of God. Eckhart does not seem to share this view, and his description of the two *esse* shows just how seriously he took the etymology of *virtuale*. For him this *esse* is that which gives power to creatures. In their *esse formale* they are weak or nothing:

> Every creature has a twofold being. One is in the causes of its origin, ultimately in the Word of God; and this being is strong and solid. This is why the knowledge of transitory things is not transitory, but strong and stable; the thing is known in its causes. There is another being of things in nature which things have in their proper form. The first is called virtual being, the second is formal being which is generally weak and inconstant. . . .
>
> Again it should be noted that being in its power or virtual being is by far more noble and outstanding than the formal being of things.[38]

In his *Book of the Parables of Genesis*, which deals extensively with the act of creation, Eckhart gives his most thorough explanation of the formal and virtual being of creatures.[39] He explains that when a being endowed with intellect makes something, the idea of the thing must exist in the intellect before the thing itself. The idea is more perfect than the existing thing because the thing is transitory while the idea of it is eternal. The idea is pure and unmixed. The existing thing is mixed with matter and imperfect. For example, pure gold is never found in reality, but only in the mind as an idea. Circles pass away; the idea of a circle is eternal. The ideas of things cannot be considered simply as God, since this would compromise God's unity and the utter simplicity of his nature. Nor are they simply identical with things, since they are not touched by the imperfections, transitoriness, and mixed nature of these. Things had an *esse verum* (true being) before they came to be, as paradoxical as this sounds. The *esse virtuale* does not cease when a thing comes to be and receives an *esse formale*. It continues to be the "higher reality" of the thing, as opposed to the nothingness conferred by the *esse formale*. The *esse virtuale* or *ratio* is rather completely within and completely outside the existing thing, preserving itself in transcendence while uniting with the created thing to make it more than the nothingness it is, insofar as (*in quantum*) it is a creature.

The *ratio*, which is the *quod quid est*, or essence, is not something that is created or able to be created because it belongs to the realm of the intellect. Applying the thought patterns most in evidence in the *First Parisian Question*, we could say that it belongs in the realm of *intelligere* (understanding), while the *esse formale* of the creature remains on the other side of the insurmountable barrier where *esse* is the first of created things but is limited to the realm of creatures. *Ratio* or essence is *non ab alio*, that is, it is in need of no external cause for its "existence" as a third area of reality that is neither simply God nor creature. It is only the *esse formale*, that constitutes things in their distinctness from God and in their nothingness, which, paradoxically, is in need of God's efficient causality. It is only as existing creatures that things are *ab alio*, as the words of the Book of Wisdom attest: "He created all things so that they might be" (*creavit ut essent omnia*; *In Sap.* n. 20; LW II, 340–342). The essences of creatures, therefore, the *what* they are as opposed to their *esse* or *that* they are, are related to the *esse formale* of creatures, of creatures as such, in much the way that the *esse* which is God is related to the *esse formale* of creatures. The essence or *ratio* transcends the creature as such and, existing in God (*virtualiter*), is firmer and nobler there than in the creature. At the same time, it is within the creature but remains untouched by the weaknesses inherent in really existing creatures. The relation of the *ratio* to creature is the subject when Eckhart interprets John 1:5, "and the light shines in the darkness, and the darkness did not grasp it." The light is the *ratio* which alone shines in the darkness of creatures, allowing them to be known; but it is not completely contained within the creature or by the creature, nor is it mixed with or grasped by the creature. Eckhart then quotes the *Book of Causes*, which states that the first cause of things rules them without mixing with them. And the first cause of a thing is its *ratio*, its *logos*, its *verbum in principio*.[40]

Verbum in Principio: The Word in Its Principle With *logos* and *verbum in principio* we pass from a consideration of the relationship of the ideas to created things to considering the ideas in their relationship to God. It is the Son, the Word in the Principle (Father), the *ratio*, as Augustine says, which is "full of all the living and unchangeable ideas that are all one in it."[41] This preexistence and continued existence of things as ideas in the Son is the source of all their nobility, which stands opposed to their nothingness. It is also the necessary precondition for actual creation because "without him [the Son] was made nothing that was made" (John 1:3), and the Son is the principle in which God created heaven and earth (*In principio creavit deus caelum et terram*, Gen. 1:1; *In Joh.* nn. 57–58; LW III, 47–48). Although Eckhart does not belabor the point, as strictly Neoplatonic authors often do, the actual creation of things—the act that confers on them their *esse formale* and that alone requires God's action as efficient cause—is described as a negative event. The act of creation involves a falling away from unity, which is God (*In Gen.* I, n. 26; LW I, 205). And duality or division is always a fall or a falling away from *esse* itself (*In Gen.* I, n. 90; LW I, 248).

In a more positive vein, creation is described as an *ebullitio* (a boiling over). The *ebullitio* of God, which establishes creatures in an existence distinct from that of their creator, is different from what Eckhart terms *bullitio*, that immanent boiling or activity within the divine being which constitutes the three Persons in their relationship to each other. However, he also stresses the close connection between the two. Both the generation of the Son and the creation of creatures are the result of one divine action (*In Joh.* n. 73; LW III, 61). It is especially the Son, as principle of the essences of creatures, who provides the connection that creatures have with the life of the Trinity.

The generation of the Son takes place outside of time in eternity. Eternity is not simply time extended infinitely both into the past and into the future. It is the fullness of time, an everlasting instant where experience is not divided, a point without extension containing all activity and undivided by the succession that vitiates temporal existence. Eternity is an important aspect of the perfect oneness of God. In an eternal instant the Father generates the Son. The temporal distinction between an action going on and an action completed has no meaning in eternity. The Son is always being born and is always already born (*semper nascitur, semper natus est; In Joh.* n. 8; LW III, 9). Creatures too are eternal as well as temporal. As indistinct from God, as *rationes* contained in the Word, they share the existence and activity of God in the *nû* (now) of eternity.[42] As distinct in their *esse formale*, they are subject to time and its consequences: division, change, and transitoriness.

Summary

What God and creatures are, what joins and separates them, was difficult for the popular preacher to convey to his audience for several reasons. First of all, Eckhart was not a popular preacher in the sense that he accommodated his audience by simplifying spiritual truths to make them more intelligible; rather, he was usually quite willing to sacrifice simplicity and intelligibility in favor of richness and vividness. Second, the sermons are not theological treatises but are really sermons. Thus the theological facts in them are not ends in themselves and are explained *ad hoc*. Third, as we shall presently see in more detail, theological terms in themselves are for Eckhart an inadequate means of explaining religious truths, and one has a sense that they lag behind the preacher's total religious consciousness. Finally, what distinguishes Eckhart's thought from more traditional Christian thought is, in particular, his insistence that neither the division nor the union between God and creature had been sufficiently expressed. Indeed, he himself cannot do both elements justice in a single utterance, and he attempts to remedy this in part through dialectical juxtaposition of statements. One cause of confusion concerning his total view is that in many contexts he treats only one side of his thought: either the unity of creature and God or their separateness from each other.

The philosophical doctrine best expressing separateness is that of analogy. Eckhart's view of analogy is definitely his own and, despite his assertions to the contrary, it differs essentially from that of Thomas. For Eckhart, to say that God and creature are analogous to each other is to say that there is no single positive quality, be it existence, goodness, truth, justice, or any other, which they both possess. The being that creatures possess bears no essential similarity to anything in God. If creatures can be said to be, then some entirely different term must be used to refer to God. In a verbal context where creatures are being, God is above being, the purity of being. Or, more frequently, God alone will be said to be being. Creatures, in themselves or insofar as (*in quantum*) they are creatures, are simply nothing. However, since nothing exists outside God, besides being "analogous to" or separate from God, creatures are also indistinct from or one with him. What has become distinct from God through creation remains at the same time indistinct from him with regard to everything that raises it above its own nothingness. As separate from God, a creature is just a sign pointing to what is real. As one with God, a creature really is, is good, is just, and the like. As separate from God it is subject to change and is extended in time. As one with God, it immutably is, was, and will be eternally.

The nature of a creature, therefore, is to have two natures or, perhaps better, to exist in the tension between nothingness and infinite divinity. This duality or tension penetrates to the core of a creature and is its core. Eckhart makes use of different comparisons and metaphors to illustrate this. The creature is like the passive principle of potency which is nothing in itself, and can be considered real only when it is fulfilled by or transformed into act. Or the creature is like the passive principle of matter, which is nothing in itself and cannot be said to exist until it is joined to its active coordinate, form. And just as a body, when separated from the soul, lacks any basis for being considered human, so creatures separated from God lack being and are nothing. God is separate from creatures while sinking himself into their essences. Just as light is utterly one with the air it illumines without taking root, so God penetrates creatures and yet retains his transcendence. Creatures are so dependent on God's being that, while eating and drinking from it, they never rest satisfied but continually hunger and thirst for it. Their being is not their own but is loaned them. As individual beings they add absolutely nothing to the perfections they share in their indistinctness from God. In themselves they are as empty as the mirror, whose capacity exhausts itself in capturing the image of the reality placed opposite it. If being is God and if nothing exists outside God, creatures are best seen not as a separate reality situated between God and nothing but as drawing their nature from both. Because it is nothing in itself, a creature is not simply God. Because it is indistinct from God, and because its nobility derives completely and immediately from him, it exceeds in nobility something conceived as existing separately from God with qualities in its own right. The intensity with which Eckhart grasped the ambivalent nature of creatures provides the force animating the call in his sermons that his hearers realize what they are and can become.

III

THE NATURE OF LANGUAGE

Although the foregoing inquiry into Eckhart's ontology has famil-
iarized us with the basic concepts necessary to understand most of
his favorite spiritual themes, another topic must be addressed before
we can proceed to them. We must consider his conception of language. Eckhart's view of language not only sheds additional light on
his ontology and the puzzles still remaining, but also provides a context for understanding such themes as the birth of the Son, the just
man, detachment, and the like. In addition, an understanding of his
attitude toward language should better enable us to comprehend his
use of it, why he often chose to express his thought not only through
the language of the schools, but also through various rhetorical and
poetic means. Underlying all of Eckhart's attempts to describe God
and what is divine in the world is the question of language. What can
it do? What are its limitations? The question of language, more particularly the question of the relation of universals or general concepts
(e.g., man, table) to the individual concrete objects (e.g., Peter, this
table) already had a long history by Eckhart's time. In the time of
Abelard, at the latest, as a result of his disputes with William of
Champeaux, medieval philosophers had been relieved of any naiveté
they may have had and could no longer simply assume that words cor-
responded to things, and that that was the end of the matter. Thomas
Aquinas offered a *via media* or common-sense solution which tried
to resolve the differences between the order of things and the order of
the mind, while preserving the validity of language as a generally adequate medium for expressing truth about things. That this solution
did not put an end to the problem is evidenced by the writings of
Eckhart's contemporary, William of Ockham, and by the philosophy
of our own day.

For Eckhart too the question of language, its nature and its limitations, had to be of great concern. However, for him it was not so much a question of how general attributes relate to concrete things as it was one of how the human mind with its limitations can deal with the infinite. If one can conclude from his teaching on analogy and on the unity of being that everything is in a sense infinite, it is equally clear that he considered it illegitimate to apply the same terms both to the realm of the infinite and to the realm of creatures as such. The unbridgeable gap between God and creature must have a corresponding equivalent in language.

The question is by no means tangential. Implicit in the question about language is this question: Exactly what value does Eckhart put on his philosophy? What does he think he has achieved when he tells us that being is God, that creatures are nothing, or that there is nothing so distinct and indistinct as God and creature? The clearest indications of what he thinks human thought and its concepts can achieve are contained in his deliberations concerning the names of God. How are we to understand the various names given to God by the authors of the Bible? Do such names really reflect something truly divine, truly in God? Or are they simply the subjective imaginings of the impotent human intellect?

As might be suspected, we are embarrassed by a wealth of conflicting statements and positions if we survey the works as a whole. It becomes clear, when we examine the various statements, that in affixing to his *Tripartite Work* the uncompromising dictum *esse est Deus*, Eckhart was aware of the questionable character of what he had thereby achieved. This *esse* that is God—can it really be grasped by the human mind through human language? Or does it not rather resemble the x in an unsolvable mathematical equation? How can the nothingness that creatures are grasp the immensity of the God-being? Eckhart admits readily and often that creatures cannot, but because man's awareness that he cannot comprehend God is in itself a kind of knowledge, and because knowledge does not have to be adequate knowledge to be knowledge of a sort, and finally, because men, including biblical authors, do talk about God, the value of applying names to God has to be discussed.

In both the Latin and the German works the point is frequently made that God is beyond description. Eckhart's favorite ways of expressing this in Latin are to call God *innominabilis* (unnameable), *indicibilis* (unable to be spoken of), *ineffabilis* (inexpressible), *innarrabilis* (indescribable), and *incomprehensibilis* (incomprehensible). Eckhart sides with those who reject the idea that God is actually "seen" in theophanies, because such an apparition must take place through some kind of medium and is not a direct or immediate experience of God. Because no means or (created) medium has any real similarity to God, he agrees with those who maintain that God cannot be adequately grasped through such revelations (*In Sap.* n. 284; LW II, 616–617). God is unnameable because he cannot be measured (*pro immensitate*), and we are given some indication of him only through his external works, but these are far removed from him, in the realm of dissimilarity (*longe in regione dissimilitudinis; Serm.* IX, n. 96; LW IV, 92). The Israelites were forbidden to make "any likeness of anything in heaven or on earth beneath" (Exod. 20:5), and, Eckhart tells us, the more learned opinion of the day holds that God cannot be represented through similarity with inferior things in such a way that the divine essence can be seen in and through itself (*In Exod.* n. 111; LW II, 109). In the vernacular sermons we find him saying much the same thing, quoting with approval a *meister* who said, "Whoever thinks that he knows God—if he knows anything, then he does not know God,"[1] or, in his own words, after mentioning that scripture contains many names for God: "Whoever perceives something in God and attaches thereby some name to him, that is not God. God is above names and nature."[2] God is *sunder namen* (without names) and *ain logenung aller namen* (a denial of all names) and *nie namen gewan* (never acquired a name; Pr. 15; DW I, 253, 3–4).

Naming God

In the *Commentary on Exodus*, Eckhart makes the names of God the subject of a long inquiry.[3] However, in contrast to his frequent practice of boldly stating his own thesis in opposition to the opinions of learned professors, he devotes much space to refereeing the teachings of various authorities. This makes more difficult the task of discerning his own opinion. A possible reason for his reserve is that one of the authorities he referees is Brother Thomas, with whom he tries to disagree as seldom and as unobtrusively as possible. Nevertheless, if one has the patience to follow him, one finds that he does arrive at definite conclusions, conclusions which, as Koch has pointed out, are much more in tune with the sober conclusions of Maimonides than with those of the more optimistic Thomas.[4] Indeed, the opinion of Maimonides is given more space than that of any other thinker— ancient, pagan, or Christian. Because the matter of naming God is so crucial, we shall examine Eckhart's elaborations in some detail.

In medieval philosophy there are five ways of applying concepts or names to God. The first way, that of univocation or its opposite, equivocation, is generally rejected because univocation would mean that the name employed had exactly the same meaning when applied to God as when applied to creatures. This, of course, must be rejected by anyone whose notion of God contains any philosophical sophistication. Equivocation is equally unsuitable since it postulates that the name contains two completely separate meanings. Hence, even though we understood the name when it referred to creatures, it would offer us no real knowledge when we applied it to God. The second way, that of negation, starts with a concept deriving from the realm of creatures and, because of the limitations or imperfections implied, denies that the concept can be applied to God. We do not learn what God is, but we have not merely performed an unproductive mental exercise since we thereby remove certain false attributes from our idea of God. We learn, for example, that God is *not* matter (which is all that "spiritual" really means), that he is *in*finite, that he is *un*divided and *in*divisible. The third way, that of causality, like the negative way, urges caution in attributing names to God. If we find, for example, that what God has created is good or true, we should not immediately conclude that God is good or true, but only that he is the cause of goodness and truth. From effects one can draw conclusions about God only insofar as he is their cause, not about what he really is in himself. And God's effects, as Eckhart has told us, are far from him in the realm of dissimilarity. The fourth way, that of eminence, begins with a positive attribute observed in creatures, like wisdom or goodness, and maintains that this same quality really exists in God but in a higher manner than in the limited and imperfect creature. The fifth way, that of analogy, is similar to the way of eminence but uses the language of analogy. The two ways have in common that they maintain the validity of attributing the same positive term to God and creature as long as it is kept in mind that each possesses this quality in different ways.

Eckhart begins his treatment of God's names by stressing that several philosophers find God not so much unnameable as beyond names. Because God contains the perfections of creatures in a more excellent way, his name is rather *omninominabile*. This apparent endorsement of the way of eminence is immediately clouded by quotations from Augustine to the effect that all things can be said of God, but nothing worthy or fitting can be spoken of him (n. 35, pp. 41–42). After some remarks on Avicenna's calling God *esse*, which are not pursued in any detail, Eckhart launches into a long discussion of Maimonides's advocacy of the negative way and his claim that all positive words applied to God are partly equivocal. In giving the Jewish philosopher's arguments against positive names, Eckhart adds one of his own, one that is worth noting because it reveals the perspective from which he is arguing for the priority of negative names. Maimonides states that one way of applying positive names, namely, that based on a relationship like father or companion, is illegitimate because such a relationship rests on similarity; but there can be no similarity between God and creature, which makes this mode of attributing a positive name improper. Eckhart remarks that perhaps a more ingenious reason for this could be pointed out by noting that a relationship requires that the things related be two and distinct; but, as distinct from God, a creature is nothing and thus lacks any basis for a relationship (n. 40, pp. 45–46). He then observes that Maimonides grants that one type of positive attribution is possible: that of viewing God as a cause. However, God's effects, as Eckhart has assured us, are far from him in the region of dissimilarity. Since this type of attribution does not touch God as he is in himself but only as seen through effects, names of God thus derived announce properly only his works and are not suitable for God himself. The startling conclusion is that positive names, which would be perfections in creatures, such as merciful and generous, are not more so in God than their opposites, such as anger and hate. These are all derived from God's external activity, from his actions toward creatures, and thus do not posit any attributes of God as he is in himself (nn. 41–44, pp. 46–49). Part of the reason for this conclusion is no doubt the necessity of justifying those passages in scripture where God is described as angry, hating, and the like. Nevertheless, to the extent that Eckhart is agreeing with his Jewish colleague here, he is leaning toward a position which severely limits the validity of attributing positive qualities to God.

In the following sections, in which he takes up the opinions of Christian thinkers, his attitude seems to be more open toward positive names. Yet there are also signs that he wishes to exercise caution and to maintain some distance from advocates of positive names and that his agreement is more seeming than real (nn. 54–78, pp. 58–82). Much of the argumentation need not detain us, and in any case would have to be reproduced almost in its entirety to be understood. However, it is essential to try to determine the extent to which Eckhart considered positive names to be applicable to God. Three points deserve our attention.

First, in laying down some ground rules he stresses the limitations of human knowledge and the differences between concepts and the things they represent. Statements are said to correspond primarily to the concepts contained in them and only secondarily to the things represented by the concepts. Such concepts arise from accidents or characteristics of the thing and not from the thing as a substance or what it actually is (n. 55, pp. 60–61). Perhaps more important to remember when talking about nonmaterial reality is that all human knowledge has its origin in the senses. The way we know something and name it depends on our sense perception of it, so that if we lack one of our senses the corresponding knowledge is also lacking. What we perceive as multiple and distinct, however, must be utterly one in God (n. 57, p. 62). The conclusion we are supposed to draw seems to be that we must be careful not to assume that we know more than we really do about a reality like God, who is so far removed from the humble origins of human knowledge.

This leads Eckhart to a second important question: When we give God various names which are distinct from each other in our minds, is there something in God which justifies the multiplicity of attributes, or is this multiplicity due solely to our way of knowing? Thomas had taught that this multiplicity had a basis in God himself and not just in the human intellect in the sense that God's infinite perfection cannot be captured in any single human concept, and that this justifies our use of several attributes.[5] Eckhart, however, denies that there is any basis outside the human mind for the multiplicity of concepts applied to God and considers it to be entirely due to our human way of gathering knowledge from and through creatures. Quoting Maimonides, he declares that God is one in every manner and in every sense. There is no real or conceptual multiplicity in him. He then adds, "Whoever sees two or distinction does not see God."[6] Probably because of the implications of such statements for Christian doctrine on the Trinity, this text found its way into the bull of condemnation under the articles that were suspected of heresy but, with much explanation, capable of an orthodox interpretation.[7] Again, Eckhart's arguments seem to be leading him toward a kind of agnosticism, but he assures us that despite God's infinity such distinct attributes are not false or empty of content when predicated of God, because something real in God does correspond to them.[8] Nevertheless, he seems much less optimistic than the Angelic Doctor about what such attributes tell us about God.

Finally, the fact that he thinks he can reconcile the opinion of Thomas with that of pseudo-Dionysius gives further clues to his own position on positive names. Pseudo-Dionysius, an advocate of the primacy of the negative way, is quoted as saying that negations are true of God while affirmations are unsuitable (*incompactae*). Eckhart explains that what pseudo-Dionysius meant to say was that the *way* we attribute affirmative perfections to God is unsuitable since they are perceived in the imperfect manner in which they are found in creatures, but that the perfections themselves, like goodness, life, knowing, and the like, are suitable and true.[9] As the editors point out, Eckhart's argument is simply an excerpt from Thomas.[10] One should not too readily assume, however, that in borrowing his fellow Dominican's words he, like Thomas, has become an advocate of the primacy of the way of eminence over the way of negation. First of all, such a reversal contradicts the general tenor of his argument both before and after this passage. It seems much more likely that Eckhart achieved the reconciliation by doing more violence to Thomas than to pseudo-Dionysius. The modest concession that applying distinct attributes to God is not totally wrong hardly qualifies Eckhart as a proponent of the superiority of the way of eminence. We have already seen him incorrectly assuming that his colleague Thomas agreed with him in the question on analogy.[11] Second, immediately after turning pseudo-Dionysius into a Thomist, he brings his consideration of the matter to a temporary conclusion by balancing this reconciliation with quotations from Augustine and Paul to explain that, in another sense (*aliter*), affirmations about God are false and unsuitable. Augustine is shown to argue that anyone believing that one's thoughts about God grasp him as he is, is worshiping a false god and that such thoughts must be abandoned as deceiving. Paul (1 Cor. 13:12) speaks of our seeing now only in a puzzle (*in aenigmate*) and only partly (*in parte*; n. 78, pp. 81–82).

To understand why Eckhart's posture toward affirmative attributes is so reserved and his endorsement of negative attributes so eloquent in contrast to Thomas, who states that the way of eminence gives us more knowledge of God, we must become aware of what philosophical doctrine provides the basis for their choices. This doctrine can be none other than that of analogy. Thomas can say that we attain more knowledge of God by conceiving him as good, wise, and the like, than by the negative way, because his doctrine of analogy stipulates that the qualities of goodness and wisdom really and properly inhere in both creature and God, though more properly, of course, in God. Therefore, when we attribute goodness to God through the way of eminence, that same goodness which we observe in creatures is really and positively in God, although in a more eminent or higher manner, that is, lacking the imperfections and limitations caused by its being joined to creatures. Thomas would agree with Eckhart that all human knowledge arises from the senses, but the implications of this are not as far-reaching for him. His view of analogy allows him to consider this fact a reason for qualifying such a transfer of attributes from creatures to God by saying that they are in God in a higher way. But the origin of human knowledge will not present him with such a formidable barrier for knowing God affirmatively as it will Eckhart. For the latter the attribute will really be in only one of the objects related by analogy. Health will no more be in urine than it will be in a stone. And since human knowledge forms concepts with positive attributes from its perception of creatures, it would seem that Eckhart must conclude that such positive attributes cannot validly be applied to God. Thus, when he borrows Thomas's distinction between that which is attributed (*id quod*) and the manner in which it is attributed (*modus quo*) to show in what sense positive attributes are true and in what sense they are false (n. 78, p. 81), he seems to be assuming, as he does elsewhere, a nonexistent agreement between Thomas and himself. For Eckhart the *modus quo* modifies essentially the *id quod. That which* is attributed is for him really in only one of the analogates, and to call God good is like calling the sun black.

This helps clarify why Eckhart does not share Thomas's optimism concerning positive knowledge of God, but it also seems to offer reasons why Eckhart should reject the possibility of such knowledge utterly and completely. Yet we have evidence in this very discussion of the names of God that Eckhart was not willing to do this.[12] And how are we to understand his frequent avowal that God alone is, properly speaking, being, one, true, and good?[13] In searching for solutions to these remaining problems, we must admit that it is difficult to find texts that address them directly, but from the evidence available we can put together plausible explanations.

To begin with, although Eckhart frequently states that being, one, true, good, and the like are properly said of God alone, this does not necessarily mean that he thought that we are able to grasp the essential meaning of these terms as they are applied positively to God. The core of Eckhart's conception of analogy is that God and creature, as distinct, are too different to be in any proper sense included in the same term. Whatever goodness or truth creatures possess is nothing compared to the goodness and truth of God. Since such terms are formed by us by means of creatures and apply properly to creatures, they would seem to lose all value when transferred across the unbridgeable gap to God. Thus, although at the very beginning of his discussion of the verse from Exodus, *Omnipotens nomen eius* (15:3; Almighty is his name) Eckhart asserts that God is in the proper sense (*proprie*) almighty (n. 27, p. 32), it is quite a different question (nn. 34ff., pp. 40ff.) to ask to what extent a human concept is able to comprehend this truth. In those texts, therefore, where he maintains that God alone is one, true, good, just, and the like, we should not assume that he thinks we have an adequate comprehension of these attributes. Everything said of God affirmatively is therefore an improper attribution (*improprie*; n. 44, p. 48), as Maimonides had written. Even though God alone is really and properly being, one, true, and good, human concepts are too feeble for us to say that such concepts give us knowledge of God that even approximates the faint intimations of divinity garnered from negative or apophatic attribution.

When, in concluding, Eckhart returns to the question of positive attributes, he simply gives three reasons why it is false and wide of the mark (*falsum et incongruum*) to apply them to God. First, they are not in God according to their forms (*formaliter*) but only through his power as creator of their forms (*virtute*). Thus they contain nothing that is formally in God (n. 175, p. 151). Second, perfections do not exist in things. To attribute to God perfections gleaned from things is to reduce him, who is pure intellect, to a thing (n. 176, p. 152). Third, in the order of human thought—and that is what this whole discussion is all about—the *esse* which actuates an *essentia* has no positive attributes added to it. The same must be true of God who is simply *esse* (n. 177, pp. 152–153).

Is there any validity at all in applying such concepts to God? Or are they simply false, like calling the sun black? There are indications of a softening of this seemingly categorical rejection. First of all, as we learn from his position on analogy, such human concepts are, at least, signs pointing to an incomprehensible reality beyond. Like urine pointing to health and the tavern wreath pointing to wine, the positive contents of concepts are symbols of the divinity. Only if we think they are somehow adequate is it like calling the sun black. And yet, if affirmations about God are merely symbolic, if they are *just* signs, are they really in any sense analogous terms? Or are they simply equivocal, having no more real connection to God than their opposites?

There is some evidence that Eckhart does not think that affirmations exhaust their function completely as signs of the divinity, although this is clearly a large part, perhaps the largest part, of what they do, and although he considers them of less value than apophatic or negative attributes. Positive attributes are equivocal, but only partly so. They are partly equivocal and partly spoken of God imperfectly (*in imperfectione*; n. 178, p. 153). How, one might then ask, does this view really differ from that of Thomas, who says that God is good, just, and the like in a higher manner (*eminentius*) than creatures? The difference is apparently great, because Eckhart borrows this line of argument from Maimonides in order to show that positive attributes are inappropriate when applied to God and not, as Thomas maintains, to show that they give us more knowledge of God than negative attributes. However, he does assign positive concepts a role in our knowledge of God, modest though it be. They provide the knowledge that must be overcome in order to achieve negative attribution. Borrowing the phrase from Thomas that all negation must have a basis in affirmation, he explains that we must know what a body is before we can intelligently say that God is noncorporeal or spiritual (nn. 181–183, pp. 155–158). Positive concepts furnish the content that is then denied God in apophatic attribution. Thus, positive attributes contribute in an essential way to human knowledge of the divine, but not in the same measure as negative attributes. They are the smaller of the two steps of a dialectic in which we posit them only to deny them, in order to achieve some hint of what the divinity is.

What about general perfections, that is, positive attributes that do not imply negation? God is in a proper sense almighty, good, just, and the like, but because of Eckhart's conception of analogy he must conclude that, to the extent that these are positive attributes and not merely concepts which deny limits or imperfections in God, we have no access to their essential meaning because our concepts of goodness and power are derived from creatures. Knowing God as good or true does not remove this barrier blocking our view of him. We remain, as it were, on one side of a wall with only the faintest indication of what is on the other side.

Unum and *Esse*

Eckhart often shows a preference among the general perfections in naming God. In such cases it is either *esse* or *unum* that is so honored. In the *Commentary on Exodus* we are given a reason for this preference. It is not so much as positive attributes that they name God. Rather, they function more properly and bring us further in our search for knowledge of the divinity when employed according to the negative way. This is clearly stated in the case of *unum*, though the brevity here requires that we first examine more elaborate comments in the *Commentary on Wisdom* (nn. 144–149; LW II, 481–487), where Eckhart concludes by maintaining that "one" is more appropriately attributed to God than "good" or "true."[14] The attribute *unum* is indistinct from number as well as distinct from number. That is to say, it is not a number. Hence, both as distinct and indistinct, *unum* is determined by negation. It is infinite and, in contrast to *verum* and *bonum*, adds nothing positive to *esse*, not even conceptually (*secundum rationem*), but only a negation (*secundum negationem*). *Unum* signifies the purity, the core, or the summit of *esse*, which the word *esse* itself does not do. What is negated when one applies *unum* to God? Nothing. One negates that the nothing (*nihil*) which is the opposite of *esse* can be predicated of God in any way. In excluding the predicate *nihil* from God, *unum* denies that there is any lack in God. *Unum* therefore expresses the highest possible form of the negative way. It negates the possibility of there being anything negative or lacking in God. This is the famous negation of negation which comes closest of all to saying something about God (*In Sap.* n. 148; LW II, 486). This *negatio negationis* is the only possible negation of God and is identical with *unum* when *unum* is employed according to the negative way. Here negation turns into its opposite and becomes "the purest and fullest affirmation: 'I am who am.'"[15]

This last sudden transition to pure and complete affirmation might at first glance seem to indicate that the leap from *unum* to *esse* is at the same time a conversion from the negative way to that of positive attribution, but this is not the case. As we have explained above, *esse* is properly attributed to God rather than to creatures, but because of his conception of analogy, Eckhart must conclude that the positive content of *esse* as understood by the human intellect from its knowledge of creatures has only a slight connection to God's *esse*. What he wishes to say by calling *sum qui sum* the purest affirmation is something else. Just previous to this paragraph he states as a condition of human knowledge the Aristotelian dictum that the truth of an affirmative proposition consists in the identity of terms (n. 73, p. 75). Thus when God says of himself *ego sum qui sum*, the reduplication of *sum* or, in other words, stating that *esse* is *esse* expresses the perfect identity of himself with himself and is the purest affirmative statement possible. This *statement* or affirmation is true regardless of whether *esse* is a positive or negative attribution.

One might also ask whether the pure affirmation attained through the negation of negation is not really just another way of stating the way of eminence which Eckhart is, in fact, here endorsing. After all, his claim that God is not *esse* but rather the purity of *esse* seems difficult to distinguish from the statement that God is *esse* in a more eminent manner than creatures are. The difference is crucial for understanding what Eckhart attempts to express through the negative way. The way of eminence, as we have seen, depends for its validity on both the objects joined by analogy really possessing the quality in question. This quality must be in some sense the same in both as well as different. This requirement does not hold true for the affirmation gained from the negation of negation. In negating the limitation of distinctness in calling God one, or in denying the *esse* of creatures to God when calling him the purity of being, one does not maintain that a positive quality found in creatures is in God in any real sense. The imperfections and limitations found in creatures, and thus in their positive attributes, are removed from the notion of God but are not replaced by any other positive attributes.

When we come to examine just what kind of word Eckhart considers *esse* to be in stating *esse est Deus*, we note that he gives clear indications of considering *esse* much more effective as a negative attribute than as a positive attribute in giving some sense of the divine reality. In the *Commentary on Exodus*, when he returns to the question of naming God and turns his attention to the Hebrew names and their implications (nn. 144–184; LW II, 130–158), he reopens the discussion of the relative merits of positive and negative attributes, this time giving only reasons that speak against the former (nn. 144–177) and for the latter (nn. 178–183), as we have mentioned. Two names receiving special consideration are the tetragrammaton, the name of four letters,[16] and the name *qui est* (he who simply is) or *esse*, which emerged from Christian interpretations of *ego sum qui sum*. The fact that they are discussed without criticism in such close proximity to his clear statements on the merits of negative names is reason enough to assume that Eckhart considered them to be negative. This interpretation is further supported by the way in which he describes them. The tetragrammaton, he tells us, "whatever it is and whatever the four letters might be from which it has its name, is hidden, secret, and is itself the inexpressible name of the Lord. This tetragrammaton is not the name itself about which we are now talking, but is rather a circumlocution of four letters for a certain name which is a holy mystery." It is never spoken aloud, but is "inexpressible by nature and because of its purity, as is the substance of God which it signifies."[17] Since this name signifies the divine substance, its meaning is not shared in any way with creatures (n. 147, p. 132). From all this it is clear that the justification of the tetragrammaton as an apt name for God is based upon its remoteness from positive speech.

A few pages later he begins his remarks on the preeminence of "who is" or *esse* and cautiously suggests that perhaps *esse* is the name of four letters since it actually has four letters and many hidden (actually *hiding*) properties and perfections. It does not derive from God as cause, nor does he share this name with anyone.[18] Eckhart just briefly mentions this tantalizing possibility of the identity of the two names and prefers to take the case no further. However, this echoes the view he expressed in the *First Parisian Question*—that in saying *sum qui sum* and thereby, through reduplication, affirming that he is the purity of being, God was actually hiding his identity rather than revealing it.[19] To support the claim of preeminence for *esse*, Eckhart offers another argument which would seem to indicate its nature as a negative name: *esse* is indistinct from all other names. Just as creatures, as distinct from *esse*, are nothing and *are* insofar as they are not distinct from God as *esse*, so the names of God can only overcome the impotence of their positive, analogous meanings when they are predicated of God by being subsumed into *esse* conceived negatively as indistinct from them (n. 166, p. 146). Only in its function as a negative attribute is *esse* able to include all other names. Precisely as *innominabile* does *esse* become the *nomen omninominabile* proclaimed of God at the beginning of the discussion (n. 36, pp. 41–42). Thus Eckhart is quite consistent when he concludes by stating the general consensus among authorities that we cannot know what God is, but only that we do not know him (n. 184, p. 158).

In summarizing Eckhart's conception of what the term *esse*, the most central in his thought, means for man in his attempt to know something of God, we can say that he considered it both a positive and a negative attribute. However, the value of *esse* as a positive attribute of God is less than *esse* as a negative attribute. As a positive name for God, it is weak. Just as is the case with the other general perfections such as true, good, and just, it is most properly a sign or symbol pointing to a quite different reality, like the tavern wreath pointing to wine. The reality symbolized is immense and beyond human comprehension. Hence it is difficult to attribute to the human concept, drawn entirely from a knowledge of creatures, a function beyond that of arbitrary sign for this infinite reality. And yet Eckhart seems unwilling, in spite of his doctrine of analogy, to see in such a concept only a sign and nothing more. It does express something that is in God at least by virtue of his creative power (*virtute*) even if it does not touch what he really is in himself. And through being posited of him in order to be rejected as a means of attaining essential knowledge, it does seem to attain a slight grasp of him beyond the merely symbolic.

What then does it mean to say *esse est Deus*? It may be true that *esse* is God and creatures a mere nothing, but this reflects the true state of things rather than our positive knowledge of God. Our positive knowledge of *esse* corresponds more to the nothingness that the being of creatures is. Understood in this sense, *esse* is something one must try to get beyond. As a negative attribute, *esse*, the *nomen innominabile* (unnameable name), must be conceded greater validity. Precisely as *esse* does God remain hidden within himself beyond our reach, and *esse* is the name which as nondistinct from other names contains the hidden perfections of God. Taken positively and negatively at the same time, it becomes the *nomen omninominabile* (name including all names) which points paradoxically to what is best approached by saying what it is not.

Further Evidence of Eckhart's View of Language

There is a wealth of evidence that the conclusions reached in the *Commentary on Exodus* concerning the preeminence of the negative way and the basic impotence of positive concepts of the human mind when applied to God are decisive throughout Eckhart's works, even though some passages might remain puzzling. In the *Commentary on John*, for example, Eckhart assures us that we have a much better idea of what God is not and where he does not dwell than what he is and where he dwells. This statement is followed by some examples of negative determinations: that God is not in time, that he is not in division, that he is not in quantity, that he is not in anything that is distinct, and so forth (*In Joh.* n. 206; LW III, 173–174). God is one because he is known by negation and is indistinct. He is incomprehensible (*Serm.* XXXVII, n. 375; LW IV, 320). One also finds in the Latin sermons references to God's being unnameable (*innominabilis*; *Serm.* LV, 4, n. 547; LW IV, 458) or, because of his nature, unable to be spoken (*ex sui natura indicibilis*; *Serm.* IV, 2, n. 30; LW IV, 31). He is above every name, reason, and intellect (*super omne nomen, rationem, et intellectum*; *Serm.* VIII, n. 84; LW IV, 80). He is unnameable because we cannot measure him (*pro immensitate sui*) and because he reveals himself to us only through his works, which are far from him (*longe*) and bear no similarity to him (*in regione dissimilitudinis*; *Serm.* IX, n. 96; LW IV, 92). At the same time, God can be called all names (*omninominabilis*) because he is above all names and above all "one," that is, he is indistinct from everything else, and thus precontains every name (*praehabet omne nomen*; *In Gen.* I, n. 84; LW I, 243–244).

Two vernacular sermons contain particularly interesting passages concerning "one" as applied to God. In the first, after explaining that the human intellect perceives God as he is pure being (*ein lûter wesen*) and transcendent being (*ein überswebendez wesen*), Eckhart adds that being, goodness, and truth are equal in the breadth of their application, that insofar as something is being, it is also good and true. He then continues:

> They [the professors] take goodness and put it on top of being: this covers over being and makes a skin for it, for it is an addition. Then they take him [God] as he is truth. Is being truth? Yes, for truth is bound to being, for he said to Moses: "He who is has sent me" (Exod. 3 : 14). St. Augustine says: the truth is the Son in the Father, for truth is bound to being. Is being truth? If one were to ask many professors about this, they would say "Yes!" If one had asked me, I would have said "Yes!" But now I say "No!" For truth is also an addition. Then they take him as he is one. One is more properly one than what is united [i.e., "united" implies the joining of *two* things]. That which is one has had everything else removed. Yet what has been removed has been added in the sense that it determines something as other.
>
> And if he is neither goodness nor being nor truth nor one, what is he then? He is nothing of anything (*nihtes niht*), he is neither this nor that. Any thought you might still have of what he might be—he is such not at all.[20]

The preacher is here trying to clarify our notion of God by purifying it of all additions and, as we might expect from his conclusions in the *Commentary on Exodus*, he elevates "one" above "good" and "true" because it removes all (positive) additions. But here "one" is understood to imply a possible positive quality in that it posits the object to which it is attached as different from all else (*divisum a quolibet alio*). Hence he finds it necessary to distinguish this concept of "one" from the purely negative "one" or negation of negation (*nihtes niht*) by which one achieves a higher notion of the divinity.

In a second sermon, Eckhart emphasizes the "one" of the way of negation and the resulting indistinctness of God as the basis for the oneness of creatures with God:

> A learned teacher says: one is a negation of negation. If I say that God is good, this adds something to him. One is a negation of negation and a denial of denial. What does one mean? One indicates that to which nothing is added. The soul perceives the divinity as it is pu-

rified in itself where nothing is added, not even in thought. One is the negation of negation. All creatures have a negation within them. One creature denies that it is another creature. One angel denies that it is another. But God has a negation of negation. He is one and negates everything else, for outside God nothing is. All creatures are in God and are his very divinity, and this means the fullness I mentioned before. He is one Father of the whole divinity. I say, therefore, one divinity because nothing has as yet flowed out, and nothing has at all been touched or thought. In denying something to God—for example, if I deny him goodness—of course I cannot deny anything to him—in denying something to God I grasp something of him, namely, what he is not. Even this has to be removed. God is one, he is the negation of negation.[21]

Turning from his remarks on *unum* to some concerning *esse*, we find Eckhart, in a variant version of the *First Commentary on Genesis*, taking the position that *esse* does not reveal but rather hides God's nature. After discussing the paradox which Augustine had called attention to—that in calling God ineffable we in fact do say something about him—Eckhart creates a paradox of his own. It is remarkable that we should seek God's name, because his nature is hidden *esse* (*cuius natura est esse absconditum*; nn. 298–300; LW I, 95–96). In German Sermon 83 he calls God nameless and denies that he can be called good, better, or best because "these words are far from God." For the preacher to say that God is wise is untrue. He himself is wiser than God. He then introduces the term *wesen* into the discussion, claiming it is untrue that God is *ein wesen*. In an almost untranslatable formulation which combines metaphysics, rhetoric, and poetry, he describes God as "ein vber swebende wesen vnd ein vber wesende nitheit" (literal translation: an oversoaring being and an overbeing nothingness). Leaving aside the verbal effects achieved by the repetition of *vber*, the parallelism with contrast of *swebende* and *wesende*, and the climax-anticlimax effect of *nitheit*, we see that he first raises the *wesen* of God to let it soar above all else and then immediately calls this phrase into question by raising him yet further above *wesen* to nothingness. Shortly thereafter he repeats the juxtaposition of being and nothingness, adding a negative modifier to both. The goal he urges his audience to reach is to understand together with God his (God's) "vngewordene istikeit vnd sin vngenanten nitheit" (literal translation: uncreated is-ness and unnamed nothingness; DW III, 441,1–443,7). Such descriptions gain in force what they lack in precision. Nevertheless, their meaning is clear enough. For us, God in his being remains hidden and essentially unnameable.

One finds passages in the vernacular sermons which seem to indicate that the soul can achieve a more vital and intimate knowledge of God than what can be achieved through the way of negation. Such knowledge is often connected with the highest power of the soul. In Sermon 11 this power is described as "so lofty and noble that it perceives [*nimet*] God in his own bare being" (*in sînem blôzen eigenen wesen*) and "in his dressing room" (i.e., naked, *in sînem kleithûs*; DW I, 182, 10; 183, 4). A closer look at these formulations reveals that they are based on the way of negation. God is seen stripped of the clothing of positive terms which more hide than enhance his being. At the same time, it must be admitted that such descriptions of the soul's knowledge imply an intensity of experience beyond what one would normally attribute to the mind's activity in logically removing positive qualities applied to God. There seems to be an intuitive side to such knowledge which in some sense crosses the barrier erected by Eckhart's view of analogy and his predilection for the way of negation. In Sermon 9 he states that the intellect "pulls off God the covering of goodness and perceives him bare, as he is stripped of goodness and being and of all names."[22] In Sermon 7, where knowledge is subordinated to *barmherzicheit*, which is not mercy or compassion but rather the union of God and soul beyond knowledge, he describes such activity as a breaking through: "Knowledge breaks through truth and goodness and falls upon pure being and perceives God bare, as he is without names."[23]

If the theologian and professor shows a clear preference for the way of negation, the popular preacher frequently shows a preference for images in order to convey his notion of God; and these images frequently perform functions similar to terms used for the way of negation. In describing God as the final end and place of rest for all being, he calls God "the hidden darkness of the eternal godhead" which "is unknown, was never known, and never will be known" (*diu verborgen vinsternisse der êwigen gotheit und ist unbekant und wart nie bekant und enwirt niemer bekant*; Pr. 22; DW I, 389, 3–8). The loftiest power of the soul does not seek God as he is goodness or truth: "it seeks in the depths and keeps on seeking and perceives God in his oneness and in his solitude; it perceives God in his desert wilderness and in his own ground."[24] This combination of *einunge* (oneness) and *einoede* (solitude) is certainly intentional. One can hardly imagine a more striking word for the concept *unum* than *einoede*, with its mixture of oneness and emptiness. *Wüestunge* (desert wilderness) reinforces the negation that *oede* effects. *Grunt*, a favorite expression of the preacher to describe the place of union, while not without some positive connotations, has no strict equivalent in scholastic Latin and has the advantage of remaining general, or indistinct, and concrete at the same time. But to balance any positive connotations *grunt* might have, we can return to the passage from Sermon 7 quoted above, where the intellect is said to attain God as pure being and without names. On the one hand, Eckhart wishes here to praise the excellence of the intellect over the will, which in loving God perceives God covered over with a skin or piece of clothing, whereas the intellect perceives God "as he is known to it," that is, as pure or bare being. To make clear the limitations of human knowledge, however, he admits that it can never grasp God "in the sea/ ocean of his bottomlessness" (*in dem mer sîner gruntlôsicheit;* DW I, 123, 1–3). If God has a *grunt,* it can only be described as *gruntlôs.*

What about knowledge in a mystical state? What about Paul, who by grace was raised up to the third heaven and saw things that one cannot and may not express (2 Cor. 12:2–4)? Eckhart assures us that Paul was not able to put into words what he saw. One can only understand something through its cause, through its limited manner of existing, or through its external effects. God is neither caused, nor is he limited, nor in his hidden stillness does he work; that is, the immanent activity/stillness within the divinity has no external effect. Therefore God remains unknown (*unverstanden*) and without names (*sunder namen;* Pr. 80; DW III, 381,1–382,1). Whatever Paul experienced changes nothing about Eckhart's basic thesis that God, as he is in himself, cannot be named.

Summary

In summary we can note that, concerning the nature and validity of concepts and language, Eckhart shares the starting point of Aristotelian scholastic thinkers that all human knowledge begins with the apprehension of material things through the senses. However, since there is no real positive similarity between God and creatures, and since there are therefore no concepts that express a positive quality that is really in a proper sense in both, our words are doomed to utter inadequacy in trying to express something about God. Even such simple terms as "good," "just," and the like, which might seem suitable for building a conceptual bridge, contain more error than truth when applied to God. At the same time, Eckhart can maintain that only God is being, truth, goodness, and that creatures as distinct from him are none of these. Our creaturely and distinct language shares our nothingness. Concepts like being, truth, and goodness in no way express what God is really like. Rather, they merely point to or hint at what he is, just as a tavern wreath points to wine without having any similarity to wine. Because of the overwhelming disproportion between what our concepts express and what God is, it is literally true to say that calling God good is like calling the sun black. Because the positive concepts we apply to God have no foundation in the utter oneness of God and are derived from God's effects in creatures and not from his nature, one positive name will not necessarily exclude its opposite.[25] As a consequence, one can accomplish more by establishing what God is not, by removing imperfections and limitations from our notion of him. This frees a positive core which we cannot grasp.

When all this has been said, does Eckhart really present us with a unified and coherent view of language which clearly defines its capabilities and limitations? More particularly, does his view of language when applied to God in any way get beyond a kind of agnosticism about God's nature? Does his view of analogy not logically lead to our having to consider words applied to God and creature as being, in fact, equivocal and thus really meaningless in what they tell us about God? Two ways of treating this question seem appropriate. First of all, to grant that the Dominican thinker did not completely solve the problem of speaking about God in human language is hardly to admit something shameful. The question could be posed (and often has been posed) whether his colleague Thomas was any more successful in dealing with the problem. Many scholars would answer that, in stipulating in his doctrine of analogy that both God and creature really (*formaliter*) possess the quality expressed in a word like "good" or "true," Thomas had merely shifted the problem to different ground: *How* is it possible for both an infinite God and a lowly creature to possess what is, in any real sense, the same attribute? Moreover, the related questions raised by philosophers in subsequent centuries, and particularly those raised most recently about the nature of communication and the impotence of language, indicate that the dimensions of the problem have grown, but not our capacity to solve it. But to respond only in this vein is to practice evasion. We must therefore, in concluding, state his view briefly but with balance.

What evidence is there, then, for saying that for Eckhart words like "good" or "true" really do have some meaning when applied to God? Two lines of thought in his works indicate the illegitimacy of concluding that he considered positive terms absolutely meaningless or nothing but purely arbitrary signs when used to show something about God. First, as already mentioned, positive terms provide the basis for apophatic description by furnishing the quality to be denied God. While this does not take us far, it does seem to mitigate the strictness with which Eckhart considered positive terms equivocal. Second, we have seen that Eckhart does admit that positive terms correspond to something in God. Because of the importance of this admission, it does not seem superfluous to quote from a Latin sermon in which it is repeated:

> In summary, note that everything which is written or said about the blessed Trinity is not at all really that way or true. [And this is so] first of all, because of the nature of the division between especially distinct and indistinct, between the things of time and those of eternity, between sensible and spiritual heaven, and between a material and a spiritual body. Second, [this is so] because God is in and of his nature inexpressible. This is why the psalmist says: "Every man is a liar." It is true, however, that there is something in God that corresponds to the Trinity which we enunciate and also [something that corresponds] to other similar things.[26]

This final sentence clearly expresses the preacher's unwillingness to consider positive terms absolutely meaningless when applied to God. Something in God *does* correspond to them. But beyond this Eckhart is unwilling to go. Because of the overwhelming dissimilarity between God and human language, no further claims can be made for positive terms. While not utterly meaningless when we use them to describe God, they transcend the state of complete impotence only to an infinitesimal degree.

As a consequence, our search for God is paradoxical. Utterly one with him and utterly nothing apart from him, we seek him but have no adequate means of grasping him. And although he can be imagined as pure and infinite light, he is, as the Hebrew scriptures teach, a hidden and mysterious God. Let us give the preacher, and not the thinker, the last word in the matter:

> God is a word, a word unspoken.
>   Augustine says: "All writings are in vain. If one says that God is a word, he has been expressed; but if one says that God has not been spoken, he is ineffable." And yet he is something, but who can speak this word? No one can do this, except him who is this Word. God is a word that speaks itself. . . . All creatures want to utter God in all their works; they all come as close as they can in uttering him, and yet they cannot utter him. Whether they wish it or not, whether they like it or not, they all want to utter God, and yet he remains unuttered.[27]

Consequences

Eckhart's evaluation of the possibilities and limitations of language left its imprint on his works in many ways and helps explain many puzzling aspects of structure and content. Further, it can be shown to be a determining factor in the personal expression of his ideas which we usually call style. Not that the preacher mentions his conception of language as a consciously perceived force influencing him, but the consistency between his expressed view of language and several elements in his practice is so striking that his conception of language offers the best explanation for many aspects of his style.

One consequence of his view of language can be seen in the form he chose for his major professional work. In contrast to many of his colleagues, Eckhart chose to write an *Opus tripartitum* instead of the popular *summa*. In other words, he seems to have been less interested in leaving behind a system of philosophy or theology than in offering his insights into various philosophical and theological questions. The systematic section of this major work, the *Work of Propositions*, was indeed to provide a foundation for what was to follow, but it enjoyed no particular preeminence over the *Work of Questions* or the Bible commentaries and sermons of the *Work of Commentaries*. These latter two parts make no attempt at systematic wholeness, and it is the Bible commentaries with their lack of system and scholarly method which the author chose to work on and some of which he actually brought to completion. The open-endedness of what he produced coincides well with what he thought philosophical language can and cannot achieve. The reality of anything which goes beyond creatures, insofar as they are creatures, cannot be grasped by such language in a way approaching wholeness. What language is able to express about a divine object or an object which is indistinct from the godhead will be less than what it omits. Words take on the nature of symbols that indicate their objects from without much more than from within. As a result, attempts at completeness lose much of their charm, since for someone with Eckhart's view of language any system will have a much weaker connection to its object than it does for the philosopher who is convinced of the priority of the way of eminence. An advocate of the priority of the negative way like Eckhart must, rather, rest satisfied with making some good points about God and about creatures insofar as the latter transcend themselves. One can point in the direction of truth but can do little more.

Eckhart's view of language also explains his great professional tolerance of other thinkers and other traditions. A certain amount of tolerance was widespread among medieval Christian thinkers who respected Islamic, Jewish, and classical philosophers and borrowed from them freely. What characterizes Eckhart within this tradition of tolerance is his apparent lack of concern about those opinions that might well conflict with established Christian thought. If one considers the amount of positive religious truth which a doctrine contains to be less than what it omits, the conflicts between doctrines do not have to be taken as full-blown, irresolvable contradictions. At least with regard to many statements about God, Eckhart held that, although valid, they were no more so than their opposites. One can consequently devote one's attention to the truth in them and worry less about conflicts.

Taking this line of thought a step further, we notice that the preacher as well as the professor finds it necessary, due to the nature of human language, to make use of opposition and contradiction to describe God. "One" is his preferred name for God because it describes him as both indistinct and distinct. This attribute overcomes with some success the limitations of words because it contains opposites and includes within it a dialectical process. Although his explanation of *unum* and his use of the pairs "indistinct"-"distinct" and "dissimilar"-"similar" are the clearest examples of this dialectic, its application is also implied in his execution of both sermons and commentaries. In both, a text of scripture will often be interpreted in several ways that defy any attempt to bring them into harmony. The implication is that such an approach yields more than that offered by the logic and concepts of the schools.

If concepts leave out more than they contain, and if words are at best external signs for truths, then philosophy and natural theology can claim no preeminent position for themselves in attaining these truths. While Eckhart was obviously convinced that his profession was capable of reaching valid and significant results, the frequency, as well as the quality, of rhetorical and poetic features in his sermons is striking and distinguishes him clearly from the other preachers of the day who used scholastic thought as the basis for their sermons.[28] Although one should not exclude pastoral intentions as a reason for the use of rhetorical and poetic devices, it must be admitted that the devaluation of philosophical language that his views imply provides the theoretical justification for his practice of often turning to rhetoric and poetry to express religious truth. Indeed, we often find that it is through images that he is able to convey to us most satisfyingly his most idiosyncratic and difficult thoughts. As we have seen in the case of his conception of being, scriptural images, such as the sun sending out rays that do not take root or hungering and thirsting in spite of eating and drinking, are of perhaps more use to the thinker in explaining his thoughts than is the language of the schools.

Two consequences of this devaluation of conceptual language must be pursued in detail. We shall examine first some of the preacher's most personal and characteristic thoughts, themes that occur repeatedly in his works, and we shall have to examine them in the light of his view of language. Second, we shall subject his modes of expression, his rhetorical and poetic style, to analysis in this same light.

Clearly, a result of an analysis of Eckhart's treatment of the divine names is that he was very critical of the ability of language to express what is truly important. Yet we should not emphasize only his consciousness of the inadequacies of language, philosophical or otherwise. For in reading his works we sense the appropriateness of the adage that in recognizing the boundaries of language and human thought one can in some sense transcend them. The finer passages in his works move at the edge of human experience. One is shown vistas of a union with God which takes place beyond the boundaries of experience. Both in his interpretations of scripture and in his use of language in general, there is an underlying attempt to uncover what lies hidden in words. One is given intimations of a core hidden from normal perception. Eckhart leaves no doubt about the power of words or about what he considers to be the source of this power: "Wort hânt ouch grôze kraft; man möhte wunder tuon mit worten. Alliu wort hânt kraft von dem êrsten wort" (Words also have great power; one can work wonders with words. All words have their power from the first Word; Pr. 18; DW I, 306, 5–7).

IV
CHARACTERISTIC THEMES

What we have learned about Eckhart's conception of human language and its limitations in expressing what is divine should help to clarify how he understood such favorite themes as the just man or the birth of the Son and how he wanted his audience to understand them. If part of Eckhart's difficulties with those judging his orthodoxy revolved around the question of analogy, a false assumption, on one or both sides, that they agreed on the related question of what words mean would certainly have compounded his problems.

If one assumes that God is nameless, that our hold on him through words is more tenuous than supposed, say, by those following Thomas, then in attempting to describe him and one's union with him through what is divine in oneself one will lay much less claim to being "dogmatic." One will not suppose that one's formulations of religious truths attain a degree of accuracy and completeness which requires that they be considered somehow exclusive. In losing their dogmatic character they become more personal. By making more modest doctrinal claims for them, one also attains greater freedom of expression. If one views the way that philosophical and theological language expresses truth as being thus limited, one will be more at liberty in using it to emphasize the point one wishes to make with less concern for giving the total picture. And since its correctness and adequacy in expressing religious truth is so limited, philosophical and theological language will approach more closely poetic expression and the language of nonscholarly piety. It is just this mixture of scholastic theology, poetry, and nonscholarly religious language that we find in Eckhart's vernacular sermons.

To understand the themes the preacher returns to again and again, we must view them in this linguistic context. They are emphatic declarations of religious truths that attempt what is, by definition, impossible. Still, they try to offer us a glimpse of the truth that at least surpasses the state of utter ignorance. However, one formulation will not exclude the possibility that a quite different, even apparently contradictory, formulation may be equally appropriate. This is a necessary consequence of the view that there is more discrepancy between human language and the divine, and thus infinite, nature of the reality it wishes to communicate than there is congruence. Only by seeing such themes against this background will we be able to appreciate the subtle modesty of what Eckhart attempts as well as his more obvious daring. And it is the modesty of the attempts which justifies his daring.

The Just Man

Eckhart's elaborations on the theme of the just man provide an appropriate starting point because of the proximity of this theme to the conception of *esse* already discussed, because it leads us directly to the central theme of the birth of the Son, because it receives detailed attention in both the Latin and the German works, and because the preacher himself assures us, "Whoever understands the difference between justice and the just man understands everything I say."[1]

We shall put aside for the moment the question of how one becomes the just man, what psychological or ascetical steps the achievement of such a state requires. At present we shall analyze only descriptions of the just man as a goal already attained. It should be noted, however, that in most contexts Eckhart is not primarily concerned with the exact nature of justice as a virtue. He is, of course, aware of the traditional definition that justice gives to each his due.[2] Characteristically he is not satisfied with the conventional definition, but continues by giving a definition of his own: ". . . and in another sense those are just who receive all things alike from God whatever it may be, large or small, pleasant or painful; [they accept it] all alike neither less nor more, one thing just like the other."[3] But this approach is rather ascetical, more in the realm of *gelâzenheit* or *abegescheidenheit*. Clearly Eckhart is not really interested in defining one of the four cardinal virtues here. The point he usually wants to emphasize, rather, is how justice, as a general perfection, is related to the just man or how "just" exists in a creature. Goodness and the good man or wisdom and the wise man would serve as well. In fact, he sometimes bunches all these virtues together for this purpose without showing interest in how such qualities differ from one another.[4]

To understand exactly what Eckhart wishes to say in his frequent elaborations on the theme of the just man, we must keep in mind two things that are important presuppositions, although the preacher does not always see fit to express them. These presuppositions are his view of the relationship of justice to the just man and the *in quantum* principle as it applies here.[5] As so frequently, it is in a Latin scriptural commentary that he makes the most lucid presentation of these two factors.

In explaining the text from the Book of Wisdom (1:15), "Iustitia enim perpetua est et immortalis," he states that there is an essential difference between the relationship of material qualities to their subjects (e.g., of "white" to "wall") and that of spiritual qualities to their subjects (e.g., of "just" to "man"). Material qualities cease to exist when their subjects do. They have one and the same *esse* with their subjects. Quite the contrary is the case with spiritual qualities or general perfections. These are not subject to the limitations of the creatures that receive them, nor do they receive anything from these. Justice exists prior to the just man, and it is more correct to say that the just man is in justice than to say justice is in the just man (*In Sap.* nn. 41–42; LW II, 362–364). Eckhart considers the point so essential even for lay audiences that he begins his *Book of Divine Consolation* by explaining it in detail:

> First of all we ought to know that a wise man and wisdom, a truthful man and truth, a just man and justice, a good man and goodness, have a mutual relationship, and depend on one another in this way. Goodness is not created, not made, not born; rather it is what gives birth and bears the good man; and the good man, insofar as he is good, is unmade and uncreated, and yet he is born, the child and son of goodness. In the good man goodness gives birth to itself and to everything that it is.[6]

General perfections like *esse*, *bonum*, and *iustum* that in themselves are not limited to just part of reality are more real than the beings that are informed by them. The just man does not, by acting justly, cause some justice to come into existence. Rather, by uniting with justice, which is infinite and eternal, he, the creature, escapes from the nothingness which he is in himself and becomes one with justice which alone, as divine, really is. The just man does not make justice a reality. Justice makes the just man real.[7]

Eckhart notes further that it is one and the same justice in which all just men reside, like accidents residing in one substance (*In Sap.* n. 44; LW II, 366–367). The just man takes on the same form as justice (*conformatio*) and as God himself. Continuing to emphasize the concept of form, Eckhart finds backing in Paul (2 Cor. 3 : 18), who says that "we are trans*formed* into the same image." While thus underlining the sameness of justice in God and creature, he also uses the words *conformatio* and *configuratio* to stress equally the shaky hold the creature has on justice: Justice is only a transitory configuration in the creature. It is not something residing permanently in the just man nor, as Eckhart had said about the *esse* of creatures, is it something rooted in him. Rather, it is like light (sun) in a medium or like the image in a mirror (*In Sap*. n. 45; LW II, 367–369). The instant the object causing the image disappears from opposite the mirror, or the instant the light ceases to shine, all traces of the image or the light disappear from the mirror or the air. Thus, also, can justice disappear from the creature.

Despite this last qualification, what nevertheless startles the reader is the utter oneness of God (justice) and the just man. To understand Eckhart correctly on this point we must be clear about what he really means by the just man. Here the second principle, *in quantum*, comes into play. This qualifying phrase (*in quantum iustus*: insofar as he is just) or its equivalents (phrases like *utpote*, *ut sic*, or *ut talis*) appear frequently in his Latin works, so that there is justification for assuming that it is in force in other passages, even when unexpressed, especially in vernacular sermons where fine distinctions are less appropriate.

In most scholastic thought the phrase *iustus in quantum iustus* (the just man insofar as he is just) would focus attention on the *man* to the extent that the man could be called just, to the extent that he exercises the virtue of justice (excluding from consideration, for example, that he happens to be a plumber and has a broken arm); but in Eckhart's view such a way of using *in quantum* is not valid. In his view "just" comes entirely from justice and is not really a quality possessed by the man; rather, "just" takes possession of the man. What he thus wishes to concentrate on through the use of *in quantum* is not the *man* to the extent that he is just, but on "just" insofar as this form—deriving from and completely one with justice—exists in conjunction with a creature.

In the Latin Bible commentaries, to make his meaning clearer, he distinguishes the just man as just from the just man in himself (*in se*). If the just man as such seems to be described as indistinguishable from the divinity, the just man *in himself* is eminently distinguishable. In commenting on the true light that shines into this world, Eckhart explains that, in himself and as inferior, the just man, like

John the Baptist, is not the true light but is filled with darkness. However, in his principle (*in principio*, John 1:1), which is justice, the just man shines and justice shines in him.[8] As in the case of the *esse* of creatures, the spiritual qualities that can be attributed to them are not really their own; they are, rather, divine qualities filling up the emptiness or darkness which creatures are in themselves. Creatures are both more and less than they seem.

While these principles remove some of the incomprehensibility from the theme of justice and the just man, they do not dilute its boldness. The teaching has its basis in Eckhart's thought, not merely in his rhetoric. For him, when viewed from one perspective, God and the just man are absolutely one. Some examples of how he expresses this oneness are worth relishing.

The *in quantum* principle is not always absent from the German sermons. In fact, the preacher finds two ways of expressing it. In elucidating the text "qui sequitur iustitiam, diligetur a domino" (Prov. 15:9), he describes God's relationship to the just man thus: "What does God love? God loves nothing but himself and *insofar* as he finds something like himself in me and me in himself."[9] The *als vil*, once one is aware of its implications, confers on the traditional Christian thought—that God's love of self is the basis of his love for creatures—the extremeness typical of Eckhart. In a more ingenious vein, revealing to us perhaps something of how he viewed the nature of language, Eckhart notes that the adjective "just" in "iustus in perpetuum vivet" (Wis. 5:16) has no noun to qualify: "He does not say 'the just man' or 'the just angel,' he simply says 'the just.'"[10] Eckhart takes this to mean that the just man here is considered solely under the aspect of his participation in justice, or insofar as he is just.[11]

Justice should not be considered some mere abstraction that can be attributed to the just man. It is God himself, as the preacher makes explicit. The just man as such has justice alone as his father, ". . . and God and justice are completely one."[12] It is pure justice, justice as form, that Eckhart claims is God: "Therefore, consider justice simply as justice, for then you are considering it as God."[13] And one becomes just by assuming the form of justice. It is an *în- und übergebildet werden in die gerehticheit*, a having the form of justice envelop one's created nature, reforming it to pure justice.[14]

Eckhart's ultimate claim for the just man is simply to identify him with God. He formulates this identity in several ways. Since justice is God, the just man and son of justice "has the same being that justice has and is, and enters into all the qualities of justice and truth."[15] This being (*wesen*) bestowed upon the just man is divine:

"God gives the just man a divine being and calls him by the same name which is proper to his own [God's own] being."[16] The just man thus achieves equality with God: "Thus shall the just soul be with God and next to God, completely the same [or equal], neither below nor above."[17] In addition, Eckhart also stresses the just man's oneness with the divinity and thus his being loved by God as God loves himself: "The just man is one with God. Likeness [sameness] is what is loved. Love always loves what is like itself. For this reason God loves the just man just as he loves himself."[18]

Finally, for those who would find distinctions in such formulations which compromise the identity of God and the just man, the preacher states this identity in a way that allows no such niceties. Taking the just man as the Word, he quotes John 1:1 that the Word was with God and then continues: "He [John] says 'with,' and the reason the just man is like God is that God is justice. Therefore, whoever is in justice is in God and is God" (. . . *Und ist got*).[19] The just man, insofar as he is just and derives totally from justice, is simply God.

Before leaving the theme of the just man, we might at least touch upon a question that must occupy us at length later: How does a person progress from being a creature, a just man in himself, and attain the goal of being the just man as such (*in quantum iustus*)? In answering, Eckhart twice says, "He who loves justice, justice takes possession of him and he is embraced by justice, and he is justice."[20] Love of justice causes this union of creature with the divine. He then continues in a heightened Augustinian vein to show that the exercise of true freedom on the part of a creature can occur only when the creature achieves equality with God. The closer one comes to becoming justice, the closer one comes to achieving freedom. Creatures in themselves are slaves and are not free.[21] For the moment it will be enough to understand that Eckhart's description of the just man's becoming just assumes not merely a certain condition of existence on the part of the creature but a course of action or development as well.

The Birth of the Son

In his efforts to breathe verbal life into his thoughts on the union of creator and creature, Eckhart turns most frequently to the image of the birth of the Son in the soul. Though he makes limited use of this image in his professorial writings,[22] it is as preacher that he returns to it again and again to give it new dimensions, thus enabling the image to enrich the minds of his listeners in ever fresh ways. He is not the originator of the birth idea in Christian theology. It could be found especially in the Greek fathers and thus had an aura of orthodox respectability, though hardly a mainstream idea in the West in Eckhart's own day.[23] However, we must not allow similarities between Eckhart and earlier theologians to cloud the fact of his originality or to predispose us in determining his meaning. The best approach for comprehending Eckhart's idea of the birth of the Son is to examine it in his own various formulations and against the background of the rest of his thought.

For orientation, let us first look at a passage from Sermon 6, where the birth is the focal point, and then attempt to clarify the issues it raises:

> The Father gives birth to his Son in eternity, equal to himself. "The Word was with God, and God was the Word" (John 1:1); it was the same in the same nature. Yet I say more: He has given birth to him in my soul. Not only is the soul with him, and he equal with it, but he is in it, and the Father gives his Son birth in the soul in the same way as he gives him birth in eternity, and not otherwise. He must do it whether he likes it or not. The Father gives birth to his Son without ceasing; and I say more: He gives birth not only to me, his Son, but he gives birth to me as himself and himself as me and to me as his being and nature. In the innermost source, there I spring out in the Holy Spirit, where there is one life and one being and one work. Everything God performs is one; therefore he gives me, his Son, birth without any distinction. My fleshly father is not actually my father except in one little portion of his nature, and I am separated from him; he may be dead and I alive. Therefore the heavenly Father is truly my Father, for I am his Son and have everything that I have from him, and I am the same Son and not a different one. Because the Father performs one work, therefore his work is me, his Only-Begotten Son without any difference.
> "We shall be completely transformed and changed into God" (2 Cor. 3:18). See a comparison. In the same way, when in the sacrament bread is changed into the Body of our Lord, however many pieces of bread there were, they still become one Body. Just so, if all the pieces of bread were changed into my finger, there would still not be more than one finger. But if my finger were changed into the bread, there would be as many of one as of the other. What is changed into something else becomes one with it. I am so changed into him that he produces his being in me as one, not just similar. By the living God, this is true! There is no distinction.[24]

The birth of the Son is spoken of as taking place both in eternity and in my soul. It is not a voluntary act on God's part. I am this same Son. In giving birth to me (himself) he gives birth to himself, his being and nature. The internal workings of the Trinity seem inseparable from this giving birth to the Son in the soul. Perhaps most striking in the historical setting is the claim that we shall be transformed into God just as the bread becomes God in the eucharist. Such is the oneness without distinction that the preacher swears takes place. He is careful to quote Paul in introducing the idea, and this comparison is certainly not being made by a Christian writer for the first time. But in the scholastic works of Eckhart's time the comparison implied a substantial union between God and creature and had pantheistic implications. Both the commission in Avignon and the papal bull single out this passage as heretical.[25]

To solve some of the puzzles arising from this and similar passages, it will help to remember that Eckhart's view of language requires that we do not consider his various themes to be separate scholastic theological doctrines but rather to be what have been aptly called "verbal strategies."[26] We must remember too the appropriateness of Quint's comment that the Dominican's greatness consists in his having subordinated all his efforts to exploring and articulating the depths and sublimity of the birth idea.[27] Some of the answers are thus most likely to be found in other themes, and still other themes will receive illumination when related to the birth of the Son.

Of obvious close proximity to the birth idea is that of the just man. Repeatedly, Eckhart will glide from one idea to the other effortlessly and without demarcation. Sermon 6, which we have just cited as containing a "classic" passage on the birth, takes as its scriptural point of departure "iusti vivent in aeternum" (Wis. 5:16). The birth theme is introduced with no transition after the biblical text has been treated. Another sermon actually states the identity of the Son and the just man: "The Father gives birth to his Son the just man and to the just man his Son."[28] The *Commentary on John* makes this identity almost as explicit.[29]

One crucial question is whether the *in quantum—in se* distinction in force in Eckhart's treatment of the just man is also operative in his development of the theme of the birth of the Son. There are clear indications that it is. First, in the sermons the proximity of the elaborations on the just man to those on the birth idea has the effect of making them appear to be alternate descriptions of the same reality. Second, while Eckhart frequently describes the birth of the Son as an accomplished reality and views the union of creature and Son as perfect, there are occasional passages where the birth is not pictured as a state of complete union and thus where the difference between us and the Son is clearly stated. Let us see whether such passages can be equated with Eckhart's description of the just man in himself (*iustus in se*).

We are told that the time is coming and is now upon us when we shall worship in spirit and truth. The preacher then explains that we are not the truth; that is, we are certainly true, but there is also something not true in us. This is not the way it is in God.[30] And immediately following this statement he urges his hearers to "bring forth" the Word. Since for Eckhart the truth is the Word, this admission of nonidentity is significant. More directly applicable is an admission in Sermon 42: "Truly, if my soul were as prepared as the soul of our Lord, Jesus Christ, the Father would work in me as purely as in his only-begotten Son and not less, for he loves me with the same love with which he loves himself."[31] The contrary-to-fact condition reflects the sad truth that we are not as prepared for divine activity, as we are in ourselves (*in se*), as Jesus is. But it also implies the sameness of divine activity in Jesus and me to the extent that (*in quantum*) I am a suitable place for God to work.

The *in quantum* factor of our becoming the Son is most clearly expressed in the *Book of Divine Consolation*, where it is said that the Son is born in us and that he (the Son) flows out from those who are sons of God "to the extent that they are *more* or *less* purely born of God alone."[32] Oneness with the Son makes us happy. Thus, "the farther we are from this oneness, the less we are sons and Son . . . and the closer we are to this oneness, the more truly we are the sons and Son of God."[33] There are, then, two aspects to being the Son. In his *Commentary on John*, when treating the lines stating that the Word gave the power to become sons of God to those who believe in his name (John 1:12), Eckhart singles out "become" (*fieri*) and "sons" (*filios*) to clarify his meaning. "Becoming" implies not yet being. It is an imperfect condition. One is not yet the Son. One has not yet reached fulfillment. However, all things are possible for one who believes.[34]

If the theme of the birth of the Son, or that of our possible oneness with the Son, bears such striking resemblance to the elaborations on the just man, right down to the distinction between *in quantum* and *in se*, one might ask why Eckhart found it necessary to state his thoughts in these two ways. What does the idea of the birth of the Son add? In reply we can baldly say: very much. Although its relationship to the just man and the concomitant *in quantum–in se* distinction are essential for a correct understanding of the birth, its meaning is by no means exhausted thereby. Eckhart is able to provide it with a variety of contexts, thus enabling it to express union with a vitality and depth far beyond what is accomplished when he bases the God-creature union on simple perfections, such as justice or goodness. To see why Eckhart gives it such a central role, let us examine the various facets of the birth theme in some detail.

The Birth and the Trinity One startling characteristic of the birth is that it is inextricably bound up with the workings of the Trinity.[35] The preacher equates the Father's generation of his eternal Son and the procession of the Holy Spirit with the birth of the Son in man. The traditional distinction between God's immanent activity as expressed in the doctrine of the Trinity and his activity *ad extra* is virtually ignored. And in a theologian as knowledgeable as Eckhart this has to be considered intentional.

Most frequent, of course, is the identification of the soul with the only-born eternal Son. We are "here in this Son and we are the same Son."[36] Since no one knows the Father except the Son and only the Son knows the Father (Matt. 11:27), one "must be a single Son of the Father with Christ. . . . You must be one Son, not many sons, nay more: one Son."[37] This spiritual birth is more important than the Son's corporeal birth from Mary. We must understand "that we are a single Son that the Father has begotten eternally." I flowed out with all creatures, "yet remained in the Father."[38] Even here in this world we have the power to become sons of God, "even only-begotten sons; or rather the only-begotten Son."[39] Man should so live "that he is one with the only-begotten Son and that he is the only-begotten Son. Between the only-begotten Son and the soul there is no difference."[40] Finally, taking basic terms from scholasticism, the preacher states, "I cannot be the Son of God unless I have the same being that the Son of God has, and from having the same being we become like him, and we see him as he is God." But saying we are like God does not strike the preacher as being apt enough: "Therefore I say that in this sense there is no 'like' and no difference; rather, without any difference (or distinction) we become the same being and substance and nature as he is himself."[41] One wonders whether a scholastic thinker could have found any stronger language with which to emphasize the utter oneness of the divine Son and the soul.

The unity between God and creature in the birth is not, however, limited to our union with the Son. We also share in the activity of the other divine persons. Man must unite with the Father in begetting: "What good does it do me that the Father gives birth to his Son if I do not give birth to him also? It is for this purpose that God gives birth to his Son in a perfect soul and lies in childbed, that it [the soul] give birth to him in all its works."[42] Thus united with the Father, I too cause the procession of the Holy Spirit: "There I am one with him [Father], he cannot exclude me, and in this work the Holy Spirit receives his being and becoming from me as from God."[43]

The mysterious nature of the Trinity, however, is that it consists somehow of three distinct persons existing dynamically in a being that is utterly one. If we are united to such a being, are there other appropriate ways of describing this union besides those already mentioned, ways that approximate this union or imitate its characteristics? One way of showing how man shares God's oneness is to describe him as united at one and the same time with more than one divine person. Thus we find man simultaneously one with the Father begetting and the Son being born. The soul which is not just a married woman but also a virgin is "fruitfully co-begetting" with the Father "out of the same ground out of which the Father is bringing forth his eternal Word." And "this Jesus is united with her [the virgin-soul] and she with him, and she shines and illumines with him as a simple oneness and as a pure bright light in the heart of the Father."[44] The soul as Father and Son shares in the mystery "preceding" this eternal generation as well as in its eternally happening: *'in principio'* (John 1:1). Here we are given to understand that we are an only son whom the Father has eternally borne out of the concealed darkness of the eternal concealment, remaining within in the first beginning of the first purity, which is a plentitude of all purity. Here I had my everlasting rest and sleep, in the eternal Father's hidden knowledge, remaining unspoken within. Out of the purity he everlastingly bore me, his only-born Son, into that same image of his eternal Fatherhood, that I may be Father and give birth to him of whom I am born."[45]

If the soul both gives birth and is born, it can with equal justification be equated simultaneously with the Son born and the Holy Spirit proceeding from the union of Father and Son: "the Father's essence is that he give birth to the Son, and the Son's essence is that I be born in him and like him; the Holy Spirit's essence is that I be consumed in him and be completely fused in him and become love completely."[46]

Finally, the soul in its similarity to God can be described as one being engaging within itself in vital immanent activity like that occurring in the oneness that is God. Attributing the statement to an unidentified teacher, Eckhart says, "The soul gives birth to itself into itself and gives birth to itself out of itself and gives birth to itself again into itself."[47]

That the soul is taken up into the immanent activity of the Trinity itself should not come as a surprise. Although the preacher clearly wished such passages to shock his audience, he was doing so not merely through rhetoric, but rather by stating the truth. The unity implied between the soul and the different persons of the Trinity in such passages is simply a clear consequence of his *in quantum* distinction and his conception of *esse*. To the extent that a human person has become the Son there is no difference between God and that person. Consequently there is no reason to use the plural to distinguish man's sonship from that of the divine Son. Nor in this same context is there any reason to separate God's activity into that which is immanent and that which is *ad extra*. Also, number has no meaning in the oneness of the divinity. Nor can there be any external goal for the infinite internal life of God. And this is the life the soul-become-Son lives.

So that the event/state of the birth of the Son be understood correctly, Eckhart felt it must be presented in its true context, namely, with all the attributes of that divine event. Two characteristics of human events, characteristics which also circumscribe our ability to imagine events, are that they take place at a definite time and in a definite location. These are, however, characteristics arising from our limited natures, dependent, as they are, on matter. The birth is not tied to a place, nor does it really happen in time. Eckhart is constantly at pains to make this clear. When does the birth occur? In the eternal *nû* (now), independent of time. In Sermon 10 he explains the eternal *nû* in some detail, calling it the "day of God": "There it is the day of God where the soul stands in the day of eternity in an unchanging now and where the Father gives birth to his only-born Son in present now and the soul is born into God. As often as the birth takes place, it [the soul] gives birth to the only-born Son."[48] Immediately following this the preacher reiterates his claim that only *one* son is born in eternity. Neither number, as we have seen, nor repetition of an event has meaning in eternity. Repetition adds nothing to the event because eternity has no duration. It is instantaneous. What would appear from the point of view of creatures to be several births to several souls at various times is really one birth happening once.

Place too, coming as it does from the realm of creatures and their nothingness, must be eliminated from our idea of the birth. The preacher achieves this destruction of place by affirming two locations for the birth: "As he [God] gives birth to his Only-Begotten Son into me, so I give birth again into the Father."[49] If expressing the transcending of place in this passage is diminished because he simultaneously gives expression to the dynamism between God and the soul, another passage is clearer. The following lines, where union of wills is stressed, are more explicit: "When the will is so united that it becomes a simple one, then the Father of heaven gives birth to his only-begotten Son into himself into me. Why into himself into me? There I am one with him."[50] Just as the timelessness of the event is most aptly expressed in human language by paradoxically joining its uniqueness to the idea of repetition, so its spacelessness is well formulated by having it happen in two places that have become one.

Another one of the preacher's assertions—that God has no choice but to give birth to the Son in my soul—might appear to be a radical departure from traditional Christian thought, but it is plausible when viewed in the context of his conception of *esse* and his employment of the *in quantum* principle.[51] Christian thinkers had taken great pains to preserve the voluntariness of creation. To demarcate clearly the boundary between the Christian concept of creation and Neoplatonic theories of emanation, in which the world flows out of the divine being by some kind of necessity, it was important to insist that God created the world not out of any compulsion or necessity of his nature but freely. Eckhart could not but be aware of this tradition since his two favorite authors, Augustine and Thomas, both treat the point in detail. Again, the intent to shock is apparent, but so too is Eckhart's wish to clarify for his hearers the oneness man has with God. If God's begetting the Son in the soul is, as we say, part of God's immanent activity, then it is governed by the "rules" governing the divine nature. Here it is a question not of voluntary actions but of activity arising necessarily out of the infinite dynamism and perfection of God. In Sermon 49 Eckhart takes the time to clarify this point:

> The Father speaks in his intellect and produces his own nature completely in his eternal Word. Not of his will does he speak the Word as an act of the will, as though what is being spoken or done is from the power of the will; in this same power he can also not do it, if he so wishes. This is not the way it is between the Father and his eternal Word; rather, whether he wants to or not, he has to speak the Word and give birth unceasingly. . . . In this Word the Father speaks my spirit and your spirit and the spirit of every human being like this same Word. In this same [act of] speaking you and I are a natural Son of God just as this same Word is.[52]

The birth of the Son in the soul is divine activity, not that of creatures. Nor is it divine activity directed toward creatures. The birth as such cannot be separated from and is totally one with the rich life of the Trinity, a life so intense and yet so unified, simple, and one that thinking of it as having dimensions like time or space distorts it. In the birth the soul is also raised above that contingency of which freedom of the will is part and which the freely created world must endure.

The Birth and the Incarnation If the birth theme allows Eckhart to display the richness of union by incorporating the life of the soul into the life of the Trinity, it also provides him with a framework in which to discuss another pivotal mystery of Christianity, the doctrine of the incarnation. Much of what he says about creatures, for example, their relationship to being (*esse*) and goodness, while predicated primarily with man in mind, obviously extends to all created things. In a sense, one could imagine all creatures, animate and inanimate, sharing in the life of the Trinity. What is it about man which makes it possible for him to transcend this basic relationship to God enjoyed by all creatures and share in the riches of the divinity in an essentially higher manner? Part of the answer is to be found in the article of faith that God became man. And while this is hardly something new in Christian thought, Eckhart's elaborations on the role of the incarnation do bear his personal imprint. Even more than in the case of the birth and the Trinity, we notice a tendency in him to use philosophy and concepts achieved through reason to reach into the heart of theological mysteries. While this tendency characterizes the efforts of several of his scholastic contemporaries, Eckhart often takes the philosophizing of theology a bit further.

The preacher poses a question: What is the purpose of all human religious striving? And what was the purpose of that most important divine and human event that God became man? He responds, "To this purpose: that God be born in the soul and that the soul be born in God." This is the meaning of all of scripture and the goal of creation.[53] The response to God's becoming man is that man become God: "Why did God become man? That I be born God the same."[54]

As certain passages make clear, however, Eckhart is not unaware of the differences between the God-man and creature. In his *Commentary on John*, in treating the words "et vidimus gloriam eius, gloriam quasi unigeniti a patre" (John 1 : 14) with typical ingenuity he takes *unigeniti* (only-begotten) as a nominative plural modifying the creaturely "we," subject of *vidimus* (saw), thus turning the human witnesses of the Son's (*eius*) glory into only-begotten sons themselves. But he then uses *quasi* (as it were) to distance these only-begotten sons who are similar to, but not the same as, Christ. He continues: "He is the Only-Begotten, coming from the Father alone; we are begotten, but not from one father. He is a Son through the generation that leads to existence, species, and nature, and therefore he is the natural Son; we are sons through the rebirth that leads to conformity with this nature."[55] Christ is the natural Son; man has to be *re*born in order to *con*form with this nature.

Earlier in this same commentary, Eckhart distinguishes clearly between Christ and man by noting that what Christ is by nature (*per naturam*) man may be by adoption (*per gratiam adoptionis*).[56] But before assuming that such traditional wordings allow us to reduce Eckhart's position to a safely traditional thought, we must investigate other passages which appear to stand in opposition to the foregoing. We have heard the preacher maintain in Sermon 6, for example, that the Father begets me as his being and his nature (DW I, 109, 8–10). And just as the Son is one with the Father according to being (*wesen*) and nature, "so are you one with him according to being (*wesen*) and nature."[57] And in being one with the Son beyond mere similarity, "we become without any differentiation the same being and substance and nature that he is himself."[58]

What is the role of the incarnation in this sharing of a single nature? And what is this nature that is shared? The preacher takes, as his starting point, the dogma that Christ assumed human nature and explains how this affects humanity:

> The eternal Word did not assume this [individual] man or that [individual] man, but rather he assumed a free, undifferentiated (*ungeteilte*) human nature that was bare of definite characteristics (*bilde*), for the simple form of man is without definite characteristics. Therefore, in this assumption human nature was assumed by the eternal Word simply, without definite characteristics, and the image (*bilde*) of the Father, which the Son is, became the image of human nature. Just as it is true that God became man, so it is true that man became God. Therefore, human nature has been reconstituted (*überbildet*) in that it became the divine image, which is the image of the Father. And therefore, if you are to be one Son, you have to separate yourself from and abandon everything that causes individuation in you. For man [as an individual] is an accident of [human] nature. Therefore, abandon everything in you that is accident and conduct yourselves according to free, undifferentiated human nature. For just as this same nature according to which you then conduct yourselves has become Son of the eternal Father because the eternal Word assumed it, so you become the Son of the eternal Father with Christ because you conduct yourselves according to the same nature that has become God.[59]

Leaving aside for the moment the question of *how* one is to attain this goal in living a human life, we must try to penetrate the metaphysical implications of this passage. *What* happens to a person to the extent that this goal is achieved? What change has occurred? Certainly the passage is puzzling, but some conclusions can safely be reached.

In becoming man the eternal Word did not take on a new personality, a personality that was human. Rather, according to the traditional teachings the divine person, the Word, took on a new nature, human nature. If this event truly touches the core of the divine Word, it must be an event taking place in an essential way in eternity as well as in time. But eternity is the realm of *esse*, where even creatures overcome the nothingness that they are in themselves and transcend those characteristics which cling to creaturely existence as such—time, location, and multiplicity. In eternity there can be no real difference between the Word and its human nature. Eckhart's conclusion is that through God's becoming man human nature became (and in eternity always was) divine.

What individual characteristics does this divine human nature have? Eckhart tells us that the individual characteristics (*bilde*, image or likeness, as we learn in Genesis) are those of the Father whose image the Son is. This divine image which informs (*überbilden*) human nature through the incarnation is what human beings become in divesting themselves of those individualized, accidental characteristics that keep them in the realm of creatures in themselves, creatures as nothing. Because God created man in his image and himself assumed human nature, the process of becoming the Son can be described as an uncovering of the divine image already existing *by nature* in individual human beings: "When a man lays bare and uncovers the divine image that God created in him *naturally*, God's image becomes evident in him."[60] Human nature as divinely informed is the means by which men become one with God. This is the role of the incarnation for Eckhart.

One consequence the theologian saw arising from this, one that disturbed his colleagues, was the identity in substance of God and man. Sermons 6 and 76 have already been quoted to this effect, but they are not isolated examples. It is significant that he makes the point several times in his Latin works, in other words, in addressing an audience that would be more aware of the meaning of the term "substance."

In Eckhart's terms the birth of the Son is not an act of creation but an act of generation or transformation. In contrast to mere change (*alteratio*), which only affects the object undergoing change as to its accidents, *generatio* has an effect on the substance or substantial form.[61] In other words, a new kind of being comes about through *ge-*

neratio, not just a modification in something already existing. Two examples of substantial change used frequently in the schools were food changing into the substance of the one eating it and wood, in the act of burning, taking on the being or substance of fire. The food and wood are no longer such but have become one with an animal organism or with fire respectively. The latter are clearly different beings from the food or the wood which then no longer exist as such. These examples are exactly the ones the preacher uses in a Latin sermon to explain Paul's words "Christ lives in me" (Gal. 2:20). The soul "is transformed into that divine being (*esse*) by which God himself exists and lives."[62] Eckhart even states that the soul's being turned into God is more of a change because it involves spiritual beings.[63] If part of his wish was to startle his audiences and jar them out of trite ways of thinking, he certainly achieved this by suggesting that one who has become the Son attains substantial identity with God. Although we have already provided most of the context for understanding this claim, we should first explore a more traditional explanation.

The Role of Grace   One might pause at this point, after being confronted with the various claims about the birth of the Son—identity of Christ and creature, that the birth unites one with the immanent activity of the Trinity transcending time, space, and contingency, the claim of oneness in substance, and the many implications of these claims—and one might consider them in the following light. Certainly they are startling and, to those of Eckhart's contemporaries concerned with orthodoxy, even disturbing. But should they have been? Does not Christian thought make many similar claims that are just as startling, especially Christian thought as found in the writings of John and Paul? And did these doctrines not provide much of the foundation for the spiritual or religious life of Eckhart's clearly orthodox contemporaries? Christ as the vine and his loyal followers as the branches: is this not a claim of substantial union? How else is one to understand the mystical body, or now no longer my living but Christ living in me? How else should one understand the putting on of the Lord Jesus Christ? Does not the preacher himself repeatedly justify his claims by referring to scriptural passages of this kind?[64] Cannot many of the difficulties regarding the orthodoxy of his thought be solved simply by appealing to the well-established doctrine that God allows the faithful to share his own divine life and be united to him in some incomprehensible way through grace?

Unfortunately, Eckhart's views on grace have never been given the detailed scrutiny they deserve. When grace does occur in second-

ary literature, the assumption is frequently made that his views fall
well within the general framework of orthodoxy or even that his
views are very much the same as those of his fellow Dominican
Thomas. The function of grace in such studies is often to shore up the
theologian's orthodoxy against those with misgivings, and passages
are cited in which Eckhart mentions grace in a very traditional way.[65]
While the goals of this study do not permit an extensive treatment of
Eckhart's conception of grace, we must examine it at least in sufficient detail to make the following two points. First, while the nature
and functions of grace in general are ill-defined in Eckhart, thus
making it of doubtful value as a measuring stick of his orthodoxy,
Eckhart's notion of grace clearly departs from that of Thomas in
at least one important respect. Second, seen in its proper context
against the background of his thought, his conception of grace does
not miraculously resolve all doubts about whether or not the nature
of the union envisioned in the birth of the Son falls completely
within the confines of orthodoxy.

Though grace had been an essential part of Christian doctrine in
both the East and West since early times, Thomas gave it a more
focused role than it had before. Augustine, the *doctor gratiae*, had
stressed its necessity and gratuity, especially in the wake of original
sin. Without it man was incapable of performing meritorious acts and
living as a child of God. Thomas sees its necessity stemming from
the goal to which man is called. As a Christian in possession of revelation, Thomas believed that man's ultimate end was not just some
state of natural happiness, but was to share in a divine life that raised
him above the capabilities of his nature. The question of man's final
goal is an instance where Thomas the philosopher had to capitulate
to Thomas the theologian. The philosopher, examining with his unaided reason the nature of man, can never come to the knowledge of
what man's destiny is in the divine plan. Man has no real end or goal
commensurate with his nature, but was created to achieve a supernatural end, one that God does not owe him simply because of giving
him his nature, and one that man can neither discover on his own nor
achieve merely by living in full accord with his nature. This goal, the
supernatural gift of human participation in God's own life, could be
incipiently achieved in this life through the instrumentality of the
sacraments which give human life and actions supernatural dimensions. However, the ultimate result of this gift, the beatific vision, is
reserved for life hereafter. This gift of sharing God's life is essentially
what grace is. The most important point to be made in juxtaposing
Thomas's view to Eckhart's is that for Thomas grace is a state of exis-

tence superimposed upon human nature. It is something added which raises a human being above his nature. Grace does not supplant human nature; it presupposes human nature as a necessary foundation. But grace takes man beyond himself and *is* the new, supernatural life which is man's ultimate goal.

Just as there are countless statements about *esse* in Eckhart's works which give us no hint that he deviates in the slightest from Thomas's views, so too in the matter of grace the majority of texts give no indication that Eckhart's views are noticeably different. Most frequently, perhaps, his references are prescholastic in the sense that they reflect that broad Christian tradition regarding grace that attributes so much to grace and uses it in so many varying contexts that the term becomes too diffuse for use in an individual theological system. Thus we are told that grace makes us children of God. It alone enables one to be without sin, to be ready and pliable for all divine operations. It flows from the divine spring, is similar to and tastes like God, and makes the soul like God. Finally, it makes us capable of exercising the divine virtues of faith, hope, and charity (Pr. 33; DW II, 151,4–153,4). More often the preacher focuses on grace in the essence of the soul rather than on how it affects our actions. Grace, we are told, does not bring about a work. Rather, it flows out of the being (*wesen*) of God and into the being of the soul, and not into the soul's powers (Pr. 11; DW I, 177, 6–8). The emphasis in this and similar contexts is on grace's function of uniting the soul with God, bringing about a union based not merely upon common activity: "Grace is a dwelling of the soul in and with God." Works, both external and internal, are too weak to serve as a foundation for such cohabitation or indwelling.[66] Using alternate terms in a Latin sermon, Eckhart calls grace a strengthening (*confirmatio*) or changing (*configuratio*) or a transforming (*transformatio*) of the soul into God or with God. It gives the soul one being (*esse*) with God, which is more than mere similarity (*Serm.* XXV, 2, n. 263; LW IV, 240). Though some of these formulations may seem extreme, they are not unusual. They demonstrate, rather, the heights to which Christian thinkers dare to soar when the subject is grace.

In other instances, however, grace is an extremely broad concept and becomes for Eckhart a term for almost everything. While one kind of grace makes us pleasing to God and gives us divine being (*esse*), everything that God works in a creature is grace. This is justifiable usage, because *gratia* is related to *gratis*. Thus grace is everything that we receive freely, undeserving though we be (*In Sap.* nn. 272–273; LW II, 602–603). This thought that every work of God in a creature is grace or a gift occurs again in one of two Latin sermons treating Paul's "gratia dei sum id quod sum" (1 Cor. 15:10). Both sermons are completely taken up with the question of grace. We are not, however, presented with a clear and unified doctrine of grace, its divisions and functions, but rather with a homiletic mélange. The individual points are often cryptic and better formulated elsewhere, but one distinction is worth noting. The preacher distinguishes between first grace, which is creation or a certain flowing out of creatures from God, and second grace, which is given only to creatures endowed with intellect and is the means by which they return to God.[67]

More in line with the role of grace as it functions in man's redemption through Christ and in his achieving a supernatural goal is the statement that man, after Adam's fall, has been reordered to God through grace (*per gratiam*; In Gen. II, n. 145; LW I, 613). And frequently the clear distinction is made between the sonship of Christ and that achieved by man by references to our becoming through the grace of adoption (*per gratiam adoptionis*) what Christ is by nature (*per naturam*).[68] Some passages sound like echoes of Thomas. We read, for example, how noble man was created in his nature and what he can attain by grace, or that grace "breathes into" (*inspirat*) nature, or that grace does not destroy nature but rather fulfills it.[69]

In view of all these references, we have no choice but to conclude that in this Dominican's view, as in the view of Thomas, grace has an essential function in explaining how the divine plan works. It must also be admitted, however, that these same references taken together show us that the word itself does not have a clearly definable core meaning in his thought. Context may clarify it some, but we most comfortably turn to a broad conception of grace in most instances when attempting to determine its meaning or function. Still, in the light of the preceding references to grace by Eckhart, we would have little reason to suppose that he viewed grace at all differently from the common tradition, or from Thomas for that matter. It is to passages that do give such indications that we now must turn.

One hint that Eckhart conceives grace differently emerges from passages dealing with the light of the intellect. While he stresses the superiority of the light of grace over the light of the human intellect, even though the latter far surpasses in nobility all corporeal things (Pr. 73; DW III, 260,6–262,8), there seems to be for man something more sublime than the light of grace. In a sermon about the birth of the Son where we are urged to reach the Son who is a light that has shined eternally in the heart of the Father, he puts it thus: "If we are to come there [to the heart of the Father], we have to climb from the natural light into the light of grace and in this we must grow into the light that is the Son himself."[70] Having attained this, we partake of the life of the Trinity. Similarly, when Eckhart tries to reconcile Paul ("The lord dwells in inaccessible light," 1 Tim. 6:16) with John ("We shall see him as he is," 1 John 3:2), the position of grace seems to be an intermediate one. After declaring the light of the intellect to be superior to the light of the sun, and the light of grace to be above the light of the intellect, he continues: "However great the light of grace is, it is still small compared to the divine light. . . . As long as one increases in grace, it is small and is just grace in which [light] one knows God from afar. But when grace is brought to its highest completion, it is no longer grace; it is a divine light in which one sees God."[71] While much in such passages is puzzling, the preacher definitely posits something above grace, something divine which man in some sense attains.[72]

Equally idiosyncratic are certain statements about grace and union. In speaking of that "something in the soul" in which God is eternally, and with which the three persons are one in principle (*nâch dem grunde*), he declares that grace has no function here because grace is a creature and creatures have no part in this (Pr. 24; DW I, 417,8–419,5). Perhaps clearer is the following passage addressing the same subject: "Grace does not bring about any work; rather, it pours all embellishments completely into the soul; that is a fullness in the realm of the soul. I say: grace does not unite the soul with God. It is a bringing to [the point of] fullness; that is its function, that it bring the soul back again to God. Then it [the soul] receives the fruit from the blossom."[73]

In passages, therefore, where Eckhart is disposed to describe it in a more specific sense and in a sense more properly his own, grace is seen as an intermediate stage or as a means by which the human soul achieves the goal of union with, or sharing in, the divine existence. It is not, as in the case of Thomas, the divine life itself seen from the point of view of man being raised above his nature to share in it as his ultimate goal. Grace is a creature enabling man to reach his goal but separate from that goal. It is the adornment, the blossom, and should not be confused with the fully ripened fruit.

If we keep this conception of grace as a means clearly in mind, other statements can be seen in clearer focus. Since the theologian most frequently insists that grace pertains to the essence of the soul and does not flow out into the powers of the soul in order to perform external works, one could assume that grace itself is this divine life in the soul. But grace does work (*operatur*) in the soul. And rather than being this divine life, grace is the means by which we receive it (*per se dat esse divinum*). If such an interpretation seems strained, it helps to realize that the occasion for Eckhart's remarks is the Gospel verse (John 10:41) which states that John the Baptist worked no unusual signs. John is taken to mean "the grace of the lord," and John, of course, is the *precursor* of Christ, not the divinity itself.[74]

The frequency with which grace occurs as a means is striking. Although there are instances where grace—especially when conceived as an indwelling in God—is not clearly distinguishable from the divine life, such phrases as *gratia per se, per gratiam*, and *per gratiam adoptionis*, where grace functions grammatically as a means, are what we find predominating. Indeed, grace as an ablative of means has great significance for Eckhart. Let us examine two passages where the preacher applies his interpretive skills to Paul's "by the grace of God I am what I am" (*gratia dei sum id quod sum*; 1 Cor. 15:10). In a Latin sermon he takes advantage of the ambiguity of *quod* in medieval syntax. *Quod* can be construed as a relative pronoun (by the grace of God I am that *which* I am) or as a conjunction (by the grace of God I am *that* I am). He concedes that both give a proper sense to the text, but points out that taking *quod* as a conjunction allows a more sensitive reading. In other words, *by means of* grace I am so purified of my individuality and am able to live so for God alone that it is no longer I who live but rather I have become one with the *esse* that alone really is.[75]

In his well-known sermon on "poverty of spirit" the preacher is clearer still about what Paul was telling the Corinthians. After explaining that true poverty of spirit means giving up one's own intellect, will, and separate existence to be one with God, the preacher quotes this Pauline text and notes that what he has just said about poverty of spirit seems to be "above grace and above being and above understanding and above will and above all desire." How then are we to take Paul's words? He suggests the following interpretation: "That the grace of God worked in him [Paul] was necessary, for grace brought it about that what was accidental brought about being. When grace was finished and had completed its work, what remained of Paul was that he was."[76]

What Eckhart means by grace in such contexts is not man's sharing in the life of God. Its function is rather preparatory. It takes man as he is, as an individual, with his individual accidental characteristics which consign him to nothingness, far from the realm of true existence which is God; and it strips him of everything that is accidental, of everything that separates him from the pure human nature that the Word assumed. To the extent that one is then freed from the nothingness of the self, one can be united to that existence which alone truly is, namely, the divine existence. What remained of Paul was *esse*, and *esse est Deus*.

From what has been said thus far, it should be very clear that for Eckhart grace plays an essential role in man's ascent to God. Eckhart is certainly no Pelagian, but he is also not simply a Thomist. There are too many indications that, in contrast to Thomas, for whom even the attainment of the *lumen gloriae* in heaven was still grace in the sense that the glorified soul shared in the divine nature only by being raised through grace above its own being and nature, Eckhart sees man's ultimate union to be based on *esse*. And since *esse* is God, the distinction between nature and supernature does not apply in the same way. For Eckhart, grace does not raise a person from nature to supernature; grace is the *means* by which one is raised from the nothingness one is in oneself to *esse*, which is God. To explain troublesome areas of his thought by appeals to grace is misleading if, in doing so, one has recourse to Thomas, or even if one takes the broader traditional Western Christian concept of grace.[77] This latter concept of grace is general enough to excuse almost anything objectionable in the Dominican's theology; but due to its latitude, it obfuscates rather than clarifies issues. This is exactly the effect grace has when Eckhart himself appeals to it in defending himself before ecclesiastical authorities against the charge that he maintained the utter unity of Christ and creature in his teaching on the birth of the Son. Despite the numerous occurrences of such assertions throughout his works, he denies before the tribunal that such a oneness is possible. He stresses that we are one with Christ *per gratiam adoptionis* as members of the church whose head is Christ.[78] He is justified in taking this position, of course, because he is speaking of men as creatures in themselves (*in se*). This is the same clear distinction between God and creature that we have seen him make, especially in his Latin works. Of course, he is aware of the difference between God and creatures. But to say that we are united to Christ through grace clarifies things only if one is aware of what Eckhart means by grace, and only if one understands that meaning in the light of his *in quantum* distinction.

If our primary concern is to *understand* Eckhart and not to render him too easily orthodox, then, rather than attempt to fit the rest of his thought into that broad and vague framework which grace can be, it is more appropriate to find the proper place for his own particular conception of grace in the context of his own thought. This we have tried to do. Grace is not the same as union. The glory of union when and to the extent that we return to our source requires that grace has already functioned to remove from us the imperfection which impedes such a union.[79] If grace can be said to exist in this union, then we must consider it as existing *virtualiter*, that is, by virtue of what it has accomplished. It does not exist in a proper sense (*formaliter*), for here "in the region of infinite dissimilarity" nothing exists except the God beyond being, beyond our understanding.[80]

Summary Since nowhere in the works of this learned Dominican do we find a thorough and well-balanced scholarly presentation of the birth of the Son, despite its prominent role in his thinking and preaching, it is a bit presumptuous to attempt something of the sort here. Eckhart's own practice of starkly emphasizing certain aspects of the birth instead of striving for balance and a total view might well be a consequence of his conviction that human language is relatively powerless to represent religious truth with any adequacy or completeness. And certainly the doctrine of the birth, which denies all difference between the soul and the infinite God, is a prime example of human language confronted with a task beyond its capacities. Nevertheless, in concluding we should attempt to construct a fuller context for it—something the format of the sermon did not readily allow—and thus further clarify how we are to understand it.

For Eckhart, man is not a creature existing halfway between nothingness and infinite being. He exists rather as a composition of these two extremes or, perhaps better, he exists in the tension between them. So dependent is he on this interplay of *lûter nihts* and *esse divinum* that it is more accurate, depending on the point of view, to call him a nothing or an insubstantial image, or, on the other hand, to identify him with God, than to think of him as a *tertium quid*, with a being and life all his own. This view of man's metaphysical composition finds a parallel in the realm of religious truth in the theme of the birth of the Son. In contrast to lower creatures, man has the capacity to influence the interplay of these extremes within him. He can fill the void of nothingness within him that he is in himself with the richness of the *esse divinum*. This process is that of the birth of the Son. To the extent that the Son *is being born*, the process is incomplete and man has not moved completely away from his nothingness. To the extent that he has achieved the birth, he is the Son and no other.

Man as the Son is not a creature but is taken up into the triune divinity beyond space, time, and accidents. There is no difference between him and the Word. In taking on human nature, the Word became a human substance. The Word did not just take on the accidents or appearance of being human. By divesting himself of his own individual, accidental aspects, man can become one with this deified human nature, united to the Word that lies hidden beneath his individuality. In doing so, and to the extent that he succeeds, man becomes one substance with God.

Eckhart ran afoul of the authorities, perhaps primarily because of his frequent claims of the utter identity of God and the soul. If he meant this in an absolute sense, with no qualifications or conditions whatsoever, the judgments of the church authorities are hardly to be questioned. Such identity does not conform to traditional Christian teachings. Is this what Eckhart really thought? Are we simply one substance with the Word without qualification? Can man so free himself from his own nothingness that he simply and completely becomes the Son?

Despite Eckhart's frequent assertions in this vein, there are clear indications that this is not how he wanted to be understood. First of all, the distinction between *in quantum* and *in se*, which we have seen is an essential thread running through the themes of the just man and the birth, implies an insuperable duality. Given the absolute character of this dichotomy, creatures can never lose completely their *in-se*-ness, just as they can never become completely something else *to the extent that* they become it. *In quantum* implies a relative success in becoming just, good, or the Son. That Eckhart understood this dialectic in this manner is a conclusion that one can probably draw from reading his more studied writings, but it is sometimes evident even in his sermons.

Concerning the question of our substantial union with the Word, a case where the preacher goes out of his way to employ an academic term in a manner calculated to astonish, we find him, in one instance at least, showing an appreciation for the necessary qualifications. In a Latin sermon undoubtedly given to an audience capable of appreciating what "substance" means, he puts the matter thus: "God put on our clothing [i.e., assumed our nature] so that truly, in a proper sense and substantially (*per substantiam*), he becomes man in Christ. The nature assumed, however, is common to all men without more or less [possessed equally by all men]. Therefore, it is given to every man to become the Son of God in [Christ] himself certainly, but in [man] himself (*in se*) [it happens] by means of grace by way of adoption.[81] Here identity in substance is claimed, but a distinction between the

Word and the creature in whom grace is operative, and hence who has not reached total identity with the *esse divinum*, is preserved as well. Eckhart's assertion of substantial oneness, then, does not necessarily remove all differences between God and creature.

But in view of the ubiquitous statements of complete union, is it not plausible to assume that Eckhart meant that *eventually* all differences could be overcome? What about man's existence in heaven? When the *lumen gloriae* is attained, which is above the *lumen gratiae* attainable on earth, are not all traces of difference then finally removed? In a passage treating the question dividing Franciscans and Dominicans, namely, whether happiness consists in loving God or in knowing (seeing) God, Eckhart gives his own twist in responding and indicates that all duality between God and the human spirit in itself (*in se*) is not overcome. He poses the question thus:

> Some teachers insist that the spirit attains happiness in love; others insist that it attains it in seeing God. But I say, it does not attain it in loving or in knowing or in seeing. Now one could ask: Does not the spirit look at God in eternal life? Yes and no. In that it [the human spirit] is born, it does not look up to nor does it look at God. But in that it is still being born, it does look at God. Therefore the spirit's happiness consists in its having been born and not in its still being born, for it [the human spirit] lives where the Father lives, that is, in oneness and purity of being.[82]

In other words, even in heaven the human spirit exists in a condition including both the birth as a state implying utter oneness with the divine existence, and the birth as an incomplete and ongoing process. Basically this is the same distinction as that between *in quantum* and *in se*. "Looking at God" implies duality, lack of union, imperfection. This cannot be the basis for happiness. Happiness lies in having been born, in being united with God perfectly.

If this interpretation is correct, why then do we find so many passages where Eckhart suppresses this duality to the point of misleading his audience and his ecclesiastical judges? Why is the union of creature with God so emphasized, to the detriment of the whole picture? An answer in the spirit and thought of the preacher would seem to be: because the reality of the birth—the fact that we are capable of achieving real union with God—is so overwhelming, so existentially vital, that all else pales beside it. Being the Son circumscribes our reality. What we are in ourselves is nothing and defines us merely negatively. Our otherness from God delineates negatively the boundaries of our being. Our being is God's being, and this is what the preacher took such pains to impress on his hearers. This was the one insight they simply had to have for true spiritual orientation.

From what has been said, it is clear that Eckhart did distinguish between the Word and a human person becoming the Son. Yet we should be careful, if we wish to call his use of the *in quantum* principle a looking at creatures from a formal or abstract point of view, not to rob his teaching of its central religious importance and not to consider it a kind of mental exercise with some basis in reality.[83] For Eckhart, man becomes the Son and *is* the Son. There is only one Son, and there is no distinction between the Son in man and the Word. The doctrine brings an immediacy of the divinity to man and, with an uncompromising radicality, reduces man's existence to the existence of God.[84] Only if one admits this does the manner in which he expressed the birth or union seem justified.

Becoming the Son

Two questions concerning the birth of the Son in the soul remain to be explored. First, how does the birth come about? What must one do to bring it about? Second, where does the birth take place, that is, what more precisely is it in the soul that enables it to receive/conceive the word and bring it forth?

We have seen that becoming the Son, at least to the degree that one achieves it, involves a transformation that is described as metaphysical. This change in the creature touches its very core, raising it out of itself toward true existence. Although the metamorphosis is in this sense metaphysical, and although God is without question its primary cause, it does not happen without human cooperation. In speaking about the birth, the preacher constantly urges his audience to become the Son, admonishing them that one *should* (*sol*) undertake steps to achieve it. We shall now investigate his conception of the process of becoming the Son. How does the cooperation of the creature in its own deification come about? What must one do to become the Son? What course of action, ethical or ascetical, must one undertake?

The fact that Eckhart, in concentrating his pastoral and oratorical efforts around the birth, neglects certain mainstream factors of Christian moral thinking and asceticism has caused some commentators to assume that he had a radically different approach to the spiritual life. While his spiritual message is certainly radical in that he, like no other, uncompromisingly applies metaphysics to a study of human spiritual progress, it would be a mistake to conclude that he rejects anything essential in traditional Christian spirituality. It is true that one finds very little concerning Christ's passion and death in his works, and he certainly does not dwell at length on such questions as sin and judgment. However, there is not the least bit of evidence that he rejects such staples. The *Book of Divine Consolation* develops as a major theme the union that one can effect with God through suffering, and sin does find scattered mention in his works. The fact is that, here as elsewhere, in discussing what Eckhart's unique contribution is, we must assume an extensive congruence of his thought with this tradition. This agreement is most in evidence in his early *Counsels of Discernment*, where he has not yet narrowed his efforts in order to concentrate on a few favorite ideas. When we judge his later works, the approach that meets with the least number of puzzles is to assume that he is presupposing the basics of Christian morality as something he shares with his audience. This shared tradition allows him to lead his hearers further, at times through startling declarations. If we do find something new or different in the path he proposes, we can best determine the extent of its newness by seeing it against the background of this shared tradition.

If there is an aspect of his ethical teaching which appears unorthodox, it is his insistence that all ethical value derives from the interior work and that the exterior work, the actual physical carrying out of an action, adds nothing of ethical worth. In a passage from the *Book of the Parables of Genesis*, which provides the material for articles 16 and 17 of the bull *In agro dominico*, he gives his reasons for this position. First, God does not formally command an external act since it can be hindered. Second, an external act is not formally good or divine, nor is it God that performs it or brings it forth. The external act can be onerous, the internal act can never be. Hence only the internal act really praises God (*In Gen.* II, n. 165; LW I, 634–636). We should not be surprised at this exclusive stress on the interior or spiritual aspect, since as we shall point out in greater detail the external work is hopelessly tied to the realm of creatures in themselves.

At the same time, one can appreciate the alarm such reasoning caused in the ecclesiastical establishment. Perhaps it brought to mind Abelard's insistence on knowledgeable consent as the essence of ethical activity, certainly a step forward in Abelard's own time, given the external formalism then prevalent in matters of morality, but also a point of view that left many problems remaining to anyone wishing to construct an ethical system that would do justice to man's composite (spiritual-material) nature. Did not Eckhart seem to be doing away with the balanced approach advocated in the ethical thought of Thomas? Or perhaps authorities were afraid that such "spiritualistic" ethical tendencies would fuel the quietism they perceived, or thought they perceived, among certain religious or parareligious groups in the Rhineland at the time. Since Eckhart most likely meant by *internal* the act done by the good man insofar as he is good and conceived the *external* act as being limited in its effect to creation in itself, his stance is really not a return to the position of Abelard. Consent or intention is not the primary issue. Eckhart's particular view of the composition of creatures is. Moreover, if rightly understood, his view does not lead to quietism. Indeed, Christ's own words and their usual interpretation notwithstanding (Luke 10:38–42), we have the text of a long sermon devoted to showing the superiority of Martha's way of life (*vita activa*) to that of Mary (*vita contemplativa*), who is still learning at the feet of the master and has yet to achieve the completeness of her sister's life.[85] We also have the evidence of his own personal activity to refute any claim that Eckhart himself drew any quietistic conclusions from his own ethical doctrine.

Although Eckhart's distinction between internal and external works plays a prominent role in the bull condemning him (articles 16–19), it does not really constitute a central concern in his works as a whole. His efforts gravitate much more toward articulating the nature of the internal work. He is frequently concerned with how this work must be constituted to fulfill the requirements for being the act of the just man or the Son. He turns his attention rather to determining what the ethical or psychological dynamics are which are necessary to turn the limited acts of a human person into acts of someone whose productivity transcends the nothingness of creatures and has relevance in the realm of infinite divine existence.

If it is a mistake to consider the preacher's emphasis on the internal work quietistic, it is equally wrong to take "interior" to mean "spiritual" in the sense that a spiritual act is one that, at least symbolically, proclaims the primacy of man's spiritual side over the material. This is a common purpose in undertaking certain ascetical practices, such as fasting, keeping vigils, wearing garments that cause discomfort, and the like. While Eckhart did not at all condemn such practices, he was endowed with enough psychological insight to warn his audience about the ambivalent role these acts can play in the search for spiritual improvement. They often give one the mistaken notion that one is in a position to bargain with God, as though such acts were independent capital providing the basis for closing a kind of business deal (*koufmanschaft*; Pr. 1, DW I, 6,6–9,6). One can hold on to them, thinking of them as things that are peculiarly one's own. They can easily become an end instead of a means. One becomes complacent, even comfortable, with acts of self-abnegation. They become an indispensable part of one's daily life, and one is no longer free to follow God unencumbered, giving them up if necessary (Pr. 2; DW I, 28,7–30,2).

Eckhart sees a much more solid goal of religious action in the union of one's own will with God's will. This most venerable ascetical idea, with scriptural backing in the Lord's Prayer and with a divine model in the Garden of Gethsemane, appears frequently as a central concern of the preacher. Since the theme itself is so well established in Christian thought, there is no need to dwell on its general characteristics. However, two points should be made about its place in Eckhart's thought. First, we have seen enough evidence concerning his view of the nature of creatures and their relationship to the divine existence to realize that he does not confine his attention to a union of wills. Certainly he considers this conformity of the human will to the divine will essential. However, both with respect to man's dependence on God in his metaphysical makeup and with respect to man's ultimate goal, the total union envisioned by the Dominican thinker encompasses much more. It cannot be conceived as just the accidental union which arises when in complete unity two wills—spiritual powers existing in separate and independent beings—will the same object. Clearly this is just an aspect of union. Second, as we might expect, the preacher is not satisfied merely with adopting the traditional doctrine. He often embellishes it and gives it his own personal imprint. One example of this occurs in Sermon 25, where he states the paradox this union entails: "Whoever gives his will completely to God catches God and binds God so that God can do nothing but what man wants. Whoever gives his will to God completely, God gives him in return his will so completely and so really that God's will is man's own . . . ; for God belongs to no one unless this person first of all becomes his [God's] own."[86] The Augustinian notion of complete fulfillment of the human will through its surrender to God is followed to its logical conclusion: Whoever so surrenders his will gets whatever he wants.

Abegescheidenheit   To discover what Eckhart thought man's contribution to the realization of union was to be, we must investigate a group of ideas usually subsumed under the heading *abegescheidenheit* or *gelâzenheit*. These terms are sometimes given more prominence than they deserve. Actually, the preacher resorts to many terms and images to express this ethical-ascetical teaching. What most of these words have in common is the idea of separation. The most frequent Middle High German prefixes for the verbal expression of this are *abe*, *ent*, and *ûz*, all of which denote separation. *Abegescheidenheit*, usually translated "detachment," is an abstract noun from a verb meaning to depart from or separate from. Eckhart frequently uses the verb and the participial forms as well. We are also urged to *abelegen* (to put off, like a piece of clothing, or to put aside) and to *abekêren* (to turn away from) and to *ûzgân* (to leave or go away from). Further, one must *entdecken* (uncover) the divinity within. One must *sich entvremden* (distance oneself or become a stranger to) *bilde* (forms or images) or, with *bilde* itself in a verb form, *sich entbilden* (divest oneself of *bilde*). Instead of developing ourselves or making ourselves "come about," we are urged to travel the opposite path: *entwerden* (to unbecome or undevelop, or perhaps to become by becoming less). Frequent adjectives used to describe the success of this process are *vrî* (free, unencumbered), *ledic* (free from, rid of), *îtel* (empty of), and *blôz* (naked, bare).

The only term among all these that is really puzzling, and the one causing the others to retain a certain unfocused character, is that signifying what we are to rid ourselves of: *bilde*. *Bilde* (picture, image, species, form) does not have a uniformly negative character for Eckhart. It has several meanings.[87] As we have seen, a favorite way he has of describing how we become the Son is to say with Paul that we are transformed into the same image.[88] In losing our own individual characteristics, we lay bare pure human nature in us which, as such, bears the image of the Word-Son. And if at times the preacher implores us to see God as he is in a realm that is described as formless (*wüestunge, einoede*, e.g., Pr. 10; DW I, 171, 12–15), we are schooled enough in his thoughts on the limits of language to realize that he is thereby asserting the superiority of apophatic language without, as is obvious from what he does in practice, ceasing to use other approaches, though their inadequacy is greater.[89]

It is this term *bilde*, as something to be eliminated, that takes Eckhart's thoughts beyond the usual ascetical dimensions of detachment and gives them a more metaphysical flavor. Its exact meaning is difficult to grasp. However, *bilde* does remove the emphasis from the concrete creature itself as what has to be left behind. Essentially, achieving detachment is a spiritual, internal event or process. Looking at it in different contexts may help us understand it better. In a Latin commentary the thinker connects it with the nature of the act of knowing. He notes that the object that one knows begets itself, or its form, in the cognitive faculty. Thus the form or image so generated can be said to be the common offspring of the object known and the cognitive faculty. The implication that the object known is indeed the "father" of the knowledge gained prompts him to conclude that we should have or know no other father than God. The knower is formed by the object and receives his *esse* (as knower) from the object, which is the *esse* of the object. Hence one who knows objects other than God cannot be the Son of God alone. Only those have the power to become sons of God who receive (only) God and are "bare of any form generated and imprinted [on the knower] by a creature" (*nudi scilicet ab omni forma genita et impressa a creatura; In Joh.* nn. 109–110; LW III, 93–94). This apparently necessary condition for attaining sonship is bewildering. Only God is to be the object of our knowledge. Knowledge derived from the forms of creatures limits one's capacity to be the Son of God.

This emphasis on the act of knowing or, rather, as expressed above, on what one knows as a determining factor in spiritual progress, in contrast to the more usual emphasis among religious writers on the will's attitude toward its objects, is certainly something that sets Eckhart apart. In the following passage from a German sermon the emphasis on knowing is less clear, but in light of the Latin passage above, there is some justification for equating *bilde* here with the Latin *forma* or *species impressa*:

> Where the creature stops, there God begins to be. Now God wants no more from you than that you should in creaturely fashion [i.e., as or to the extent that you are a creature] go out of yourself, and let God be God in you. The smallest creaturely image (*bilde*) that ever forms in you is as great as God is great. Why? Because it comes between you and the whole of God. As soon as the image comes in, God and all his divinity have to give way. But as the image goes out, God goes in. God wants you to go out of yourself in creaturely fashion as much as if all his blessedness consisted in it.[90]

The apparent rigorism of these passages is disconcerting. It seems as though we are being asked to change the very way human cognition comes about. Or at the very least he seems to be saying that human cognition of objects other than God—cognition necessary in everyday life—blocks us from "letting God be God in us." Fortunately, we find Eckhart explaining his position in a way that mitigates such rigorism. In Sermon 2 he demands that we become as free of *bilde* as we were before we existed. Being free of such forms is the meaning he gives in this sermon to virginity. The preacher anticipates the problems his audience might have with his thought and himself raises the question "How can a man who has been born and reached the stage of rational life, how might he be as free of all forms as he was before he existed? After all, he knows a lot, and it is all forms. How then can he be free?" The solution follows immediately:

> If I had such capacity of intellect that there existed in me, as they do in the intellect, all forms that all men ever received and that are in God himself; and if I had no possessiveness regarding them so that I had not grasped at any one of them in what I did or did not do, looking neither ahead nor back; but rather that I stood solely in the present—free and unencumbered—for the dearest will of God, to carry it out unceasingly, then truly I would be a virgin without the obstacles of forms, as truly as I was before I existed.[91]

The central term in this passage is *eigenschaft,* which has been translated as "possessiveness." Actually the word has three clearly different applications in Middle High German. Most frequently it denotes ownership or proprietary rights. Hence the use of "possessiveness" here. Second, it can indicate bondage, the social and legal condition of the serf. Third, even this early it can also express the idea of quality or characteristic. Thus the word in itself is not that helpful to us. We must look to the preacher's use of it. Whatever he meant by it, the audience could not help but relate it to the first possibility—that we should avoid treating these *bilde* as though they belonged to us. And they might well have concluded that we must not let the *bilde* we possess make slaves of us. But due first to the strange connection to the act of knowing, and second to the contexts of the term in this sermon, what we are not permitted to do is reduce this warning against having *bilde mit eigenschaft* to some common religious attitude toward worldly possessions. There are aspects of the Dominican's *abegescheidenheit* that clearly do not fall into the area of practical asceticism.

In Sermon 1, where we learn what must be driven out of the human temple so that God may dwell in it, Eckhart prepares us for the difficult concept *eigenschaft* by explaining first the more readily accessible idea *koufmanschaft* (business, commerce). Merchants are those who think they can make business deals with God. They are good people who avoid sin, but they practice good works for the purpose of being in a better bargaining position with God. Their mistake is that they think they have independent capital as bargaining power. Their utter dependence on God for what they are and do shows the illusory nature of their position. God has given them everything and owes them nothing. God alone and his honor must be their goal (DW

I, 6,6–10,7). This is a coarser attitude than that of *eigenschaft*, but it is found in religiously minded people who must, because of it, be removed from the temple. The dove keepers, though their offense is not as serious and who may therefore remain in the temple, must also be reprimanded. These are people who act purely for God's sake and are devoid of self-seeking, but yet whose actions are accompanied by *eigenschaft* because these actions do not leave the limits of time, place, and multiplicity. In other words, their actions are those of creatures, not those of Jesus, who is always free and not limited by the accidents of time, place, and number. Thus our actions must ultimately be divine actions. Only when we are free of these obstacles—*koufmanschaft, eigenschaft,* and the ignorance (*unbekantheit*) which is a necessary consequence of our creaturely or merely human condition—have we reached the goal the preacher envisions for us. There we stand sovereign, looking over and through everything God has created to the uncreated God himself (DW I, 10,8–13,2).

What do these passages tell us about *bilde* and *eigenschaft*? The preacher is asking us not merely to exchange our creaturely way of viewing things for another, but rather to exchange a human for a divine point of view. We are to detach ourselves not just from things or their forms, but even from the usual way men see.[92] Since Eckhart demands it, he must have thought it in some sense or to some extent possible. If we comprehend things devoid of their accidental characteristics and see them as they are in God, and hence see only God, we are not comprehending them *formaliter* but *virtualiter*, which is higher: "Whoever leaves things as they are accident, possesses them where they are a pure being and are eternal."[93] Such a person paradoxically is both virgin and wife (*wîp* here clearly with the right and ability to conceive and give birth). In ridding self of *bilde*, one attains virginal receptivity. But if one is actually to give birth to God, one must make use of the full potentialities of womanhood. Such a virgin-mother transcends mere human endeavor in her actions. Married people, those whose spiritual activity is colored by *eigenschaft*, are free to produce only one offspring a year. A virgin-mother bears nothing less than God as her fruit. She gives birth a hundred, a thousand times a day. There is no limit to her fruitfulness because it is activity united to divine activity, out of the same ground and with the same infinite qualities (Pr. 2; DW I, 28,7–31,4).

Âne war umbe Closely connected to the admonition to act *âne eigenschaft*, and an idea helping to clarify it, is the charge that we should act *sunder* or *âne war umbe* (without a why).[94] A life lived *âne* *war umbe*, like the life lived by the just man or as the Son, takes on divine qualities. Although even Eckhart does not escape anthropo-morphizing God and frequently speaks of him acting for this or that reason, he clearly believes it is more correct to say that God's activity is without a purpose. Just as it is impossible to assign some source to God out of which he came, it is equally improper to posit a final cause or purpose on account of which (*propter quam*) he exists. Rather, he is the end or purpose of all things. In him efficient, formal, and final causes are indistinguishable and internal (*In Joh*. n. 337; LW III, 285). In saying this, Eckhart is not attributing a kind of irrationality to God's existence, but rather immanent completeness or self-sufficience. In a sermon on Paul's "Ex ipso, per ipsum et in ipso sunt omnia" (Rom. 11:36) he makes it clear that one must be careful when speaking of God as final cause.[95] Paul did not add *propter ipsum* (on account of him). God is an end, and his own end *in himself*, but has no end or purpose outside himself on account of which he exists. This is the kind of existence Eckhart urges his audience to strive for: "God, and consequently man as divine, does not perform actions because of a why or a wherefore."[96] Like the efficient cause, the final cause is ex-ternal to a being and influences only change (*fieri*) in it, not being (*esse*) itself (*In Joh*. n. 342; LW III, 291). In other words, external final causes (*propter quae*) must be relegated to the realm of creatures in themselves, a realm from which we should strive to detach ourselves. As divine or just, we have no external goals to achieve: "Remember, the just man [who is born] from justice does not have a source (*prin-cipium*) or a goal (*finis*) outside himself, but rather in himself and flowing out of himself."[97]

These are the scholastic terms at the foundation of living *âne war umbe*. But when Eckhart presents this thought in the vernacular sermons, it is not usually this dry academic logic, but either a con-crete directness or a carefree lyricism with which Eckhart informs the theme. United to the ground of being, we should perform our ac-tions without any external goal or purpose to limit them:

> Out of this innermost ground you should work all your works with-out a why. I say truly: as long as you work your works for heaven or for God or for your external happiness, imposing this on them exter-nally, you are truly not right. One can certainly tolerate you, but it is not the best. For whoever thinks to get more of God in internal piety or in devotion, in sweet consolation and in unusual happenings than in kitchen work or in the barn, then you are acting as though you were to take God, wrap his head up in a cloak, and throw him under a bench. For whoever seeks God in a specific way takes the way and

leaves God behind. He is hidden from ways. But whoever seeks God without a specific way takes him as he is in himself. Such a person lives with the Son and is life itself. Whoever asked life a thousand years long: why do you live? It would say nothing else but: I live so that I might live. This is because life lives out of its own ground and spills forth out of its own self; therefore it lives without a why in that it [life] just lives itself. Whoever would ask a religious person who was working out of his own ground: why are you working your works? And if he should correctly answer, he would simply say: I work so that I work.[98]

We are not to determine the goal to be achieved or the work to be done. All this is *wîse* (limiting factors) making our actions human and robbing them of divine dimensionlessness. To act *mit wîse* is to reverse the relationship of end and means, to make a candle out of God in order to look for something else (Pr. 4; DW I, 69, 2–4). Being and life are in themselves infinite. Only our seizing them and limiting them to our own designs make them otherwise. The same is true of our actions. Performing them *âne war umbe* makes them truly *be*.

Living and performing one's actions *âne war umbe* and ridding oneself of *bilde* can now be seen to function similarly. They both perform the magic of turning the nothingness of man into true being or the Son. For *abegescheidenheit* astounding claims are made. Despite Paul's words (1 Cor. 13:1–3), it is better even than charity. Charity forces me to love God. *Abegescheidenheit* forces God to love me (*Va*; DW V, 402, 1–6). It seeks nothing that is determined (*diz noch daz*) and therefore limited. It wants nothing other than *esse* (*sîn. Va*; DW V, 406, 2–7). If the goal of detachment is unqualified being, its foundation is pure nothingness. Only by emptying oneself of *bilde, war umbe*, and *zuovelle* (accidents) is one able to "build up" a solid base of nothingness, the necessary condition for receiving *esse* (*Va*; DW V, 423,1–425,5). Even the *bilde* of Christ as he appeared on earth was a hindrance to the apostles. He had to leave them before they could receive the Holy Spirit and unite themselves to being beyond all forms (*formelôsez wesen; Va*; DW V, 430,12–431,7). Thus *abegescheidenheit* enables us to unite ourselves to the *esse divinum* both as it is the source of all justice, goodness, and other pure perfections and as it is that which is *formelôs*, which can best, though inadequately, be known by denying positive qualities in it. It extends our ability to unite with God to the limits of our ability to know him.

Mystical Detachment In the preceding treatment of *abegescheidenheit*, the center of Eckhart's teachings in the area of religious ethics and asceticism, we have attempted to present his thought in the terms he himself used. It is hoped that these remarks have clarified his perception of man's path toward union with God. But a certain indefiniteness remains. One is still justified in asking, What exactly would Eckhart have us do? What exactly takes place in the soul? While some passages are specific in their demands, others are not; and one senses that the more concrete precepts which we feel comfortable with rest upon an only partially comprehensible epistomological and metaphysical foundation that must also be "fulfilled" if we are to follow the preacher in *real* detachment.

The heart of the problem is that *abegescheidenheit* joins areas of human experience usually considered disparate. While it seems to be primarily a virtue, and as such pertains to ethics and asceticism, its relationship to the metaphysical composition of creatures and their self-awareness must also be considered essential to it. Because, metaphysically speaking, creatures are nothing in themselves, this virtue does not function to rid them of things foreign to their *selves*. It is the self which must be eliminated as far as possible. *Abegescheidenheit* does not just affect accidentally a creature already metaphysically constituted. It affects, rather, the metaphysical constitution of that creature. What might, at first glance, strike us as confusion of categories on the part of the preacher is really an essential element of his thought. The following passage emphasizing the fluidity between ethics and metaphysics stands for many. The biblical point of departure is "One God and Father of all" (Eph. 4:6):

> "One" is emphasized, first of all, because God is known by negation, for he is incomprehensible. Second, because he is indistinct [from us]. Through this his sublimity and nobility is revealed, and God's goodness and love for us is emphasized. He does not want to be separated [from us], nor can he be. . . . The nothingness of the creature is emphasized in this also: John 1: "without him that which was made is nothing." Third, because all things are one in him and he thus makes them happy. Fourth, because someone wishing to become one with God, [wishing] to find him, ought to be one, separated from everything else and undivided in himself by denial of himself.[99]

On the one hand, as indistinct, God cannot be separated from us. He is *esse omnium* (the being of all things). We contribute nothing to our being; God contributes everything. These are the metaphysical facts of the matter. On the other hand, we also have a goal to achieve. Besides the fact (*is*), our existence also includes a *should*. But this *should*, *abnegatio sui* (denial of self), also affects our metaphysical constitution. We deny the self in a much more radical sense than is usually envisioned in practical asceticism, and with much more radical results. We help bring about being—God's being—where nothingness was before. The union achieved raises us out of our creatureliness, to an existence beyond time, place, and multiplicity.

While it is reasonable to assume from Eckhart's writings that *abegescheidenheit* depends in part on the activity of our wills, it clearly encompasses much more. It touches the very core of creatures, and knowing is an integral part of it as well. Our success with *abegescheidenheit* depends on our insight into what we have called the metaphysical facts of the matter: "If the spirit recognized its pure detachedness, it could incline toward no creature; it would have to remain in its pure detachedness."[100] Just as one cannot look upon God and not love him, so one cannot know one's true self and what one's true being is without detaching oneself from everything, including self, that is other than God.

The interplay of human powers, knowing and willing, and the interplay of the creature with the divine as the human person divests self of nothingness—all this is detachment. We must change, but the most essential aspect of this change is that we recognize the truth and become what we are. Because of the way the metaphysical, religious-ethical, and cognitive factors of *abegescheidenheit* intertwine, and because of the divinization of the creature it brings about, one seems justified in reaching for the word "mystical" to describe it.

The Spark of the Soul

Part of the mystery of how we become the Son results from Eckhart's description of where the birth takes place. When cataloging the various passages where the birth is treated, one notices a certain inconsistency in terminology specifying the place of the event. Of course, as a spiritual happening the birth has no time or place in a material sense. Rather, it is located in the soul. And although the soul united to the body in its dealings with everyday creaturely existence must work within the confines of place and time, the birth happens in a "part" of the soul essentially untouched by such limiting factors. So much is clear. The question of "where," then, is really the question of the nature of the human soul. What is it that makes it possible for the soul to receive/conceive the Son? What capacities or capabilities must the soul have in order to beget the Son?

In a sense, we tried to answer the question earlier when we noted that the role of the incarnation was basic to Eckhart's notions of detachment and becoming the Son. In ridding ourselves of our individuality, we become more and more the nature, unrestricted by accidents, that is informed by the person of Christ. While this explanation is definitely one offered by the learned theologian, it occurs less frequently than the explanation we now wish to treat. What is it, more precisely, about this nature which bridges the abyss between God and creatures? Eckhart's most persistent attempts to answer this question are in his elaborations on the theme of the "spark of the soul," probably his most widely known and most misunderstood teaching.[101]

It is not without reason that there is confusion surrounding this doctrine. In comparing the preacher's frequent and varying references to it, one finds much that is bewildering. Inconsistencies and apparent contradictions abound. Clarification resembles mystification, and the reason for this appears to be rooted in the nature of what he is describing. Turning to secondary literature for help, one finds several ingenious insights but no satisfying total explanation.[102] In view of all this, it seems appropriate, even more so than up to now, to proceed in an "essaistic" spirit. Nothing approaching completeness or roundedness will be attempted, and the author will feel justified in proclaiming success if the main contours of the Dominican's thought seem to emerge.

There is little doubt that the birth of the Son is intimately connected with man's ability to know. We should begin, therefore, with a look at Eckhart's ideas on man's intellect. As in most other questions, we find him generally in agreement with the broad Platonic-Aristotelian tradition coming down to him through such thinkers as Augustine and Thomas. In commenting on the description in Genesis (3:1) of the serpent as the most subtle of all wild beasts, he has gathered together thoughts on the intellect scattered throughout his works. He mixes thoughts from both of the great Greek thinkers without concern for consistency, obviously using what he considers important to give a basis to his own thoughts (*In Gen.* II, nn. 137–153; LW I, 604–624). A summary of these sections should be helpful to us.

Man's cognitive faculty exists on three levels. These are symbolized by the animal (serpent), woman (Eve), and man (Adam). The animal represents the sensitive faculty which can speak to the woman, who is the inferior rational faculty. She, in turn, can speak to the man, the superior rational faculty. He it is who speaks to God. The sensitive faculty is not itself rational, but rather serves the rational faculties and can be called rational by participation but not by nature. Human cognition requires a sensitive faculty because man cannot know without phantasms. These are images arising from the senses and remain in the realm of the senses.

There is one aspect of the human intellect to which Eckhart gives great emphasis: its indeterminateness. He likens it to an empty wax tablet waiting to be written on. And he also compares it to prime matter, that which combines with form to result in real material objects but which itself is just potentiality or passivity waiting for a form to make it real. Another Aristotelian analogy for knowing which occurs frequently in his works, though not in this commentary, is that of the eye and color. Just as the eye has to be free of all color in order to see color, so the intellect, in order to know all things, cannot have anything in common with any things. The startling conclusions Eckhart draws from this, in the *Second Parisian Question*, are that the intellect as such is nothing and that knowing is not some form of being (n. 2; LW V, 50). But we shall return to this matter later.

The inferior rational faculty is given little attention. The superior rational faculty, which is also called the highest part of the soul (*supremum animae*) or the noble soul (*anima nobilis*), is the commentator's chief concern. He tells us that, according to Augustine, it fixes its gaze on the unchangeable rules above in God. And he goes on to note that the *Book of Causes* states that the noble soul has three activities: animal, intellectual, and divine. The divine operation occurs when the noble soul has been transformed into the same (divine) image (2 Cor. 3:18). This superior rational faculty is formed immediately by God. In sermons and commentaries, Eckhart upholds the Dominican position that the intellect is more important than the will and is what ultimately allows man to achieve eternal happiness. In a German sermon he teaches his audience the Aristotelian doctrine concerning the active and passive intellect. The passive human intellect, through its capacity to receive the forms of things or to have these forms "impressed" upon it, has the power, as Avicenna had noted, to become all things in a nonmaterial way (*geistlîche*). The active intellect, which performs the task of turning things into ideas or forms that can be impressed on the passive intellect, is similar to the Father in that it fashions a new kind of existence for all things (Pr. 37; DW II, 220,1–221,1). The intellect touches infinity (*capax infiniti*; *Serm.* XI, n. 112; LW IV, 105). In some places Eckhart refers to man as being the image (*imago*) of God, and in others, weakening this claim, as being *according* to the divine image (*ad imaginem*). When one examines the contexts, one learns that he uses the weaker *ad imaginem* to refer to man in himself or as a possessor of the faculty of reason. When speaking of *imago*, he is referring to the *ratio superior* or *supremum animae*. The higher rational faculty is what justifies removing qualifications expressed through *ad imaginem*. It is the *imago Dei*.[103] Since it is the other aspects of man which cause distinctness from God, but his intellect which underlies sameness with the divine existence, Eckhart can say "man is that which he is through intellect."[104]

It is this superior rational faculty (*ratio superior*) which the preacher so frequently mentions in the vernacular sermons and for which he uses several different terms and images. It is a power of the soul (*kraft der sêle*), a noble power (*edeliu kraft*). It is like conscience (*synteresis*). It is a piece of the soul (*stück der sêle*). It is the image of the divine nature impressed upon the soul (*ein ingedrücket bilde götlîcher natûre*). It is a castle (*bürgelîn*), a temple, a light of the spirit (*lieht des geistes*), a divine light (*ein götlich lieht*), a spark (*vünkelîn*), a beam of light (*zein*), the head of the soul (*houbet der sêle*), man (as opposed to woman and animal), a watchful guard (*huote*). It is the loftiest branch (*der oberste zwîc*), the crown of the tree (*der oberste wipfel*). Why does the preacher feel compelled to shower images upon this power? Paradoxically, because though it exists it is neither this nor that (*weder diz noch daz*), being above determination or qualification (*enboben alle wîse*).

If, as we are maintaining, the "spark of the soul" of his German works can be identified with the *ratio superior*, then Eckhart introduced into medieval psychology no really new factor regarding human cognitive capabilities. It was rather the claims he made for this already familiar intellectual faculty which gave some of his contemporaries pause. We must now examine more carefully the more important and more puzzling of these claims. They can be approached by posing three questions: (1) What is the nature of the spark of the soul? (2) What is its relation to God? (3) What can it do?

Concerning the nature of the *vünkelîn*, the preacher tells us that it is a power or faculty (*kraft*) in the soul, but he also separates it from the faculties, connecting it to the ground (*grunt*) or essence of the soul. It is completely spiritual, more unknown than known. Neither time nor flesh touches it: if one were completely in it, one could not grow old. It contains all things according to their essence (*weselîche*). It contains the images of all creatures, but these are "images without images" and "beyond images." And it has nothing in common with creatures. Even God himself cannot gaze into it insofar as he has names or is persons. It is above both the sensitive and the rational. It is often described as the place where the birth of the Son occurs and, most remarkably, it is in some sense uncreated. Its capabilities are astounding. It seeks God as its object, stripping away the covering of goodness to see him as he is in his dressing room—bare, bare being. It beholds him as he is nameless, beyond being, a vast wasteland and solitude. To say that it is united to God is too little. It is one with him with no difference or distinction. In a detached person its knowledge is exactly that of God knowing himself.

Based upon our previous experience with questions concerning the just man and the birth of the Son, we can best search for explanations not in the realm of the exotic but in the nature of the human creature. For Eckhart there are miracles enough hidden in this combination of divine being and nothingness to cause never-ending wonder. One only has to be aware of what is there. Certainly the *vünkelîn* is not simply the human intellect because he admits the dependence of human knowledge on phantasms and hence on the senses. Unlike the human intellect, at least insofar as it is human, this power has nothing in common with anything created and has God, stripped of *wîse*, as its object.

Despite the limited and imperfect intellect man is endowed with, it is nevertheless true intellect and has certain capabilities in common with all intellects, whether human, angelic, or divine. This is an important facet of Eckhart's thought, for man is in some sense in possession of a cognitive faculty which, as such, truly knows, just as God truly knows. This is what differentiates man from lower creatures. This is the most important aspect of his sharing a nature with the Word. And it is this faculty which makes possible the birth of the Son in the soul.

How can the *vünkelîn* be something uncreated? Or did Eckhart ever really make this claim? In a sermon preached in the Dominican church in Cologne on February 13, 1327, he attempts to clarify what he had preached. He denies having said or taught that there is something in the soul which is uncreated and uncreatable, because this would imply that the soul is a mixture of something created and something uncreated. This he considers clearly erroneous. However, the qualifications he makes are at least as interesting as his denial. One can, he implies, speak of something in the soul that is not per se created but that is *con-created*. Also, he admits teaching—and thinks he does so with the concurrence of some of his colleagues—that there is something in the soul that, if the soul were totally thus, it would be uncreated—*if*, that is, *the soul were essentially intel-*

lect.[105] Thus he does not categorically deny having talked about an aspect of the soul which can be termed in some way uncreated. And we have several sermons where such statements play a central role.[106] Because this question touches the very core of Eckhart's thoughts on the *vünkelîn*, we must examine the uncreatedness of this power in more detail.

We can begin by recalling that, according to the language of the *Parisian Questions*, one cannot attribute *esse* to God in a proper sense.[107] God is instead pure understanding (*intelligere*). *Esse* can only be used of created things. Later Eckhart will call God *esse*, but he will still insist that his whole *esse* is understanding.[108] As *principium* or origin, God remains pure intellect in which there is no *esse* other than understanding.[109] In spite of Eckhart's willingness to identify *esse* and *intelligere* in God, *intelligere* retains a certain primacy over *esse* in God, and *esse* can be used in some sense of lesser things. More important, there is a sense in which *esse* and *intelligere* must be considered irreconcilable opposites rather than coextensive transcendentals, whether we are considering them in God or in lesser rational beings. Knowing, of necessity, has certain characteristics. Really existing things have contrary characteristics. Thus, whether in God or in man, knowing cannot simply be reduced to a kind of being.

The most important opposition is based upon the analogy with sight, which Eckhart borrowed from Aristotle. Just as the eye must be free of color to perceive color, so the intellect must be free of the forms given in nature to be able to understand all forms.[110] Eckhart draws the most sweeping conclusion possible from Aristotle's analogy between seeing and knowing. Since being is the object of the act of knowing, the intellect must be free of being to know. This gives his concession allowing God to be called *puritas essendi* a new twist. God is the purity *of* being, not so much because he is purified being but because he is purified *of* being. The intellect, since it has nothing in common with anything, is nothing, nor does the act of knowing have any *esse*.[111] Since the occasion for Eckhart's calling the intellect nothing is a *quaestio* in which he states that *esse* and *intelligere* are not the same in angels, and since he makes the statement refer to the intellect *in quantum* intellect, he is not just speaking of God's knowing, but of all knowing. In man it is the *vünkelîn*, his highest intellectual power, that allows the soul to "work in nonbeing." (*würket in unwesene*; Pr. 9; DW I, 151, 11–12).

Must it, however, not be admitted that the objects we know have a kind of existence in our intellects? Certainly a chair in the mind *is* in some sense. Eckhart counters this objection with the following arguments. First, it is precisely as nonbeing that an image in the intellect functions to let us know the real object. To the degree that we focus on the image as something real, we are distracted from knowledge of the object which the image represents.[112] Second, universals like "chair" or "man" are the ideas that the mind produces. But universals do not exist. Only individual chairs and men do. A universal is only possible as nonbeing. Third, a really existing thing (*ens*) is determined. It has a definite size, shape, color, and the like. But both the intellect and the act of knowing, as we have seen, are of necessity undetermined (so that they can receive determination from the objects known). Therefore, the intellect and knowing are not beings but are, rather, the opposite of *esse*.[113] We must recall here Eckhart's view on analogy, according to which something attributed to two analogates (here, for example, a real chair and a chair in the mind) can only really (*formaliter*) exist in one analogate.[114]

If we are to think of the intellect as nonbeing or nothing, we must realize that it is a nonbeing above being just as *intelligere* is above *esse*. It is exactly man's possession of a real, if weak, intellect that permits us not to relegate him completely to the region of *esse* (in the sense *esse* has in the *Parisian Questions*, i.e., creatures) and also to locate him in some sense on the divine side of the boundary between *intelligere* and *esse*. Paradoxically, it is the ability to know, requiring, as it does, that the cognitive faculty be undetermined (like prime matter) in order to receive determination from *esse*, that underlies a certain capacity in man to take on the form or image of God (*quaedam deiformitas vel deiformatio; Q. Par.* III, n. 9; LW V, 60) because of God's "form" as *intelligere*.

Because the intellect and its activity stands in opposition to *esse* or creatures, it is uncreated and uncreatable. *Esse* is the first of things created (*Q. Par.* I, n. 4; LW V, 41), and there is no way that the intellect and the qualities of knowing can be assimilated into such a conception of *esse*. In this sense, knowing as such must be considered outside the ambit of being. But how does this apply to man, who is obviously a creature yet endowed with intellect? At least two possible and not mutually exclusive explanations suggest themselves. The reply of February 13, 1327, given above by the beseiged theologian, implies an application of his ubiquitous *in quantum* principle. As such, the intellect without any qualifications is uncreated. And man has a real intellect. As human, however, man's intellect must be admitted to be con-created with the soul. If the soul were pure intellect, it would be uncreated, but this is not the case.[115]

The opposition of being and knowing in Eckhart's thought is not limited just to the period of the *Parisian Questions*. We find it in the *Tripartite Work* as well, where we are told that the ideas of created things are neither created nor creatable (*In Sap.* n. 22; LW II, 343). More to the point, the reason for something's being able to be created is solely its *esse*: "Hence a thing produced by God, although it be a being which is living and knowing, is creatable for the reason of its *esse* alone. Thus if something were to be living or knowing but did not have any *esse* except for and outside of living and knowing, as such it would be uncreatable."[116] If, therefore, we are considering man's intellectual faculty separately from its place in his makeup, it is by its own nature uncreatable. But by his use of the subjunctive, Eckhart admits that, aside from God, nothing exists which has life and knowledge but no being.

Probing further, we might find an additional context for understanding this "something uncreated in the soul," although grasping the thinker's ideas in this area is particularly difficult. First, as we have seen, the stability of creatures depends upon their *esse virtuale*, which is stronger than the being they have in themselves.[117] This *esse virtuale* resides ultimately in the Word. Since there is no *esse* in God other than pure *intelligere*, this *esse*, which raises creatures above their nothingness, is really a kind of knowing and pertains to the intellect. Second, man as a living and knowing creature cannot merely have, as even inanimate creatures do, an *esse virtuale* in the Word. Especially as a knower he cannot be reduced simply to a *bilde*, the object of knowledge, but must also have a mode of existence other than this, other than the *esse* which is limited to and begins with the existence of creatures as such. In describing the life of the just man and man as Son, Eckhart takes great pains to show that such a person throws off the limitations of creatures and performs divine acts in the context of eternity. Since any activity or existence apart from creation is *intelligere*, it is man's cognitive abilities and, more particularly, his intellect as true intellect, most evident in the *ratio superior* or *vünkelîn*, that allows him to function as one with the Word and with the wholeness of the divinity as well. As indistinct from God, therefore, man's knowing can be called uncreated and uncreatable, although as human, and therefore a creature, the intellect will be referred to by the thinker under attack as con-created, even though it functions in ways not reducible to *esse*.

Man's intellect as one with God can see things from God's point of view. Characteristic of Eckhart, however, is the following passage, where his use of the subjunctive, functioning actually as the *in quan-*

tum principle, implies that the creature as such never attains the condition perfectly: "For into this power nothing enters but God and the power is always in God. And therefore: if a man were to perceive all things in this power, he would take them not as they are things, but he would take them according to how they are in God."[118] Despite the qualification, it is nevertheless correct to see the *vünkelîn*, as indistinct from God, sharing in creation. Since creation as an act can only be *intelligere* on God's part, and since the soul has intellect and thus transcends time, place, and multiplicity, God creates the universe in the soul as a continuous event: "In the innermost and highest of the soul, where time has never entered nor form (*bilde*) shined into," God created the world. Past, present, and future things are created by God "in the innermost of the soul."[119] In another sermon, the *vünkelîn* is given the same function as the Word in creation. Although a few lines earlier the preacher had stressed how perfectly the soul has been *created*, when he goes on to speak of the spark he describes it as having been *begotten* (the sentence is an anacoluthon): "When God created all creatures, and if God had not begotten something before this, which is uncreated, which carried within itself the forms of all creatures: this is the spark (*vunke*)— . . . —this spark (*vünkelîn*) is so related to God that it is a simple one, unseparated, and it carries within itself the form of all creatures, forms without forms and forms beyond forms."[120] Despite some confusion in the transmission and despite the double terms *vunke-vünkelîn*, it seems evident that the *vunke-vünkelîn* is the power in the soul and not simply the Word. Like the latter, the *vünkelîn* contains the forms of things that must precede creation if creation is the work of an intelligent cause. However, we have just heard the preacher maintain that form (*bilde*) has never entered into the *vünkelîn*. The resolution of this apparent contradiction is probably to be found in a standard scholastic solution to the problem of having a multitude of forms in the Word, something that would appear to conflict with the unity and simplicity of the person of the Word and the divine act of knowing. These forms cannot exist in the Word formally distinct from each other (*formaliter*), but only in a higher and more unified way (*virtualiter*). The point to be made here is that Eckhart conceives of the unity and simplicity of the *vünkelîn* in the same way. No *bilde* may enter in as a distinct and separate form, yet the *vünkelîn*, as one with the Word, contains all *bilde*; however, they are *bilde sunder bilde* and *bilde über bilde*.

Although the *vünkelîn* is often described as a *kraft in der sêle* where the birth occurs, there are passages that designate the *grunt* as the ultimate place of union.[121] Where God gives birth in the inner world, "here God's ground is my ground and my ground God's ground."[122] Since it is difficult to determine an exact meaning for *grunt* or to equate it clearly with scholastic Latin, this statement must remain unclear. In the following passage from a Latin sermon, we find what is probably the same idea stated more precisely: "in the substance of the soul God dwells in the proper sense. This, however, is higher than the intellect."[123] The confusion grows when, in this same sermon, the preacher goes on to interpret *domus mea* (i.e., God's house) first as the very essence of the soul into which God alone falls as he is naked, and then immediately (*secundo*) takes God's house as the superior faculty of reason, which we have equated with the *vünkelîn* (n. 249, pp. 227–228). Similarly, in a vernacular sermon he speaks of a *kraft in der sêle*, but wishes to qualify this: "There is a power in the soul, and not just a power, rather being (or essence, *wesen*), and not just being, rather: it dissolves being."[124]

The probable reason for these ambiguities is that Eckhart finds the usual scholastic distinction between the faculties of the soul (intellect-will) and its essence misleading. Of course, the distinction is necessary so that the soul does not "disappear" when we are not knowing or willing. But the "accidental" aspect of the intellect as *potentia*, the fact that it can be turned on and off, that it can be merely in potency as well as in act, robs it of the substantiality due the place where the birth occurs. Thus the birth cannot be relegated merely to a sometimes only potential power. On the other hand, the distinguishing mark of the soul, above all else, is its ability to know. It is his highest form of knowing that raises man from "made according to the image" to an "image of God" himself. Hence one may not consider the *vünkelîn* as separate from the essence of the soul. Perhaps Eckhart's most successful formulation of this position is the following note for a sermon concerning how God is revealed in us: "Note that revelation, properly speaking, is a matter of the intellect or rather in the essence of the soul, which has *esse* as its proper object. God-*esse* is naked *esse* without a covering. Or say both: the soul, in its essence as intellectual [being of an intellectual nature], is, through what is highest in it, united to God and is, according to Rabbi Moses [Maimonides], 'of the race of God.'"[125] The "essence as intellectual" (*intellectiva*) is the preacher's compromise when he tries to explain the place of the event that cannot be properly placed or described.

If we try to determine the most important function of the *vünkelîn* in Eckhart's thought, we might best say that it attempts to bridge the abyss created by the philosopher's doctrine of analogy. We have already seen that we must balance the rigorous separation of *esse* which is God from the nothingness of creatures in themselves that this doctrine of analogy posits with the dialectic of *unum*, which demands that we consider God indistinct as well as distinct from creatures. The *vünkelîn* is an additional bond between God and the soul. Because of his intellect, man shares with God the distinction of being unlike anything else: "By being similar to nothing, this power is like God. Just as God is similar to nothing, so is this power similar to nothing."[126] *Intelligere* is both *esse* in its highest and purest form and a mode of reality not reducible to mere *esse*. In contrast to non-intelligent creatures, man shares this form of existence with God. Man too is this purest form of *esse* but cannot be relegated just to the region of *esse*. As the Son or just man there is no difference between his understanding and God's: "The same knowledge in which God knows himself is the knowledge of every detached spirit. There is no difference."[127] But here too this sameness must be correctly understood.

First of all, Eckhart has expressed this sameness in knowing by stating that precisely because of his intellect man was created not merely *ad imaginem* but as the *imago dei*. The *vünkelîn* is an image of divine nature impressed upon the soul (*ein îngedrücket bilde götlîcher natûre*; Pr. 37; DW II, 211, 2). It is the paradoxical nature of an image, however, to be nothing in itself and to take its whole being from the object it reflects.[128] Thus this sameness in knowing fits well into the patterns of thought we have already established for the *magister*. Man as an image of the divine *intelligere* exists in the same ambiguous way that all creatures do when *esse* is the central term. Any real understanding he has is in God and not in himself. Nonetheless, the *vünkelîn* raises his being to a level of existence that is essentially higher than that of lesser creatures. Indeed, it is the unity of God and the human person based upon knowing that is the source of all man's prerogatives over other creatures, and even of his being the Son: "And since his [God's] knowing is mine and since his substance, his nature, and his being are his knowing, it follows that his being, his substance, and his nature are mine. And since his substance, his being, and his nature are mine, I am the Son of God."[129]

Besides describing the *vünkelîn* as an *imago dei*, Eckhart tries to clarify the oneness of God and the human soul in knowing by emphasizing the unity arising from oneness in operation (*würklicheit*). In Sermon 48, immediately before introducing the subject of the *vünkelîn*, he takes up oneness in operation in detail:

> As I was coming here today, I was wondering how I could preach to you so that it would make sense and you would understand it. Then

I thought of a comparison: If you could understand that, you would understand my meaning and the basis of all my thinking in everything I have ever preached. The comparison concerns my eyes and a piece of wood. If my eye is open, it is an eye; if it is closed, it is the same eye. It is not the wood that comes and goes, but it is my vision of it. Now pay good heed to me: If it happens that my eye is in itself one and simple, and is open and casts its glance upon the piece of wood, the eye and the wood remain what they are, and yet in the act of vision they become as one, so that we can truly say that my eye is the wood and wood is my eye. But if the wood were immaterial, purely spiritual, as is the sight of my eye, then one could truly say that in the act of vision the wood and my eye subsisted in one being. If this is true of physical objects, it is far truer of spiritual objects. You should know that my eye has far more in common with the eye of a sheep which is on the other side of the sea and which I never saw, than it has in common with my ears, with which, however, it shares its being, and that is because the action of the sheep's eye is also that of my eye. And so I attribute to both more in common in their action than I do to my eyes and my ears, because their actions are different.[130]

This passage really posits two kinds of sameness through knowing. The first is the unity achieved through the active-passive relationship of the knower and the object known in the act of knowing. Knower and object known retain their separateness and yet are utterly one in the act of knowing and being known. This is basic Aristotelian thought. The preacher then adds a wrinkle of his own: If the wood were not a material object, one could say that the two subsist in one being (*wesen*). This oneness and separateness of subject knowing and object known is next applied to what happens when the *vünkelîn* perceives God bare in the operation (*würklicheit*) of the birth.[131] Since both knower and known are completely spiritual, the implication is that this union in *würklicheit* is of an essentially higher kind than that achieved in acts of knowing in general. Nonetheless, the separateness of the knower and its object has also been stressed.[132]

The second oneness in *würklicheit* described is the activity of two powers or faculties that are basically the same but exist in beings that are not only separate but essentially different kinds of beings (sheep-man). This oneness is that of being equally noble. Despite the infinite distance separating man from God, there is a sense in which they are the same. They both really know. As part of the total creature *man*, the *vünkelîn* is no more noble than any other faculty such as vision or hearing. Seen, however, according to what it can do, the *vünkelîn* is more one with God than it is with the totality of man (DW II, 418, 4–11).

Perhaps the most intriguing and confusing statements about the *vünkelîn* are those directed to how it comprehends God. We are told that it takes God completely bare (*blôz zemâle*) in his true being (*istigez wesen*; Pr. 13; DW I, 222, 1). It grasps him in his own bare being (*in sînem blôzen eigenen wesen*; Pr. 11; DW I, 182, 10). Intellect penetrates to God's being; it sinks into being and takes God as he is pure being (*lûter wesen*; Pr. 37; DW II, 216, 5). More frequent, however, are descriptions of the intellect stripping God of the skin (*vel*) of goodness, being (*wesen*), and all names (e.g., Pr. 9; DW I, 152, 6–8).

We can best reconcile these statements by remembering the ambivalent role of *esse* for Eckhart.[133] In a passage where *wesen* is viewed on the same level as *güete* (goodness), as in the one cited above, it must be taken as a positive term that as such has only a tenuous "indicative" relationship to the infinite reality which is God. It points to God but, as a concept whose content is derived from creatures, it contains no positive content really existing in God and is, rather, something to be overcome. On the other hand, when *wesen* is taken negatively as describing the *bare* and *pure* being of God, that is, as indicating *esse* stripped bare and purified of the distorting limitations all positive terms of necessity include, then it is correct to say that the *vünkelîn* perceives God as he is *wesen*.

This reading of the texts is corroborated by the frequent appearance of *ein* when the subject is the *vünkelîn*'s power to comprehend God. God can enter into this power only as he is simply one (*einvaltic ein*), without any limitations or limiting characteristics (*âne alle wîse und eigenschaft*; Pr. 2; DW I, 43,9–44,1). "One" here is clearly a term of negation denying to God all limitations included in positive names. The *vünkelîn* can see God bare of all the distinctions that positive terms include. The intellect can see God "in his dressing room, bare, as he is one, without distinction."[134] "One," as we have seen, adds nothing to pure *wesen* in God. As the negation of negation, it denies that God lacks anything, without saying what God is.[135] Many of the images depicting how the *vünkelîn* grasps God stress the vast emptiness remaining when it has stripped away all positive forms and laid bare the naked divinity. It perceives God in his empty solitude (*einoede*) and in his wasteland (*wüestunge*). Interestingly enough, similar images are used to describe the *vünkelîn* itself: "It is an otherness (*elende*, literally, a foreign land) and a wasteland (*wüestunge*) more unnamed than having names, and is more unknown than known."[136]

When we read the accounts of how the *vünkelîn* ultimately takes hold of God, a nagging question arises: Is what Eckhart describes simply the result of the philosophical mind using the negative way of "naming" God with particular acuity and thoroughness? Or is it something more? Is what is grasped the ultimate God of the philosophers, or is it the God of the truly religious man? Is the knowledge of God achieved mystical? Does it have characteristics that are not reducible to the normal use of the highest part of the intellect?

The question is a difficult one. Clear evidence is meager. The difficulties confronting both the mystic and the philosopher are similar, if not indistinguishable. The mystic is trying to depict an indescribable realization, both hidden and ineffable, which is by definition impenetrable by human language. The philosopher, using the negative way, is attempting somehow to reach an infinite object, whose nature as *intelligere* is indeterminateness, by means of an indeterminate *vünkelîn* that is "neither this nor that." If we restrict our notion of philosophy to a process of logical analysis by the unaided human mind, then we can safely maintain that Eckhart is trying to put into words something which cannot be grasped by this type of reasoning. Indeed, we find him distinguishing between pagan *meister*, who know "in a natural light," and holy *meister*, who have knowledge "in a much higher light" (*in einem vil hoehern liehte;* Pr. 9; DW I, 152, 2–5). The image or concept of light comes up frequently and is almost always connected with knowing.[137] As something in man, it is most frequently used in conjunction with the *vünkelîn*. The Word, of course, as pure *intelligere*, is the true light enlightening all men (John 1:9), indeed, all creatures. In treating this verse, the commentator writes that the Word illumines different intelligent beings and different things in different ways. For some things (material, inanimate things), he is light under the characteristics of *esse*. Living things he illumines as life. Others (human beings) he illumines so that the light of his countenance (i.e., *imago* or true understanding, and not just *ad imaginem*) or *intelligere* shines upon them. Higher beings (angels) he so illumines that they do not need the shadow of phantasms to know. Finally (and we are clearly being given an order of increasing value), he illumines some by grace, a supernatural light (*In Joh.* n. 89; LW III, 77). As we have seen, Eckhart assigns grace an untraditional role in one's becoming the Son, but it is nonetheless a necessary factor, and it so raises one above the merely natural plane of illumination that the preacher can call the highest power of the soul a "spark of divine nature, a divine light" (*vünkelîn götlîcher natûre, ein götlich lieht;* Pr. 37; DW II, 211, 2). Thus a supernatural means appears necessary before God, and God alone shines naked into this power (Pr. 46; DW II, 382, 8–10).

These lines of thought hint that the *vünkelîn*'s perception of God is a religious or supernatural insight going beyond what philosophy can accomplish, but they do not go far in helping to determine what actually occurs in the *vünkelîn*. On the one hand, it does not appear that in the birth, when God's *grunt* is my *grunt*, the union achieved necessarily includes our consciously experiencing it.[138] The union, though a type of knowledge much deeper somehow and much more one with the core of our being, is untouched by the accidental qualities of time, place, and particularity which characterize our ordinary experiential knowledge.[139] On the other hand, the preacher's frequent descriptions of the nakedness and vast solitude of the divinity have an air of intensity and immediacy characteristic of authentic experience. Yet we must not dwell on this seeing God bare as an exotic personal "experience." The preacher never does. The extent to which his elaborations are philosophy, the extent to which they are more, what the *vünkelîn* actually sees, and in what sense man-become-Son experiences all of this remain unclear. And perhaps it must be so, for although the intellect of man is true intellect, he never throws off his limitations as creature entirely. The oneness he achieves with God as *intelligere* is real. His nothingness as merely the image of God is equally so. What the intellect *as such* can perceive directly seems to remain an enigma, an experience beyond direct human experience.

Will this condition ever change? How will things stand when the soul achieves its final end? The preacher answers: "Even God himself does not rest there, where he is a first beginning. He rests where he is an end and a rest for all being; not that this being shall pass away; rather, in its final end it will be fulfilled in accordance with its highest perfection. What is the last end? It is the hidden darkness of the eternal divinity which is unknown, never was known, and never will be known."[140]

Poverty of Spirit: An Alternate Description of Union

The themes presented in this chapter thus far have to be considered Eckhart's favorite ways of attempting to describe union with God and the means of achieving it. Thus it must come as a surprise to find the preacher striking off in quite a different direction, although obviously pursuing the same ends, in what is probably his best-known sermon, German Sermon 52 (DW II, 486–506), "Beati pauperes spiritu" (Matt. 5:3). At most, we find incidental remarks on *abegescheidenheit* and a short, veiled reference to the *vünkelîn* (496, 4), but the emphasis clearly lies elsewhere. The themes of the just man, the birth of the Son, and the spark in the soul stress what is divine in man. Although his elaborations on poverty of spirit ultimately achieve this same end, the manner in which his thought progresses is more reminiscent of the path he takes to describe *abegescheidenheit*.

What is poverty of spirit? Typically the preacher first disposes of some meanings of the phrase which he does not wish to pursue. He does not mean external poverty, though this is a good thing when undertaken freely for the love of Christ, as Christ's embracing it while on earth made clear. No, it is rather an internal poverty he intends to describe (486,8–487,4). He then also rejects the clever definition of Albert the Great, who calls those poor in spirit whom creatures can never satisfy. A truly poor person, he says, is one who does not will, does not know, and does not have anything (488, 3–6). We might paraphrase this tripartite definition by calling poverty of spirit poverty of *will*, of *intellect*, and of *being*.

After admitting that this definition is difficult to grasp, he proceeds immediately to disabuse his audience of the idea that his conception of poverty of will can be identified with the traditional notion of how one unites one's own will with the divine will. People who think that poverty of will means not seeking to fulfill one's own will but to fulfill only God's will are, he assures us, full of good intentions but have no more an idea of true poverty than a donkey does. Poverty of will is not a matter of an independent human will choosing the same object as its divine counterpart. It is something much more radical than that: "So long as a man has this as his will, that he wants to fulfill God's dearest will, he has not the poverty about which we want to talk. Such a person has a will with which he wants to fulfill God's will, and that is not true poverty."[141]

Union of wills is not enough. One must surrender the capacity to will. One cannot even retain the will as a faculty, a faculty usually considered essential to being fully human. Fortunately, the preacher immediately gives those in his audience with ears to hear a hint of how such demands are to be understood. True poverty of will is attained, he teaches us, when one is as free of one's created will "as one was, before one existed" (*als er tete, dô er niht enwas*; 491, 8–9).

The demands of the preacher, here as elsewhere, rest firmly on the thought of the metaphysician. As we have seen, Eckhart conceived of creatures as possessing a twofold being, an *esse virtuale* which ultimately resides in the Word of God and an *esse formale* residing in the creature itself.[142] The *esse virtuale* is one with God and is thus strong and eternal. The *esse formale* of creatures comes about

through the act of creation by which they assume an existence separate from God, an existence which in itself is nothingness. What the
preacher asks of us is that we give up our *esse formale*, the root of our
separateness and our impotence, and return completely to the state of
esse virtuale and thus to the state of being completely one with God.
The following rhapsodic passage celebrates this latter state, our true
or higher existence:

> When I stood in my first cause, I then had no "God," and then I
> was my own cause. I wanted nothing. I longed for nothing, for I was
> an empty being, and the only truth in which I rejoiced was in the
> knowledge of myself. Then it was myself I wanted and nothing else.
> What I wanted I was, and what I was I wanted; and so I stood, empty
> of God and of everything. But when I went out from my own free will
> and received my created being, then I had a "God," for before there
> were any creatures God was not "God," but he was what [that]
> he was. But when creatures came to be and received their created
> being, then God was not "God" in himself, but he was "God" in the
> creatures.[143]

Two paradoxes are presented here. The first is that of the creature as
God. The second is the diminution in "God" occurring through creation. Through its *esse virtuale* the creature is God and has all the
characteristics reserved for the divinity alone. The creature, in the
eternal existence of its first cause, before it existed formally, was (and
is), as God is, the cause of itself (*causa sui*). Because it was (and is)
completely one with God, its desires were (and are) completely satisfied, as God's are, by having the self as the sole object of its will. Its
act of knowing was (and is) totally engaged in grasping the infinity
that is itself. This is the eternal search for and attainment of truth
taking place in the divinity. Like God and as God, the creature, as
esse virtuale, is totally absorbed by immanent activity and has no
need to go outside itself for fulfillment. Finally, the creature in its
eternal state can lay claim for itself to that most august description
of the divinity. The creature is, simply, that and what it is (*ego sum
qui sum*).

From such a conception of the creature's existence in God, it can
only follow that the separation from God which occurs through the
creation of the nothingness of our *esse formale*—this flowing out
(*ûzvliezen*) from God—must be viewed as an event with negative
consequences, consequences that can only be made good through the
redivinization of the creature. More puzzling are Eckhart's comments
on the "effect" of this flowing out on God. Two interpretations of this
limited notion of God seem possible. First, "God" can be conceived

as that positive knowledge one can have of him in accordance with Eckhart's notion of analogy. Enough has been said of this to see why such a paltry notion of God cannot be the goal which satisfies all creation. But perhaps another interpretation of "God," one related to this first interpretation, fits the context better. God is perceived in this passage as the author of creation, not as he is in himself. The preacher makes this explicit later in the sermon: "for my real being is above God if we take 'God' to be the beginning of created things. For in the same being where God is above being and above distinction, there I myself was."[144] As the source of creation, he manifests very little of his true self and is perceived only insofar as he is distinct from creatures. Only when this half of the dialectic is supplemented by perceiving God as indistinct from creatures, and as he is above being, do we have something approaching a notion of God as he is in himself and as he is as the end and fulfillment of creatures.

After these interjections on the creature's preexistence and the opposition of God to "God," the preacher takes up his second point: poverty of the intellect. His description of this is equally radical. A person who has this kind of poverty should not even *know* that he does not live for himself, for truth, or for God: "Rather, he should be so free of all knowing that he does not know or experience or grasp that God lives in him."[145] Living for self, truth, or God implies a duality between God and the poor person that may not exist. Even a separate awareness on the part of the creature that God lives within him militates against this poverty. The only true knowledge and the only real act of knowing are purely divine. The creature's knowledge, both as to content and as to act, must so disappear that it is God alone who knows. This was the condition prevailing before creation.

Finally, the preacher describes this poverty in its extremest form: having nothing, or poverty of being. This poverty extends the emptiness of will and intellect already demanded to being itself. Those who express this union by saying that one should empty oneself completely so that God may work freely within oneself do not understand this poverty (500, 1–3). The existence of a place in creatures in which God works implies duality and a condition of imperfection. True poverty of spirit requires that "a man keep so free of God and of all his works that if God wishes to work in the soul, he himself [i.e., God] is the place in which he wants to work." In overcoming the duality of place the poor man overcomes a duality in being. This becomes evident when the preacher concludes this section by maintaining that in this poverty one achieves "that everlasting being which he was and which he is now and which he will evermore remain."[146] Such is the oneness with God gained through this poverty that, as this last quotation makes clear, Eckhart feels justified in shocking his audience by making the poor person the subject of the doxology. Such a person's *esse* is the eternal *esse* of God, that always was, is, and will eternally be.

If the major portion of the sermon consists in an analysis of the three aspects of poverty of spirit, the conclusion unites these aspects into a single term: breaking-through (*durchbrechen*). To describe the beginning of creatures' separate existence, Eckhart used the Neoplatonic concept of emanation, or flowing out (*ûzvliezen*). Through poverty of spirit the creature *returns* to the oneness of the divinity. The poor man "breaks through" into the divine being above all being. In this breaking-through, Eckhart teaches us, one is above all creatures and is neither God (as he is the beginning of creatures and cannot satisfy us) nor creature. Marvelously mixing God's description of himself in Exodus with the doxology, and applying it to the poor man, he continues: "Rather, I am what [and *that*] I was and what I shall remain, now and eternally."[147] In the breaking-through, God and creature become simply one. Again, in closing, the preacher daringly attributes divine qualities to the creature who breaks through: "Then I am what I was, and then I neither diminish nor increase, for I am then an immovable cause that moves all things."[148]

This sermon, like those describing the birth of the Son, attempts to make clear to those who can understand that our perfection and final goal consists in our being literally *re-duced* to God. However, the purpose of Eckhart's preaching is not that we grasp this intellectually. He is aware that many of his hearers cannot comprehend these thoughts. True understanding, he seems to be telling us, is something quite different from successfully following a theologically charged sermon. One who merely has an intellectual grasp of all this is still far from the truth. We have to be like this truth to understand it. It is a truth that the human mind cannot fathom (*unbedaht*) and that comes immediately from the heart of God.[149] Paradoxically, only by living in such a way that we become the truth do we understand the truth. Since the Truth is the Son coming immediately from the heart of the Father, the preacher actually concludes by making a reference to our becoming the Son. Becoming the Truth/Son and breaking through to the *esse virtuale* that we were, are, and always shall remain are actually two ways of describing one event: the deification of the creature. Both end in the unity of creature with the Word, for as we have seen, Eckhart in accordance with mainstream Christian tradition places the *esse virtuale* in the Word.[150]

Put simply, Eckhart's view of poverty of spirit is that the union with God that one should strive for is the same oneness one had with God before one existed as a creature. Perfection consists in "undoing" creation and returning to the *ideal* or *virtual* existence one enjoyed in the Word. Two questions come immediately to mind: Is such a conception of union orthodox? And did Eckhart really think such a union possible? If poverty of spirit is taken literally, it does not seem possible to make it conform to Christian teaching. Creation cannot be undone. The beatific vision in heaven implies that the duality of the creature beholding and the God beheld continues in a real sense in eternity. The creature remains creature. In this sermon, Eckhart appears to be proposing a union that does away with the creature as an independent entity in any sense. Thus it seems that the preacher's description of true poverty must conflict with Christian teaching.

Two considerations mitigate the harshness of this conclusion. First of all, what we have learned about Eckhart's view of language should make us realize that his conception of poverty is not a theological teaching in a rigorous sense. It is rather an attempt to capture in words a reality that is by nature far beyond the potentialities of human language. Language, as Eckhart views it, expresses spiritual things with great inadequacy. Thus he must assume from the beginning that poverty of spirit does not correspond directly and essentially to a real, or possible, spiritual state of affairs. This does not mean, however, that the elaborations of the preacher are meaningless. They do offer us a glimpse of a higher reality, but only a glimpse. Shocking though it is in the preacher's formulation, poverty of spirit, while offering us a hint of the truth, falls far short of the truth. Since all descriptions are inadequate and contain much that is false or misleading, one listens to the sermon in the spirit of the preacher only if one assumes the inadequacy of language and concentrates on the kernel of truth that remains.

Second, as in the case of his other favorite themes, one must weigh the possibility that Eckhart is aware of the distance between the ideal and what can actually be realized. It must be admitted that Sermon 52 presents poverty of spirit without any clear references to such qualifications. And yet, if we see this sermon against the background of his other sermons and treatises, and if we remember the central position of the *in quantum* principle in so many contexts, it does not seem unreasonable to imagine the preacher assuming something similar here. The union of God and creature envisioned through poverty of spirit conflicts with orthodoxy only if it is ever perfectly realized. As long as a creature remains in any way imperfect and retains some of its *esse formale*, no such conflict arises.[151] If we recall the value Eckhart puts on shocking his audience, the non-academic nature and purpose of his sermons, and his actual practice in other sermons, we do well in considering this way of understanding him more probable. The impossibility of a creature's achieving poverty of spirit completely does not dampen the preacher's enthusiasm and brilliance in describing it. Nor does this impossibility lessen its value as an ideal.

V

MASTER OF LANGUAGE

In the previous chapter we attempted to explain Eckhart's favorite themes by placing them in the context of his own philosophical and theological thought. Unless one views them in this manner and against the background of the schools from which they emerged, they lose much of their vigor and definition. Given Eckhart's own thoughts on the limitations of language, when it is directed beyond the creature in itself, we chose not to consider these themes as strict philosophical doctrines. The relation of human word to divine reality is too tenuous and too indirect to allow us to talk about philosophical doctrines in a narrow sense.

For Eckhart the veil separating words, those products of the human intellect, from God, the goal of all human seeking, is not directly penetrable. Words or concepts can at best only hint at what God is. However, one should not imagine that this line of thought simply removes God to a region of great distance from us. Though infinitely distant, God is at the same time immediately present to us. Creatures are in a very real sense epiphanies of the divine. If Eckhart claims that creatures in themselves are nothing, we must note that he is talking about creatures as independent from God's being and not about the concrete world around him. Things in the concrete are not creatures in themselves but are rather a marvelous mixture of finite and infinite. His fellow Dominican Thomas did not think that God's existence was a self-evident fact, but something that had to be proved by showing that the world was an effect needing an eternal and unchanging cause, which we call God. Eckhart seems to disagree. Grasped positively, the beings we see are limited, but they point to a reality that is infinite. And this infinity is within them! Seen negatively, they are indistinct from, or one with, infinite being. Thus things and not just words are poetic—hiding an incomprehensible wealth within themselves, but at the same time revealing it however slightly. Things correspond perfectly to words because things, like words, are the intimations of eternal infinity.

Since the time when he was rediscovered in the nineteenth century, Eckhart's vocabulary, the structure of his language, and his style have all been the subject of close scrutiny.[1] While many useful insights have come to light in various studies, some of the more ambitious undertakings, especially those treating structure or style, have not yielded the results they promised. This lack of productivity can at times be attributed to the method employed. If one takes as a framework the basic structural possibilities of the Middle High German sentence, one can hardly expect to find that the sermons and treatises diverge significantly from this framework.[2] Eckhart did not create a new language. Rather, he made good use of the potentialities of the language already constituted. Departures from what the accepted language structure allows must be few and must be rooted in the normal structure. Otherwise, chaos, and not creative communication, will result.

Another vitiating factor in some studies laying claim to an "objective" method is the questionable nature of such a claim: The objective structure in language perceived by one school of linguistics is, in time, replaced by that of another. Thus it is perhaps safer to view the contributions of various groups as achievements that have provided valuable insights through the construction of useful models for the study of language. Since the discovery of the ultimate structure of language or even of an individual language is indeed an elusive goal, one does well to use these linguistic models with discretion.[3] Even if such a structure could be found, one would still have to pose the question whether such a discovery would necessarily put us in the enviable position of having a secure and productive starting point from which to explore *creative* or *artistic* use of language.

In view of the difficulties connected with such approaches as those mentioned above, the path chosen here is one that emphasizes the connection between Eckhart's own ideas on the possibilities and limitations of language and what he actually does in practice. More particularly, the question is asked: Do Eckhart's theoretical views of language described in Chapter 3 bear any actual fruit? Do they have a palpable impact on the manner in which he formulates his thoughts in his sermons and other works? If, as we maintain, his favorite spiritual themes, like the just man and the birth of the Son, are better understood when placed in the context of his view of language, then it is not unlikely that this same context will also prove useful in examining his use of language. In addition, even the most cursory glance at the sermons shows that the preacher was not only very familiar with traditional rhetorical devices but held them in high esteem as well. One finds them everywhere. These two factors, therefore, namely, his view of language and his employment of traditional rhetoric, seem to hold the most promise when we analyze his actual use of language.

There is much evidence indicating that Eckhart's conception of language greatly influenced his attempt to find suitable modes of expression for religious truth. If it is true that Eckhart differs from other preachers of the day because he did not simply use scholastic thought in his vernacular sermons but used it creatively, the equally creative way in which he articulated his own thoughts is what guaranteed their survival for later centuries. And in order to understand these formulations it is important to realize that many of the most characteristic of them flow naturally from his conception of the possibilities and limitations of human language. We shall see that a judgment such as Clark's, that Eckhart was a victim of his style, requires basic revision.[4] Moreover, though during his trial he himself occasionally referred to his emphatic way of speaking as a line of defense,[5] we should not be too ready to excuse or water down his astonishing statements as exaggerations.[6] We shall discover that it is much more advisable to give his expressions full weight, assuming that we understand his notion of creatures and language.

Let us first summarize Eckhart's conception of language. Language, when it refers to God or the divine dimensions of things, has legitimate meaning in three ways. It may, first of all, be used *negatively* to describe what God is not. The negative approach removes limitations from words applied to God and purifies our notion of what is divine. Second, in a *positive* sense words can be used of God only analogously. And for Eckhart, as we have seen, the thread linking things joined by analogy is tenuous indeed. If we learn of goodness directly only through creatures—and Eckhart would say that this is the case—then this quality of goodness perceived through creatures cannot formally be attributed to God in the sense that the same goodness which is found in creatures is in any way really found also in God. His goodness is too different. Thus, positively, words are not to be taken literally of God. Positively, words are at best inadequate symbols or external signs.

Third, words can attain some truth about God by being employed *dialectically*. Although Eckhart himself does not expressly treat dialectic use of language, as he does positive and negative use, his frequent recourse to rhetorical or literary devices with dialectic as their philosophical base must indeed be viewed as a separate attempt on his part to break through the limits of language. We have observed that use of dialectic in his explanation of the term *unum*, which, he points out, expresses both God's separateness from creatures and his oneness with them. Similarly, we have seen him use pairs of concepts dialectically, as when he maintains that nothing is both so distinct and indistinct or so similar yet so dissimilar as God and creatures. While these are the clearest examples of his use of dialectic as a philosophical method, dialectical thought patterns abound in all his works, especially in the vernacular sermons.

If we examine Eckhart's language in some detail, the justification for doing so is not merely to substantiate the fact that what he does in practice follows from his view of language, though this appears to be the case. Rather, what justifies such an examination is the literary quality of his language and the frequently marvelous effects he is able to achieve. While any method of classification will to some extent be arbitrary, we can achieve some clarity by first examining Eckhart's vernacular vocabulary and then the most important rhetorical and poetic features of his style.

Vernacular Vocabulary

Extravagant claims have been made about Eckhart's contribution to the development of German as a vehicle for abstract thought and lofty speculation. Immediately upon his rediscovery in the nineteenth century, at a time when few Middle High German documents other than those of courtly literature were well known, he was often viewed as a giant standing alone, creating a *German* philosophy and a *German* vocabulary to express it. As knowledge of him and his intellectual environment increased, however, serious modifications had to be made in evaluating his effect on the vernacular. Most of the abstract terms he employs in the Middle High German sermons are, as we now know, translations of the Latin of the schools. Certainly he was not alone in his time in using scholasticism as a basis for his preaching, but he did not rest satisfied, as did many of his contemporaries, with presenting rudimentary scholastic philosophy and theology. It may well be that his influence was responsible for the acceptance of words like *Wesen*, *Grunt*, and *Bild* into the mainstream of German philosophical thought. However, the evidence for such claims is not overwhelming, and other explanations are possible.

While there is no question that even Eckhart's least philosophical forms of expression, the German sermons, are essentially speculative, the artistic or literary elements and their quality must not be overlooked. Indeed, one could even ask whether he thought more like a philosopher or a poet. Many of his incidental similes and metaphors show the freshness and vigor of authentic poetry. In describing the nature of the existence of all things in God, for example, where all things are equal and "are God himself," where God "courses through his own nature and being in this sameness," he states that God's joy in this activity is like that of "a horse running upon a green meadow that is completely flat and of even texture. The horse would naturally pour itself out in frisking about on the meadow with all its energy out of pure joy, as is natural to it."[7] The oneness of God and creature in the birth, as well as God's being everything and the creature's being nothing in this oneness, is depicted at one point by presenting a person (God) "standing opposite a lofty mountain and calling out 'Are you there?' The echo would then call out in reply: 'Are you there?' And if the person would say 'Come out!' the echo would also say 'Come out!'"[8]

Eckhart's language often shows a directness reminiscent of Luther, as when he chides people for wanting to be able to see and love God as they do a cow (Pr. 16b; DW I, 274, 1–2). As we have noted, he scolds people who seek God out of selfish reasons for making a candle out of him: once they have found what they want, they throw the candle away.[9] Such earthiness occasionally finds its way even into his professional writings. He describes people who serve God selfishly as treating him like a goat because they feed him with the (unwholesome) leaves of their (empty) words, or as treating him like a traveling player to whom they give their old and dirty clothes (*In Sap.* n. 61; LW II, 389).

In considering the concrete aspects of his language, one must also point out the very important role imagery plays in the formulation of his philosophical thought. Perhaps the clearest explanations of his conception of *esse* are those resting on imagery. In any case, scholars who have contributed much to the illumination of this concept have relied heavily on Eckhart's imagery.[10] That the *esse* of creatures can well be understood as a person who eats and yet continually hungers; or that the divine *esse* is like the sun which illumines objects without taking root in them; or, finally, that the relationship of the divine being to creature can be explained by comparing it to that between a real object and the ephemeral image of this in a mirror— such imagery clarifies his thought considerably and can be viewed as a necessary complement to his more strictly scholastic elaborations on *esse*.[11] As is clear from these examples and from his interpretations of scripture in general, he deeply valued imagery of all kinds as a means for discovering and expressing insights. And what is the birth of the Son if not an image? Through the mystery of human birth—the sudden existence of life where there was none before—we are taught a still greater mystery: our transformation from creature to God.

This having been said, it is Eckhart's success in expressing difficult philosophical and theological concepts and developing abstract thought in the vernacular that has attracted the most comment. And it is to this area that we now wish to return. To measure his accomplishment one must call to mind the position of vernacular language at the time. Certainly by the closing decades of the thirteenth century, German had been made to serve many purposes other than that of being merely the basis for communication about everyday matters. Fundamental religious documents, such as the Bible and the *Rule of Saint Benedict*, had been translated for the unlearned. Sermons were also preached in German. In addition, the amount of religious poetry from these times and even earlier is considerable. Those who clearly expanded German into a vehicle capable of expressing the loftiest human aspirations, however, were the courtly poets, who explored the many facets of human love in their lyric poetry and depicted or criticized the aims and ideals of their society in such narratives as the *Nibelungenlied*, *Parzival*, and *Tristan*. As mentioned, Eckhart was not alone in using scholasticism as a basis for his sermons. However, it is generally admitted that no one among his predecessors or contemporaries equaled him in the ability to make thought on difficult spiritual matters come alive in his native tongue. We must now try to determine more exactly the nature of this success.

While it is true that words like *wesen*, *wesenheit*, *grunt*, and *abegescheidenheit* are the essential blocks that structure his thought in the vernacular works, it is not simply the creation or use of such words that constitutes his genius. One has only to read a few pages of the Middle High German translation of the *Summa theologica* of Thomas Aquinas, a document roughly contemporary to Eckhart's sermons, to discover that it does not require an unusually gifted mind to find or create Middle High German equivalents for the refined language of the schools.[12] Eckhart's German is vital, stimulating, and, considering the difficulty of what he attempts to transmit, generally clear. The *Summa* translation seems mechanical and, without the original Latin as an aid, frequently incomprehensible to the modern reader, as it must have been in its own time. Coining words usually requires little real creativity. Enabling them to function fully does. And this is where Eckhart proves himself to be unusually gifted. His sermons are filled with rhetorical, linguistic, and what one can even call poetic devices which allow the listener to see key concepts in the correct perspective. In a word, his virtuosity lies not in creating words but in creating contexts that allow key words to come alive. It is this skill that is at the bottom of all his use of rhetorical and poetic figures. However, it would perhaps be helpful, before examining the most striking figures, to analyze some examples of words in the contexts he creates for them, contexts that guarantee their full impact on the attentive listener.

One method the preacher uses to force us to focus our attention on a word, and thus to expand our understanding of it, is to create contexts for it which make us assign opposing values to it. An example of this is his use of *berüeren* (to touch) in Sermon 10. The question is raised whether the divine light in the soul resides just in the essence (*wesen*) of the soul or in its powers (*krefte*) as well. Eckhart denies that it dwells in the powers because what touches or is touched is far from God, and the powers of the soul are touched and touch (*berüeret werdent und berüerent*) and thus lose their virginity (*magetuom*). However, they can be made capable of conception (*enpfenclich*) by means of exercises (*üebunge*) and stripping off (*abelegunge;* DW I, 162, 7–14). The two themes of *virgo intacta* and *virgo concipiet* are thus combined, but *berüeren*, which here signifies the contact of the soul's powers with the physical world, has strictly negative overtones in this instance. Later the word recurs, but this time it signifies both the action of the Holy Spirit on the soul ("A teacher says that the soul is touched [*berüeret wirt*] immediately by the Holy Spirit" [DW I, 168, 3–4]) and the union of the soul with the divinity "When the soul receives a kiss from the divinity, it stands in complete perfection and happiness; it is embraced by oneness. In the first touching [*berüeren*], where God touches [*berüeret*] the soul and is touching [*berüerende ist*] it as uncreated and uncreatable, there the soul is as noble as God is himself because of the touch of God [*nâch der berüerunge gotes*]. God touches it in accordance with himself" [*berüeret sie nâch im selber;* DW I, 172,4–173,1]). Since "kiss" is used here in conjunction with *berüeren*, we must assume that touching retains the erotic overtones of the earlier passage where *berüeren* was given a negative value. Now, however, the soul is touched not by the world of creatures but by God. Thus this loss of virginity denotes the highest kind of spiritual experience. The effectiveness of this latter passage results largely from the sudden change in the value of *berüeren*, as the preacher switches alogically and without warning from one staple of ascetic-mystical thought to another, from the *virgo intacta* theme to bride mysticism.

Another method for expanding the boundaries of a concept is to begin by using it in a traditionally acceptable manner and then giving it a new definition at odds with this first meaning. Thus in Sermon 21 the term *ein* is made to signify two logically incompatible states, both of which man must strive to attain. The starting point is the definition of *ein* in the sense of the scholastic transcendental *unum* as it is realized perfectly in God: "God is one in himself and separated from everything else" (*ein in im selben und gesundert von allem*). This is followed by the exhortation that we should try to realize this quality in ourselves, with the following content then added to the original definition of *ein*: "and we should be one with God" (*suln wir mit gote ein sîn*). With this we have moved to the preacher's own concept of *unum*, whereby everything is both distinct and indistinct from God. For Eckhart, *unum* is not complete if it refers only to the internal composition of something. It embraces the relationship to other things as well. A creature's unity is as insubstantial as its being if the creature is taken as the nothing it is in itself. Why must we be one with God? Because only God is: "Outside of God is nothing but absolute nothingness" (*Ûzer gote enist niht dan niht aleine*; DW I, 357,7–358,3).

Sometimes the preacher will juxtapose two concepts and, by stating different and even contradictory relationships between them, add unsuspected dimensions to them. For example, in Sermon 8 (DW I, 129–132), for the purpose of elaborating on the relationship of life (*leben*) to being (*wesen*), he begins with the paradox that death gives the martyrs *ein wesen*. *Leben* is then said to be more noble than *wesen*, but pure *wesen* is higher than *leben*. This apparent contradiction is still within the pale of scholastic gamesmanship since *wesen* is being taken in two different senses. In a concrete being, *wesen* is a less noble perfection than *leben*, while in the abstract, *wesen* is prior to, or a necessary condition for, *leben*. In the abstract, the full concept *wesen* includes the concept *leben*, and *leben*'s exclusion is a diminution of *wesen*, since the latter is all-embracing. Against this background Eckhart then embarks upon a short rhapsody on *wesen* and concludes with the statement "Our whole *leben* should be *ein wesen*. To the extent that our *leben* is *ein wesen*, it is in God" (DW I, 132, 2–3). In the really existing being that is God, the all-embracing nature of *wesen*, taken abstractly as the fullness of all perfections, is actually realized. In God perfect abstraction and concrete perfection coincide. Although nothing in these lines offends against logic when fully digested, the passage achieves its striking effect by the seeming illogicality of combining these basic concepts: Death gives being. Being is less than life. Being is more than life. Our life should be being. By turning our life into being, we turn it into God. Only through difficult struggle with these terms and their relationships does the hearer gain insight. But the struggle enhances and intensifies the insight. We can conclude our look at Eckhart's creation of contexts by examining two more elaborate examples, a context which he creates for *eigenschaft* and one which he constructs for *bilde*.

In Sermon 2 (DW I, 24–45) Eckhart attempts to explain a concept essential to his ascetical-mystical thought: *eigenschaft*. We are already familiar with this term from our earlier discussion.[13] Here we shall concentrate on how the term increases in meaning as the preacher structures its context in the course of the sermon, and on what dimensions the word has assumed by the sermon's close.

At the outset we are told that whoever is to receive/conceive (*enpfâhen*) Jesus must be a virgin, that is, must be as free of images as he was before he existed. How can we, who need images for human knowledge, accomplish this? By having them without *eigenschaft* (25, 8). At this point our whole attention is focused on a word that we both understand and yet obviously do not understand. The word's multivalence gives pause: possessiveness, bondage, characteristic. But what does the preacher mean by it here? Because he uses *eigenschaft* in conjunction with the verbs "to hold on to" (*begrîfen*, 25, 8 and 29, 8) and "to possess" (*besitzen*, 29, 6–7), the preacher is clearly urging us to avoid possessiveness regarding images. Yet because of his references to people who are bound by or to *eigenschaft* (28, 8 and 30, 1), we can see that the word implies bondage or servitude to these images as well.

Finally, Eckhart also forces his audience to think of *eigenschaft* in the sense of *characteristic* or *quality*. This notion is familiar to the preacher from the schools. An accident or accidental property (*proprietas accidentalis*) is a characteristic which limits a created being or substance.[14] The fruitfulness of those who are not virgins is limited in the same way that human beings are limited by these characteristics. One can be in only one place at one time, doing one thing or being influenced by a limited thing, and so on. Why is it clear that Eckhart is asking us to divest ourselves of characteristics which are necessarily connected to our being creatures? Because he urges us not to hold on to images (*bilde*) in action or passion (*in tuonne noch in lâzenne*) or limited in time (*mit vor noch mit nâch*; 25, 9). Works done by a virgin free of *eigenschaft* are not bound by time or number (quantity), and since the virgin soul has thrown off its creaturely nature and its limitations, the fruit (works) of the virgin soul is begotten out of the same ground from which the eternal Word is begotten. Indeed, the virgin freed from *eigenschaft* co-begets this fruit with God (30,3–31,4). And so the preacher utilizes all three of the disparate meanings of *eigenschaft* in urging us to throw off our possessiveness, our enthrallment, and even the limitations of our nature in order to become divinely fruitful. Thus he embraces traditional ascetical values in the term but pushes beyond them by insisting that we change not only morally but also metaphysically. All this he achieves by structuring the contexts of *eigenschaft*.

Having accomplished this, however, the preacher does not rest content. As he describes the union of the soul with God, he goes on to take the idea of eliminating *eigenschaft* to its ultimate conclusion. The *vünkelîn* with which God unites in the soul is here given its ultimate definition: "it is neither this nor that; yet it is a something that is higher above this and that than the heaven is above the earth" (39, 4–6). Every name is an *eigenschaft* in that it limits what is described and binds it. The *vünkelîn* that unites with God is without properties because, as intellect, it is above being merely this or merely that. It is above all definite manner of being (*enboben alle wîse;* 43, 1). So too God must be utterly simple in entering into this union. This is impossible insofar as he can be understood to have a manner of existence or to have the characteristics of persons (*als verre als er sich habende ist nâch wîse und ûf eigenschaft sîner persônen;* 43, 4–5). For this union, God too must be "without manner of being and without properties or characteristics" (*sunder wîse und sunder eigenschaft;* 43, 6). Even the Persons of the Trinity must divest themselves of this last *eigenschaft* of being separate persons before God can look into the temple (*bürgelîn*) of the soul.

The underlying unity of the sermon becomes apparent only when one realizes that *eigenschaft*, applied here to God at the close of the sermon, expresses the same content as when it is used in regard to the human soul in the first part of the sermon. Eckhart's linguistic achievement is precisely that with a single word he is able to span religious thought from common asceticism to the heights of mysticism, while at the same time and with the same word joining God and the human soul by means of an attribute necessary to both for their union.

This use of *eigenschaft* can be called mystical because in employing it the preacher unites areas of reality usually considered discrete. One can also claim for it a musical quality in that, like a leitmotif, it surfaces again and again in the texture of the sermon, the setting transforming its effect each time, until at the end its full significance becomes clear. A similar leitmotif effect appears frequently in other sermons. In Sermon 72, for example, *bilde* functions in this manner, although only through the first half of the sermon (DW III, 239,1–246,2).

The sermon opens with the lines from Matthew that describe Jesus ascending a hill to preach his Sermon on the Mount (5:1ff.). One way of interpreting this, Eckhart tells us, is that upon the heights of the divine nature, where all that is merely creature recedes, one knows only God and knows oneself simply as an image (*bilde*) of God (241, 1–3). After an undeveloped reference to another mountain ascent, for the transfiguration (Matt. 17:1–6), the preacher has Christ recall, presumably to his apostles, that he spoke to them and they saw neither image nor similarity (*glîchnisse*), for when one leaves the multitude God surrenders himself into the soul without image or (mere) similarity.[15] Eckhart then immediately adds the jarring observation that all things are known in image and similarity (243, 1–2).

Having startled us with this juxtaposition of discordant meanings of *bilde*, he begins the topic again, this time in more orderly fashion, with Augustine as guide. The great church father, we are told, distinguishes three types of knowledge. The first is corporeal or sense knowledge, as when the eye captures the image of an object. The second is spiritual, but originates from physical objects, as when we recall a physical object that is absent. The third type of knowledge is internal in the spirit and, like that of the angels, without image or likeness (242,4–243,4). Eckhart then cites "a teacher" who maintains that this immediate knowledge is like God's surrendering himself into the soul without image or likeness, which happens "on the heights" (*in der hoehe*; 243, 3–6).

If we think, however, that we can now rest content with the idea that this union of God and soul is without image or likeness, we are mistaken. The reference to "in the heights" provides the bridge to an ascent already briefly alluded to: the trans*figuration*. And with this the preacher again does a complete turnabout. The transformation of Christ, which the soul is to imitate, is based utterly upon image (*bilde*): The soul is to be transformed (*widerbildet*) and pressed into the image (*bilde*) and struck (like a coin) into the image that is God's Son (244, 1–2). Granted, the soul is formed (*gebildet*) according to God, but the teachers say that the Son is an image (*bilde*) of God and that the soul is formed (*gebildet*) according to this image (*bilde*). Here

the preacher interjects his own view, which resolves by means of paradox the *image–without image* opposition structuring the sermon
thus far: "But I say rather, the Son is an image of God above image
(*obe bilde*); he is an image of his hidden divinity. There, where the
Son is an image of God and where the Son is formed (*îngebildet*), accordingly the soul is formed. The soul does not remain on the edge of
the divinity where the Son flows out; rather, it is above image." Sense
faculties are limited to their formal objects, the eye to what is visible
or the sense of taste to what can be tasted. Thus they "perceive" the
same object (e.g., an apple) in entirely separate ways. "However, the
soul knows nothing but one, it is above image" (244,2–246,2).

This play with *bilde* is difficult to follow, and one might well
sympathize with those who thought the preacher was at fault for presenting abstruse matters to those who were not prepared to understand them. As linguistic artistry, however, it is a masterful stroke,
ending with the soul as a *bilde obe bilde* united by knowledge (i.e.,
the *vünkelîn*) to God as he can best be expressed, as *unum*, utterly
one with and utterly distinct from all things. The reader of the sermons will find other striking examples similar to these.[16] Clearly this
genius for structuring contexts so that key words come ever more
fully to life is a strong force attracting us to Eckhart's vernacular
works and is a salient feature of his virtuosity with language.

Major Stylistic Characteristics

Eckhart's view of human language is that it cannot, through concepts
having a positive content, formally go beyond the creature as such.
Something very important follows from this: philosophical discourse,
which uses carefully defined concepts and strict logic, will not enjoy
a preeminent position among the various linguistic strategies for describing God and the divine aspects of creatures. Since such concepts,
when applied to what is divine, leave out more than they contain, or,
as Eckhart phrases it, since calling God good is like calling the sun
black, one is free, nay, even obliged, to seek out turns of speech which
approach God by means of alogical or antilogical paths. His use of
dialectic shows Eckhart's philosophical commitment to this stance.
His vernacular sermons, however, bear much richer witness to this
commitment. Just as the most characteristic feature noted about
his creation of contexts is the juxtaposition of words in ways that
challenge traditional patterns of thought, so the most common and

obvious quality of most of the rhetorical and poetic devices that animate his sermons is that they achieve their effect apart from logic. It is certainly true that the vocabulary of scholastic philosophy provides the linguistic basis of Eckhart's thought and preaching. It is equally true, however, that Eckhart was unique among his contemporaries in that his sermons moved beyond this conceptual foundation of scholasticism. Often this originality results from his combining concepts or ideas in ways that defy logic and the scholastic method. Although there are other points to be made about Eckhart's style, this very important feature, namely, his frequent reliance on alogical and antilogical devices, provides us with an appropriate point of departure.

As we have mentioned, Eckhart is an enthusiastic practitioner of traditional rhetoric. So regular is his use of certain devices that Quint considered the presence of several of them in a single sermon to be a secondary criterion in support of the sermon's authenticity. Some of the devices appearing most frequently are accumulation, antithesis, parallelism, and hyberbole.

Accumulation, or the piling up of words or expressions to describe the same thing, allows the preacher to invest the spiritual phenomena he is describing with a richness not possible through the strictly logical use of concepts. So, for example, in explaining how "who is" (*der dâ ist*; Exod. 3:14) is to be understood as God's most suitable name, he states that in order to arrive at the negation of negations (*nihtes niht*), which alone remains of *esse* when applied correctly to the *is* that is God, everything positive must be "separated" (*abegescheiden*), "pulled off" (*abegezogen*), and "peeled off" (*abegeschelt*) from the term if one is to uncover the quality of that name (Pr. 45; DW II, 372, 3–7). Juxtaposing three verbal actions for this process of dis-covery gives it an appropriate prominence in the minds of the hearers. In another sermon, Eckhart uses this same figure of accumulation to emphasize that the *vünkelîn* must be separated from the accidents of time and place if it is to see God. Perhaps with Augustine's famous passage on the nature of time in mind he stresses how short the present is: "*Now* is the smallest segment of time; it is neither a piece of time nor a part of time. It is certainly a taste of time and a point of time and a boundary of time. And yet, however small it may be, it has to disappear."[17] While *now* is neither a *stücke* or *teil* of time, it is a *smak, spitze,* or *ende* of time. Through the accumulated effect of these five words, Eckhart expresses well the ambivalent relationship of *now* to duration. Yet though it is not really time, *now* must be transcended if we are to see God. Finally, in a well-known passage on the *vünkelîn* the preacher recalls how he has at times referred to it as a "power in the spirit" (*kraft im geiste*), as a "guard of the spirit" (*huote des geistes*), as a "light of the spirit" (*lieht des geistes*), or as a "spark" (*vünkelîn*). This time, however, he accumulates these images for the intellect only to reject them. Since the intellect must be free of all things in order to understand all things, its ultimate description is that "it is neither this nor that."[18]

Antithesis, or the contrasting of opposites, is everywhere in the sermons, as the just mentioned positive description of the *vünkelîn*, which is then rejected, makes clear. Eckhart frequently introduces his own views by stating the opposing views of some authority. The contrast functions to set off the preacher's ideas more clearly and, in addition, often places him in the role of an independent thinker going beyond the commonly held positions of his colleagues. In the exposition of the preacher's own thoughts, antithesis is prominent and frequent. So, for example, he contrasts the effects of God's activity on creatures with their inability to affect him in any way by stating that God "touches" (*berüeret*) all things but remains himself "untouched" (*unberüeret*; Pr. 71; DW III, 218, 4–5). And John the Baptist is great, we are told, because he is small through his humility. His smallness was his greatness (Pr. 49; DW II, 448, 3–4). As is clear from these two examples, antithesis is often employed in conjunction with paradox. In the following final example we find antithesis used to express his conception of *unum*, which in one sense can be linked to nothing (*niht*) since God cannot be grasped. Yet God is certainly something (*iht*) and his somethingness is different from ours because we are a mixture of the antithesis of *iht* and *niht*, but what God is he is completely: "I cannot see what is one. He [Saul, Acts 9:8] saw nothing, which was God. God is a nothing, and God is a something. Whatever is something is also nothing. Whatever God is he is completely."[19]

Parallelism in grammatical structure is a less striking but hardly less frequent device of the preacher. Thus he tells us: "Where (*Dâ*) man retains the accident of place, there (*dâ*) he retains difference" (Pr. 52; DW II, 502, 5). In explaining how spiritual things differ from what is material, he extends its use: "the (*ie*) higher spiritual things are, the (*ie*) greater they are; and the (*ie*) more powerful they are in their works, the (*ie*) purer they are in their being" (Pr. 58; DW II, 612, 9–10). He quotes a teacher as saying that God is the measure of all things: "and to the extent (*als vil*) that one person has more of God in himself than another has, to that extent (*als vil*) he is wiser, nobler, and better than the other." He continues: "the more (*ie*) of God's likeness is in us, the more (*ie*) spiritual we are" (Pr. 47; DW II, 403, 3–6). As the last two examples show, in parallelism he found an appropriate rhetorical vehicle for the expression of his *in quantum* principle.

Hyperbole is usually defined as extravagant exaggeration, and one can point to frequent claims and images in Eckhart's works which fit this definition well. In describing what it would be like if one were to look into God's *grunt* with which the soul's *grunt* unites, he assures us that to the person enjoying such a sight "a thousand marks of red, minted gold are no more than a counterfeit penny" (Pr. 5b; DW I, 90, 9–11; Colledge, p. 183). Similarly, so utterly selfless is the detached soul and so utterly intent on God's will alone that such a soul does not want God to bestow his whole divinity on it. What is more, this soul would be as little consoled by such a gift as it would if God were to give it a gnat (Pr. 62; DW III, 59, 2–6). In speaking of the faithful servant (Matt. 25:23), who is actually the just man in different clothing, Eckhart will claim: "whoever were to be so [completely] faithful, God would have within himself [because of this] such ineffably great joy that, if someone were to take this joy from him, one would be taking from him his life and being and divinity—completely."[20] These astonishing words reveal something at first glance perplexing about rhetoric when the subject is God or the divine aspect of creatures: hyperbole is not necessarily exaggeration at all but can be the literal truth. The utterly faithful servant, as one with and therefore indistinct from God, causes *divine* joy which is so essential to God's being that he cannot be separated from it and survive.

If the previous example shows that for Eckhart hyperbole can be literally true, the following passage reveals that the same figure must be viewed as understatement when he uses an image from the physical world to provide the basis for insight into the spiritual. To elucidate God's greatness he says: "The sky is so large and so vast that, if I told you about it, you would not believe it. If someone took a needle and touched the sky with the point, the part of the sky which the needle encompassed would be greater in comparison with the sky and the whole world, than the sky and the world would be compared to God."[21] So vast is the difference of the world we see—and which must provide the origin of all our thoughts—from the reality to which we must "break through," that modes of expression taken from the former to explain the latter radically change in meaning and can even turn into their opposites.

These examples suffice to illustrate the preacher's characteristic use of some standard rhetorical figures. Two further devices, however, one pertaining to content and one to external form, must be singled out for more detailed study. These are paradox and chiasmus.

Paradox

Etymologically, "paradox" refers to statements that are contrary to common opinion. That Eckhart sought to startle his hearers by contradicting common views is obvious enough, and as we have seen, one of his expressed purposes in undertaking the *Tripartite Work* was to provide new and unusual interpretations of scripture.[22] More commonly, "paradox" is understood to refer to declarations that conflict with or at least seem to conflict with ordinary logic. It is paradox in this latter sense that we now wish to address.

One does not have to look far to discover the source of Eckart's fondness for this form of expression. The Gospels abound with examples of paradox. We are told that the first shall be last and the last first (Matt. 19:30); that it is the least among us who is great (Luke 9:48); and that seeking to save one's life will cause its loss, while losing it for Christ's sake means saving it (Luke 9:24). The purpose of these paradoxes was to raise the listeners' consciousness by introducing them to new possibilities contained in words like "first," "great," and "life"—powerful words that had become harmless, misleading, or almost meaningless as a result of frequent and unthinking use. It is not sheer and complete contradiction that we find at the root of these statements, but rather a kind of dialectic. It is not the same life that will be both lost and gained. Rather, we must give up life as an experience common to all and limited in scope in order to attain life that is rich beyond imagination. The truth of this paradox is comprehended not simply by the joining of two concepts, as is done in normal logical discourse (e.g., God is good). Instead, the second, richer conception of life is grasped—insofar as it can be grasped—when one juxtaposes it to life as first conceived and then rejects this previous conception of life as insufficient. In other words, an important aspect of such paradox is that it is the rhetorical equivalent of the negative or apophatic way. We achieve here a heightened conception of life by seeing that life, as generally understood, is *not* life in the true sense of the word.

Because of its connections both to dialectic and to the negative way, we should hardly be surprised to find Eckhart using paradox to formulate many of his most profound insights. For example, his sermon on "poverty of spirit," treated above, breathes the spirit of paradox.[23] Two examples from this sermon show especially well how effectively this traditional rhetorical device serves to express the preacher's thought. True poverty, we are told, demands that we return to how we *were before we were*. How does the mind of the listener come to grips with this formulation? The first "were" is made to perform a dialectic leap. Before we feel the force of the subsequent "before we were" which qualifies it, we assume that it simply signifies our ordinary existence as creatures or, as the preacher would term it in Latin, that it signifies our *esse formale*. But we are then forced to see that the "were" in the phrase "before we were" is the term that actually denotes our creaturely *esse formale*. As our mind then compares the two "weres," the first "were" becomes our *esse virtuale* or our true existence as we are one with and in God.

This dialectic occurs through the interplay of positive and negative terms. How *were* we before we were? Our *esse formale*, which we received through creation and which makes us in some sense independent of God, is the term we can grasp positively with our intellect. Our existence as one with God, our noncreated existence, can be understood only to the extent that we can say of it that it is not existence in any sense really similar to our existence as creatures. This existence merely points darkly to the rich reality of our virtual existence in God. Paradoxically, not only *were* we *before we were*, we *were* in a much richer and more incomprehensible way than we are. Explaining the paradox, as we have done, weakens its effectiveness. Brevity is the soul not only of wit but of paradox as well. Eckhart may go on to explain to his audience what he means by existence before existence, but it is the terse expression of the thought in the form of paradox which causes us to perform the dialectical process with the instantaneity that characterizes insight.

In the same sermon Eckhart plays with the term "God" in a similar manner. We are urged to beg God to rid us of God. God can be known to us in any positive way only through what he brings about. But as the cause of creatures God does not reveal himself as he really is. Creatures are too far from him, are in the region of dissimilarity. In knowing God as the cause of creatures, we grasp something that is little more than an arbitrary sign of the reality. By getting rid of this sign, by realizing through negative attribution that our notion of God contains hardly a hint of his true nature, we pass—paradoxically—to a better understanding of the God who is hidden from us.

As the foregoing examples attest, most of the paradoxes found in the sermons are attempts to deal with two areas: the nature of God in relation to our frail capacities to understand him, and the similarly incomprehensible nature of creatures, suspended, as they are, between infinity and nothingness. Taking a quotation from Augustine as his point of departure, the preacher muses about Father and Son:

> Augustine says: "All writings are in vain. If one says that God is a word, he has been expressed (*gesprochen*); but if one says that God is unspoken (*ungesprochen*), he is ineffable (*unsprechlich*)." And yet he is something, but who can speak this word? No one can do this, except him who is this Word. God is a Word that speaks itself. Wherever God is, he speaks this Word; wherever he is not, he does not speak. God is spoken and unspoken.[24]

The context suggests more than one possible meaning for the statement that God is both *gesprochen* and *ungesprochen*. Certainly, one possibility is the contrast between the internal activity of the godhead as the Father *speaks* the Word and our inability to comprehend this activity: for us God must remain unspoken. Another possible meaning rests on the ultimate impenetrable oneness of God. Although God is utterly simple in his nature, the dynamism in the godhead is more forcefully expressed by paradoxically viewing the divinity as both speaker and what is spoken, as both subject and object, as both cause and effect. Eckhart commends highly a teacher who has said that activity in God is a *gewerden svnder gewerden* (a changing without change). In other words, divine activity can correctly be conceived only if we negate of it a quality that is a necessary component of action: change in the being in which activity occurs. Yet pure activity is precisely the dynamism making up the essence of the divinity, for the preacher continues: "vnd das gewerden ist sin wesen" (and change, becoming, activity is his nature, essence, being; Pr. 50; DW II, 459, 7–8).

Most paradoxes, though fertile, are stated briefly. However, a paradox can serve to inform an entire sermon. In Sermon 69, in order to explain both how we can see God and what can hinder this vision, Eckhart fastens upon what he perceives to be a paradox in Christ's use of the word *modicum* in the Gospel of John: "Modicum et iam non videbitis me: et iterum modicum, et videbitis me" (John 16:16; usual translation: "In a short time you will no longer see me, and then a short time later you will see me again"). With typical ingenuity the preacher construes *modicum* not as a temporal expression (a short time) but rather as "a small thing." Thus he interprets this passage to mean that a small thing both hinders our perception of God and is a necessary condition for it. As the first step in explaining this paradox, he takes *modicum* to mean the totality of creation—certainly a small thing compared to God—and says that this can hinder our seeing God. It is only when the soul has "leaped over" this *modicum* that it can find God the beloved.[25]

Relying on association more than logic, Eckhart then passes on to the disparate views of Democritus and Aristotle regarding the role of a medium for sight. Since ordinary human vision has the role here of providing an analogy for the soul's "seeing" God, the transition is plausible enough. The *modicum* which has been seen to hinder our seeing God now becomes the medium (*mittel*) which Democritus sees as a hindrance to sight, while Aristotle considers it a necessary condition. As with the *modicum* of the Gospel, the preacher sees these conflicting opinions as a paradox because he considers both authorities to be correct. Democritus is correct because a medium, such as a mist or impure air which dulls perception and separates the perceiver from the object, must be removed to improve sight. In this sense God suffers no medium. And if the soul were completely free of any medium, God would give himself to the soul as completely as the object gives itself to the perceiver. Thus we are urged to rid ourselves of all *mittel*, such as joys, sorrows, fears, and hopes, in order to "see" God (DW III, 163,6–167,1).

In another sense (that of Aristotle), however, a medium is necessary for perception. The material object must be refined, purified of its materiality, and turned into an image (*bilde*) before the eye can receive it. With this jump from *mittel* or medium to *bilde* or image, Eckhart has come around to a favorite theme. For just as the image of the material object is the necessary medium for sight, so it is the Word that is the image by which we perceive God: "The eternal Word is the medium and the image itself which is without [additional mediating] means and images, so that the soul grasps God in the eternal Word and knows him without [additional] means and images."[26] Because the intellect is an image of the Word—and Eckhart assures us we have grasped the entire sermon in understanding this—it is possible for us to be one with or see God: "Image [the Word] and image [the intellect] are so completely one and connected that one cannot understand any differentiation between them."[27] Thus does the paradox of the Johannine *modicum* lead to the theme of the birth.

If saying that God is good is like calling the sun black, there is a paradoxical irony about our knowledge of God. What we know for certain is that we have no real knowledge of him: "Whoever sees anything of God sees nothing of God."[28] The categorical nature of this formulation underlines the ironic position of the human mind in its search for God. Our only certitude is the clear knowledge that we have no real grasp of the immensity that is God. To this we must add the paradox implied in all of Eckhart's writings. Despite the shortcomings of human knowledge, despite the fact that we can much more correctly say what God is not than what he is, and despite the fact that any positive language applied to God merely points to him but does not reach him, both as preacher and as professor Eckhart clearly saw his principal task to be that of explaining God to man. Plainly he is not in the least overwhelmed by the irony of his situation. He approaches the task tirelessly, with an array of sophisticated intellectual and linguistic means at his disposal. One can sense in his words the conviction that, despite the ironies, something very important is achieved by these attempts. He has no doubt about the splendor of the divinity beyond the darkness surrounding our minds. Nor does he question the nobility of his task.

Creatures too provide the preacher with a fertile field for paradox. Their ambivalent existence, expressed in Sermon 52 as an existence both *before* and *as* creatures, can also be called both a flowing out (*ûzvliezen*) and a remaining within (*innebliben*), just as this is also a way of describing the incarnate Word.[29] The preacher is quick to add a second paradox to this: If we really understood how creatures flow out yet remain within, it would not be true.[30] Because God is one, which means that he is both distinct and indistinct from creatures, he is in all things. However, "the more he is in things, the more he is outside of things: the more he is within, the more [he is] outside, and the more outside, the more within."[31] The union of God and the soul is spiritual and thus not subject to the accident of place. This fact is also fittingly expressed through paradox: "just as God flows into the soul, so does it flow into God."[32] When its goal is achieved, the soul is completely dissolved (*vervlozzen*) in God and God in it" (Pr. 84; DW III, 465, 3–4). Similarly, the Son is born in us and we are born in the Son and become one Son (Pr. 41; DW II, 293, 9–10).

One form of paradoxical expression that Eckhart employs to good effect is the oxymoron, which heightens the effect of the paradox because the contradictory terms are placed immediately next to each other as adjective and noun. In a context already mentioned, he calls God "an unspoken word" (*ein ungesprochen wort*; Pr. 53; DW II, 529, 2). And how can one describe the being of God that is signified by the mysterious tetragrammaton, that word of four letters which might be the Latin *esse*? If God is being (*wesen*), Eckhart tells us, then he must be described as "a being above being."[33] Or if we think of *wesen* as essence, that negative principle limiting *esse*, or if we take *wesen* to be an *esse* that can be understood in some real sense by the human intellect, then perhaps an even more appropriate oxymoron will be to call God a being without being or essence (*ein wesen weselôs*) who must be loved in a manner (*wîse*) that is without manner or limitation (*wîselôs*; Pr. 82; DW III, 431, 3–4).

To explain the pervasiveness and effectiveness of paradox in Eckhart's thought, it is not enough merely to recall his linguistic cleverness or his familiarity and skill with rhetorical figures. Paradox functions for him not simply as a decorative effect but as an eminently suitable means for expressing something true about the nature of God and creatures, as we perceive them. From our vantage point, God and creatures are paradoxes. Single concepts must of necessity leave out more about God than they contain. Paradox, in a sense, captures what is left out by such concepts. If one says that calling God good is like calling the sun black, one is really calling attention to this inadequacy of single concepts. God's goodness has very little in common with goodness as we understand the term. It is essentially different from our concept of goodness. And God's *wesen* really is *weselôs*. When applied to God or creatures, contrary or contradictory concepts will not really conflict with the laws of logic, because they do not contain enough truth to exclude their opposites. One will come closer to expressing a truth by combining such concepts than by using them individually. Thus we come much closer to understanding what creatures are by viewing them simultaneously as distinct (*ûzvliezen*) and indistinct (*innebliben*) from God, than by considering them just as pure nothing (*ein lûter niht*), as they are separate from God, or by considering them only as divine, as they are one with him.

Paradox thus takes us to the limits of our knowledge and helps us to define these limits in our search to know ourselves and God. What is beyond these limits is darkness and, paradoxically, a splendor beyond all our capacity to imagine.

Chiasmus

Perhaps the preacher's most striking rhetorical configurations are the many examples of chiasmus. This device presents two or more words or phrases and then repeats them in reversed order. Thus, in a passage already cited, to explain that God is both inside things and outside them he states: "God is in all things. The more he is in them, the more he is outside them: the more within, the more outside, and the more outside, the more within."[34] *Ie mê inne, ie mê ûze, und ie mê ûze, ie mê inne*: why Eckhart found this figure so appealing is readily apparent. On the purely formal level it is a means of taking differing concepts and, by intertwining them, making them one. Thus it does not seem amiss to consider chiasmus, or at least Eckhart's use of it, as a mystical figure, since by means of it two things are made one in an alogical manner.

Another characteristic of the chiasmus advantageous for the preacher's aims is the ease with which it can be made to serve paradox. The union of God and the soul can, in Eckhart's view, be grasped by paradox or, in other words, by juxtaposing contradictory statements or concepts. Chiasmus intensifies the expression of this supralogical union and underlines the paradoxical nature of the thought. So, for example, in describing the life of the soul in heaven he says: "It is dissolved in God and God in it" (*Si ist vervlozzen in gote und got in ir*; Pr. 84; DW III, 465, 3–4). The repetition of God and the soul in inverted order intertwines them and joins them as co-subjects of the state of *vervlozzenheit* as well as co-locations of it. If this example indicates that the union of God and the soul transcends the philosophical category of place, it also implies, by association with another chiasmus occurring some lines earlier in the same sermon, the overcoming of another boundary: the antinomy of state and activity. In speaking of the birth of the Son in the soul Eckhart says, "And just as God flows into the soul, so does it flow back into God" (*und als got in die sêle vliuzet, alsô vliuzet si wider in got*; Pr. 84; DW III, 463, 5). In this instance he pictures God and the soul as flowing into one another, whereas in the first chiasmus he describes the flowing as an accomplished state. One should notice also how Eckhart increases the chiasmus to three terms (*got, sêle, vliuzet* :: *vliuzet, sêle, got*), thus making it a more sophisticated figure. Making *got* the outside member of the chiasmus here provides a nice contrast with the first example, where the soul is the outside member and God is the inside member.

In other passages Eckhart combines chiasmus with other structures or complicates the order further. For example, in describing the "something in the soul" where union occurs, the preacher mixes chiasmus with its opposite—parallelism: "and there is a something in the soul in which God lives, and is a something in the soul in which the soul lives in God" (*und ez ist ein etwaz in der sêle, dâ got inne lebet, und ist ein etwaz in der sêle, dâ diu sêle lebet in gote*; Pr. 42; DW II, 301, 5–6). Again through contradiction the location of the union is abolished. This calls into question the duality of the first and second *etwaz*. At times the intertwining of concepts characteristic of the chiasmus becomes even more intricate. In the following passage Eckhart demonstrates an artistic solution to the problem that our minds can approach God only by means of an array of concepts, while God himself is utterly simple. By rearranging the order of concepts, the preacher merges them into one reality: "All of God's commandments are from love and from the goodness of his nature; for if they were not from love, they could not be God's commandments; for God's commandment is the goodness of his nature, and his nature is his goodness in his commandment. Whoever then lives in the goodness of his nature lives in God's love" (*Alliu gotes gebot diu sint von minne und von der güete sîner natûre; wan enwaeren sie niht von minne, sô enmöhten sie niht gotes gebot sîn; wan gotes gebot ist diu güete sîner natûre, und sîn natûre ist sîn güete in sînem gebote. Wer nû wonet in der güete sîner natûre, der wonet in gotes minne;* Pr. 28; DW II, 59, 4–7).

An ingenious combination of chiasmus and parallelism occurs in one of Eckhart's descriptions of Father and Son: "The Father is a speaking work, the Son is speech working" (*Der vater ist ein sprechende werk, und der sun ist ein spruch würkende;* Pr. 53; DW II, 529,7–530,1). The Father's operation is to speak the Word, which is the Son. The Son, who is the result of the Father's action, is the Word through which all things were made (John 1:3) as a result of his working. Their juxtaposition (*sprechende werk—spruch würkende*) is artistically fashioned, each Person being represented by a noun with an accompanying participle—the nouns inside, the participles outside. This chiasmus on the formal level is contrasted to parallelism on the content level—*sprechende-spruch* and *werk-würkende*—which skillfully presents by association the unity of Father and Son despite their diversity.

While the complexity that characterizes many examples of chiasmus demonstrates linguistic virtuosity, it is perhaps when reducing this figure to its simplest form that Eckhart is most effective. In interpreting the statement (1 John 4:9) that God sent his only-begotten Son into the world, the preacher first reduces the historical event to a symbol for the more important and purely spiritual birth of the Son which takes place in the inner world of the soul. How better then to stress the unity achieved in the birth than to continue: "Here God's ground is my ground and my ground God's ground" (*Hie ist gotes grunt mîn grunt und mîn grunt gotes grunt;* Pr. 5b; DW I, 90, 8). The possessives (*mîn, gotes*) surrender their separate identities through being formed into a chiasmus. And the idea of oneness conveyed by the relentless repetition of the substantive (*grunt*), alternating with the possessives, has an intensity very appropriate to the theme of the birth.

The birth of the Son in the soul is frequently the topic we find being expressed in the patterns of chiasmus. The relationships between Son and soul in this union make this figure especially apt because its nature is to express the reduction of separate things to unity. However, the birth of the Son is not brought about by two separate and equal agents. Hence the parallelism or balance usually found between the two halves of the figure is not always appropriate. Taking the example of the son of the widow of Nain as someone in whom the Word has given birth to himself (Luke 7:11–15), Eckhart retains the basic pattern of the chiasmus but not the equality of its members: "When the Word speaks into the soul and the soul answers or echoes in the living Word, then the Son becomes alive in the soul" (*Swenne daz wort sprichet in die sêle und diu sêle widersprichet in dem worte, dâ wirt der sun lebende in der sêle*; Pr. 18; DW I, 305, 3–5). The Word speaks *into* the soul. True life through the birth of the Son comes from without and precedes the union. The soul's speaking is a *widersprechen*, a response that merely echoes the Word. And this response of the soul does not occur from without into the Word, but rather from *within* the Word, where the soul must be in order to echo the Word.[35]

When the unity of Word and soul is the point to be made, however, a simple, balanced chiasmus can well form the structural center to express it: "er [der vater] gebirt mich sînen sun und den selben sun. Ich spriche mêr: er gebirt mich niht aleine sînen sun, mêr: er gebirt mich sich und sich mich und mich sîn wesen und sîn natûre."[36] Juxtaposing *mich* and *sînen sun* with nothing intervening expresses the essential unity of *me* and the *Son*. The following *mich sich und sich mich* chiasmus goes even further. First of all, it implies a union of creature with the Father as the subject giving birth because, second, it is identified with the reflexive *sich*, which is the object (and subject) of the action. To help clarify the extremely telescoped content of this chiasmus he then identifies *me*, again with nothing intervening, with God's being and nature. There is no English equivalent for the chiasmus and the appended *und mich sîn wesen und natûre*. The use of "as" in translating, which is needed for clarification, palliates the effect of the original. Eckhart uses the most extreme linguistic means possible to express union.[37]

Chiasmus occurs frequently in the vernacular sermons, so much so that it must be considered an essential part of the preacher's pattern of expression. And he takes delight not only in using it himself but in discovering it elsewhere. In the example just mentioned he introduces the birth idea with a chiasmus-like expression he found in John (1:2–3): "Daz wort was bî gote, und got was daz wort." At times we find him approaching the forms of language as though they were somehow magical. His exegesis of the Latin word *ecce* illustrates this. As indeclinable, and thus in need of nothing for its perfection, *ecce* signifies the Word. It is also a chiasmus and signifies the union of God and the Word: "*Ecce* [Behold], this little word contains within itself everything that belongs to the Word. One cannot give it anything more. Word, that is God; God is a Word, God's Son is a Word" ("*Ecce*": *daz wörtelîn hât in im beschlozzen allez, daz ze dem worte gehoeret; man enkan ihm niht mê gegeben. Wort, daz ist got, got ist ein wort, gotes sun ist ein wort*; Pr. 44; DW II, 344, 4–6). At other times there is a playfulness evident, as in Eckhart's explanation of the Latin *mutuo* (mutual, reciprocal) by *meo tuo et tuo meo* (mine yours and yours mine) and support of this with a passage from John (17:10), "*omnia mea tua sunt et tua mea sunt*" (*In Gen.* II, n. 152; LW I, 622).

Although one must be careful not to overemphasize any thought that the Dominican approached language as something magical, it is clear here, as in his comments on the interpretation of scripture, that he sees much hidden in it which logical discourse alone cannot unveil. If *ecce* with its completeness and balance signifies the Word, we can well imagine that part of Eckhart's fascination with *esse*, another indeclinable chiasmus, was not merely philosophical. We have seen him speculate that it might be the most sacred word of all, the tetragrammaton.[38] And when pondering the motto under which he wished his whole *Tripartite Work* to be understood, we might recall that his *esse est deus* can well be thought of as a response to the more traditional *deus est esse*.

Word Games

A stylistic phenomenon similar to Eckhart's broad use of traditional rhetorical figures, but not susceptible to strict definition, is the word game, a device that appears in various forms and in which their author takes manifest delight. At times these games seem to be nothing more than the product of a playful sense of humor, but then again we see them serving didactic purposes, often enriching a scriptural quotation through the addition of a useful but unsuspected meaning. Finally, such playfulness occasionally yields very lofty results, something akin to poetry. For purposes of examination we can divide such word games into puns, word play with sounds, word play based on grammar, and finally, simply other similar displays of wit with words.

The preacher shows that he appreciates the value of a pun when he quotes a phrase from Augustine, "O munde immunde" (*Serm.* XXXVIII, n. 385; LW IV, 331), which the bishop had used to castigate a *world impure*, implying it is not the world that it should be. Eckhart also then avails himself of the ambiguity of *mundus* (world, clean) in interpreting 1 John 4:9, that God sent his only Son *in mundum*. By taking *mundus* as the adjective and assuming the noun *cor*, he interprets the passage as stating not that the Son was sent into the world, but that he was sent into a pure heart (*Serm.* VI, 2, n. 57; LW IV, 56). In another Latin sermon he poses the question about God: Whose God is he? He then answers that God is the God of those who love *bonum absolute*. The adverb *absolute* can modify both the verb "love" and the adjectival substantive *bonum*. Hence he is the God of those who love good absolutely, without qualification, and he is the God of those who love what is absolutely good, or God. Both meanings are clearly appropriate. A more involved play on the verb *praedicare* occurs at the beginning of Latin Sermon XXV, 1 (n. 251; LW IV, 230–231). He begins by saying that every *quod quid est*, or essence, praises (*praedicat*) its *esse* or *quo est*. Thus *esse* is never subject but rather predicated (*praedicatum*) and is, according to Boethius, of the order of things predicated (*de ordine praedicatorum*). Hence the praiser or preacher (*praedicator*) of truth (Paul) says, praising (*praedicans*) the grace of God, "By the grace of God I am what I am" (1 Cor. 15:10). One wonders whether Eckhart, in addition to the mixing of scholastic terminology with the more usual meaning of *praedicare* as to preach or praise, was not also having some fun by implying that *esse*, by Boethius's own admission, was of the Order of Preachers, his own religious order.

Even in the vernacular sermons we find Eckhart playing with the meaning of Latin words. Speaking on the feast of Saint Benedict, for example, he tells his audience that the reading for the day from Ecclesiasticus (45:1ff.) fits the saint well because it states that his memory is *in benedictione* (a blessing; Pr. 73; DW III, 259,6–260,2). The angel's greeting to Mary—*ave*—is simply transformed on the basis of sound to the Middle High German *âne wê* (without pain or grief), which is taken to describe the condition of those who, having turned their backs on the world of creatures, are *âne crêatûre* (Pr. 38; DW II, 240, 7–8).

In other instances Eckhart resorts to word play in the vernacular for various purposes. He does this in one sermon, for example, to startle, calling God *daz aller gemeineste*. The meaning of *gemein* which would most readily occur to his audience would be "common," "ordinary," or "lowly"—at any rate a word applied to something of no particular value. He then goes on to explain that anything that things have in common they have from some higher being. The preacher actually wishes to say that all universal or transcendental qualities come from God. By calling God *gemein* to express this idea, he certainly gains the attention of his listeners (Pr. 9; DW I, 149, 5–7). *Gemein* also means "lowly" when used to refer to social class, and hence the preacher contrasts it with *edel* (noble), claiming that the state one achieves through detachment is both *edel* and *gemeine*— noble, yet so common/transcendental that it does not cost a penny (Pr. 29; DW II, 80, 5–6).

Eckhart also uses homonyms to expand language beyond the usual. Taking *wîse* as his focal point, he quotes Bernard to the effect that to love God is to love *wîse âne wîse* (in a manner without measure, *modo sine modo*; Pr. 9; DW I, 144, 8–9). Shortly thereafter he quotes Augustine as saying that God is *wîse âne wîsheit* (wise without wisdom) and follows this immediately with the thought that, in the schools, being is divided into ten *wîse* (categories or modes of being) and that none of them applies to God (Pr. 9; DW I, 147, 1–4). The similarity of the first and third mention of *wîse* rests on the opposition of finite to infinite. Our love of God must be infinite, just as he is infinite and cannot be grasped through the various categories of substance and accidents. The second occurrence of *wîse*, however, which refers to God's being wise without wisdom, is upon examination related to the other two by much more than just sound. For God is wise in a sense that transcends our way of attributing the quality of wisdom to something. Wisdom is not an aspect of God. It is God. Another identification by homonym occurs at the conclusion of the sermon on *The Nobleman*, where Eckhart quotes from Ezekiel (17: 3ff.) the description of how a large eagle comes to Lebanon and plucks off the top branch of a cedar. This eagle is then equated with the nobleman (Luke 19:12), since a variation of the Middle High German *adeler* (eagle) is *edeler*, which also signifies a nobleman (DW V, 118,20–119,4).

We can conclude our look at the preacher's employment of this kind of play on words with two examples that are richer in meaning. In Sermon 2, where he is making the point that the person who is to receive/conceive Jesus must be both a virgin and a wife, the preacher explains why this must be so and why a wife (one who can rightfully give birth) is more noble than a virgin: "That a man conceives God in himself is good, and in his conceiving he is a maiden. But that God should become fruitful (*vruhtBAERlich*) in him is better; for the only gratitude (*dankBAERkeit*) for a gift is to be fruitful (*vruhtBAERkeit*) with the gift, and then the spirit is a wife in its gratitude giving birth in return (*in der widerBERNDEN dankBAERkeit*), when he for God gives birth again (*widergeBIRT*) to Jesus into the heart of the Father" (DW I, 27, 4–9; Colledge, p. 178). In the context of conception and birth, the root *bern* (to give birth) must be clearly felt in the repeated *vruhtbaerkeit* and *dankbaerkeit* as well as in the actual "giving birth again" (*widergebern*). The whole passage has the denseness and intensity of lyric poetry, and the rhythmic repetition of *baer/bern* adds much to its effect.

We have seen that Eckhart elevates the term *unum* even above *esse* in its aptness for describing God. But how can the vastness and impenetrable simplicity of the term be made real in language? To the extent that *unum* describes something true about God, it is both overpowering and yet empty of content for the human mind. At least twice Eckhart tries to deal with the problem by joining *ein* (one) to *einoede* (desert wasteland). The *vünkelîn* is said to penetrate somehow to the first breaking-out (*ûzbruch*) of God and sees him, but not just as he is good or true. It seeks the foundation (*gründet*) and keeps seeking and takes God in his being one (*einunge*) and in his desert wasteland (*einoede*); it takes God in his empty vastness (*wüestunge*) and in his own ground (*grunt*; Pr. 10; DW I, 171, 11–15). In concluding his sermon on *The Nobleman*, the preacher joins this combination of *ein* and *einoede* to a repetitive use of *ein*, thus achieving a formulation of great power. Expanding on a passage from Hosea (2:14), he states how the Lord wishes to lead the noble soul "in *ein ein*oede, und ich wil dâ sprechen in ir herze *ein* mit *ein*em, *ein* von *ein*em, *ein* in *ein*em und in *ein*em *ein* êwiclîche" (into a desert, and there I will speak to her heart, one with One, one from One, one in One, and in One, one everlastingly; DW V, 119, 4–7; Colledge, p. 247).

Similar to puns based on homonyms are certain alogical connections that the preacher makes based on sound. In the following example he "improves" the meaning of scripture at the same time. Starting with Paul's command to put Christ on (like a garment; Rom. 13:14), he takes *induimini* (to put on) and through sound association renders it in German *întuot iu Kristum*—make Christ interior to yourselves. He then continues with this sound association, contrasting *Kristum întuon* with *sich entuon* (ridding self of self; Pr. 24; DW I, 414, 1–7). He makes a similar transition in Latin by taking the apostle's exhortation to Timothy to proclaim the word (2 Tim. 4:2). *Praedica* becomes *praedic*, which he interprets to mean "say beforehand interiorly." This he then changes to *prodic* (speak outwardly), which then becomes *produc* (bring forth; *In Eccli.* n. 69; LW II, 299). With this transformation we are close to a favorite theme. In a German sermon on the same text he is more explicit. The steps in the phrase's transformation are "sprich daz wort" (speak the word), "sprich ez her ûz, sprich ez her vür" (speak it openly), "brinc ez her vür" (bring it forth), and "gebir daz wort" (give birth to the Word; Pr. 30; DW II, 93, 3-4). The basis for these words in the vernacular sermon would seem to be the similarity in sounds (*praedica, praedic*, and so on), which exists only in Latin.

Some passages seem to be formed with lyrical intent, in the sense that sounds appear to predominate over meaning. Consider, for example, this concluding sentence of a description of the life the *vünkelîn* shares with God: "In disem leben sint alliu dinc ein, alliu dinc gemeine al und al in al und al geeiniget" (Pr. 76; DW III, 317, 2; translation: in this life all things are one, all things in common, united all and all, in all and all). The interweaving of the predominant sounds *al* and *ein* joins the intellect with the divine *intelligere* more intimately than is possible through logical structure. In asserting that the love of God for the soul involves the very existence of the Holy Spirit, the preacher plays with the sounds of *minne* (love) and *inne* (within, in). Through sounds all love becomes one love: "in der minne, dâ sich got selben inne minnet, in der minne minnet er mich, und diu sêle minnet got in der selben minne, dâ er sich selben inne minnet, und enwaere disiu minne niht, dar inne got die sêle minnet, der heilige geist enwaere niht" (Pr. 10; DW I, 168, 4-7; translation: in that love in which God loves himself, in that love he loves me, and the soul loves God in that same love in which he loves himself; and if this love did not exist in which God loves the soul, the Holy Spirit would not exist). A logical understanding of these lines seems of secondary importance if not superfluous.

More frequent than such melodic flights are passages where the structure of language, or grammar, becomes content as well as form. In many other instances where it is not strictly the subject matter, grammar is the means of interpretation, so that Eckhart the grammarian often dictates the thought of Eckhart the interpreter of scripture. To begin with a straightforward example: In urging his audience to give up all things, even spiritual things, to achieve perfect detachment, he rests his argument on the distinction between believing God when he tells us something (*gote glouben*) and believing in God (*an got glouben*), which is greater. He finds it ironic that some people can believe in God yet do not really believe God when he tells them they shall receive a hundredfold in return for leaving all things (Pr. 62; DW III, 56,1–59,2).

The preacher often interprets individual words strictly according to their grammatical function or according to all their potentialities, giving no attention to the context, literal or otherwise. In a sermon on the introduction to the Simeon episode ("et ecce, homo erat," and behold there was a man; Luke 2:25), Eckhart devotes his attention almost exclusively to exploring the grammatical implications of these four words. Thus *et* means "a union and a binding together and an enveloping. Whatever is completely bound together and enveloped means union. Here I interpret it that man is bound together and enveloped and united to God."[39] Certainly a heavy load of meaning for this particular *et*! In notes for a Latin sermon on the Pauline text "Nunc vero liberati a peccato" (Now, however, you have been set free of sin; Rom. 6:22), the preacher devotes all his efforts to explaining the eight possible interpretations for the word *vero*. First, it is a conjunction like "but," and this is the way it is usually understood. Second, it can be taken as an adverb like *vere* and means that we have *truly* been freed from sin. Third, it can be taken as an adjectival noun meaning "by truth," as when we are told in John (8:36) that the truth shall make us free. This is also true philosophically because the potencies of the soul are all limited and, as it were, captives of the objects that bring them into act. The intellect, however, in which truth resides, is not limited by objects and is therefore free. Fourth, taking *vero* as modifying the preceding *nunc*, we see that we are freed from sin *by the true now*, that is, by the now of eternity which the freed soul shares with God and compared to which the now of our existence in time is nothing. Fifth, it can mean that we are truly freed from the now of time. Sixth, we are freed from being true merely through participation. Seventh, we must be freed from truth itself because the idea of truth is purer than truth itself, or, eighth, from truth as we can conceive it, because it is only bare being (*ens nudum*)— freed from all constrictions necessarily accompanying our ability to conceive of ideas like truth—that can make us happy (*Serm.* XVII, 2, nn. 168–169; LW IV, 160–161).

If what appears to be a mere adverb contains such wealth, the meaning and tense of a verb can also be made to yield unsuspected riches. In analyzing John 1:1, "In the beginning was the Word," the preacher instructs us that the verb "was" (*erat*) requires three different interpretations before we can understand all its implications

about the Word's relationship to its beginning/principle, which is the
Father. "Was," because of its relation to *esse*, denotes substance and
shows that the *Word* is the very substance of the Father. Because
"was" is a past tense, it points to the eternity of the birth: the Word
has always been born in the Father. However, because *erat* is the imperfect tense and thus points to incompleted action, it also describes
the eternal dynamism of the birth; the Word is always being born.
Thus only *erat* is suitable to describe both the substantial union and
the dialectic of the birth in the Trinity as something both eternally
complete and still going on.[40] In commenting on Exodus 3:14, "He
who is sent me" (*qui est, misit me*), Eckhart will be equally emphatic
in stating that the present tense (*est*) alone is appropriate for God,
since what was (*fuit*) or will be (*erit*) is not. "Is" (*est*), therefore, alone
is appropriately applied to God and must be applied to him exclusively, for he alone truly *is* (*In Exod.* n. 22; LW II, 28–29).

In the well-known German Sermon 9, the part of speech a word
from scripture is again becomes the starting point for interpretation.
The passage to be illuminated is "Quasi stella matutina in medio
nebulae . . . sic iste refulsit in templo dei" (Like the morning star
among the clouds . . . did he shine in God's temple; Eccli. 50:6–12).
Focusing on *quasi* (like), which he calls a *bîwort*, and recalling that
God is a *wort*, Eckhart urges us to become a *bîwort*. Etymologically,
bîwort denotes a word that is dependent on another word and can
mean adjective, adverb, or possibly other parts of speech conceived of
as having a subordinate role. Thus he is exhorting his audience to become dependent on the Word (DW I, 154,7–155,3). But his use of
bîwort here is perhaps more complex than this. The word can also
mean allegory, and the preacher continues his sermon at this point
by explaining the allegory of the morning star (which we should
be), which always stays equally close to the sun (God) and allows
nothing to separate it further from the sun (DW I, 155, 3–11). Thus
Eckhart is able to draw two parallel relationships from the text, one
based on allegory (morning star, sun) and one based on grammar
(*bîwort, wort*).

The preacher is not above changing scripture or misrepresenting
syntax to achieve his purposes. For example, he sees fit to change the
"thy will be done" of the Pater Noster, which he feels expresses only
the wish to submit one's human will to the divine will, to something
expressing the complete union of these wills through the creature's
giving up his own will: "wille, werde dîn!" (Will, become yours [God's]!
Pr. 30; DW II, 99, 2). In another sermon, based on the passage where
Peter exclaims when escaping from prison, "Nunc scio vere, quia

misit dominus angelum suum, et eripuit me de manu Herodis" (usual translation: Now I truly know that the Lord has sent his angel and snatched me from the hand of Herod; Acts 12:11), he changes the obvious meaning of *quia*. We might lament Jerome's departure from classical syntax, but *quia* really does mean "that" and does introduce a clause telling us what Peter truly knows. Eckhart, however, wishes to interpret the passage according to his conception of human cognition and turns the *quia* into a conjunction introducing a causal clause: "Wan mir got sînen engel hât gesant, dâ von bekenne ich waerlîche" (*Because* God sent me his angel, I know truly; Pr. 3; DW I, 48, 6–7).

One valuable distinction Eckhart makes in translating results from the lack of a definite article in Latin. How, for example, is one to translate "Deus caritas est?" (1 John 4:16). Is it *got ist diu minne* or *got ist minne*? If one says that God is *diu minne*, he muses, one could ask what love among all the kinds of love God might be. By saying *got ist minne*, he asserts, one remains by God as he is simply one (Pr. 63; DW III, 74, 5–8). The passage is not completely clear, but it seems that by leaving love indefinite Eckhart wished to have us consider God, as he is love, to be indistinct from all love, so that all love must be considered divine.

The indefinite aspects of Latin are several times a basis for original interpretations. We have mentioned that the adjective *iustus* with no accompanying noun allowed Eckhart to see in it the scriptural vindication of his *in quantum* principle, whereby the just man insofar as he is just is one with God.[41] The indefinite "certain man" (*homo quidam*) who gives a banquet for ungrateful guests (Luke 14:16–24) offers another opportunity for the preacher's creativity in interpretation. He is certainly not unusual in considering the host to be God. However, he takes the indefinite *quidam* as a confirmation of the legitimacy of describing God apophatically. *Quidam* implies that this "man" is without a name, "for God is unnameable for us because of the infinity of all being in him."[42] Similarly, in his exegesis of the pivotal *ego sum qui sum* (Exod. 3:14), he considers *qui* (who) as a word without limits. It is appropriate in this context, he maintains, because it is the indefinite or infinite subject of an *est* which signifies God's *esse*, an *esse* that is infinite and immeasurable (*infinitum et immensum*; In Exod. n. 15; LW II, 20).

Inflection, especially of pronouns, is another aspect of language which Eckhart exploits, as the following interplay of genitive and dative makes clear: "Dû solt sîn sîn und solt im sîn und ensolt dîn niht sîn und ensolt dir niht sîn und ensolt niemannes sîn" (You should be his [God's] and should be for him and should not be your own and should not be for yourself and should be nobody's; Pr. 16b; DW I, 271, 2–4). The interplay of genitive and dative, coupled with the repeated constants *solt* and *sîn*, gives an effect that a translation cannot reproduce. Simpler, yet at the same time more astonishing, is the following play with the inflection of pronouns in an attempt to apprehend something about God, not as he is in his antechamber (being) but as he is in his temple (knowledge): "Got in sîn selbes bekantnisse bekennet sich selben in im selben" (God in the knowledge of himself knows himself in himself; Pr. 9; DW I, 150, 7). God appears in all four cases. He is once the subject of knowing and twice the object (in the objective genitive and in the accusative). The dative phrase *in im selben*, given the context of temple and antechamber, implies a location where the knowledge takes place. More immediately, however, it translates the Latin *in se*, or God as he really is.

Some of these examples of word play are no more than conscious attempts to enlist aspects of language to achieve ascetical instruction. At times, however, they achieve something more, as the final example does. In such cases the formulation is more than a means for ordinary human discourse: form then *means*, just as content does. In this sense such passages can be called poetic.

Other Poetic Effects

Many turns of speech found in Eckhart's works defy classification, or at least do not owe their impact to being this or that recognizable figure. While it would be difficult to make a case for any of his works being literature in any strict sense, the presence of poetic qualities can hardly be denied. One poetic characteristic repeatedly in evidence is the "anti-Euclidean" nature of many forms of expression. Again and again we come upon passages or whole sermons where we ascertain that the whole is clearly more than the sum of the parts. With respect to many sermons or sections thereof, no amount of analysis, be it literary or philosophical, can either explain or equal the impact made on the attentive reader. We can conclude with a few examples that illustrate this phenomenon in various ways.

In the following passage concerning the birth of the Son, both the union of God and creature and the dynamism of this union are marvelously expressed:

> Got hât allen sînen lust in der geburt
> unde dar umbe gebirt er sînen sun in uns,
> daz wir allen unsern lust dar inne haben

und wir den selben natiurlîchen sun mit im gebern;
wan got hât allen sînen lust in der geburt,
unde dar umbe sô gebirt er sich in uns,
daz er allen sînen lust habe in der sêle
und daz wir allen unsern lust haben in im.
(Pr. 59; DW II, 627, 8–628, 1)

God has all his pleasure in the birth,
and therefore he gives birth to his Son in us,
that we might have all our pleasure in it
and that we might give birth to the same natural Son with him;
for God has all his pleasure in the birth,
and therefore he gives birth to himself in us,
that he might have all his pleasure in the soul
and that we might have all our pleasure in him.

It does not seem inappropriate to cast these lines as verse. There is an interplay of passive and active ideas (*lust hân-gebern*), with the subject alternating between God and creature. The place of the birth changes from us, to God, and back again to the soul. God gives birth to the Son in us. Then we give birth to the Son in God. Finally God gives birth to himself in us. The pleasure of all this resides in the birth, with God having pleasure in the soul and we in God. Although such analysis helps point out how the passage functions, no amount of analysis can hope to recreate its effect.

In another sermon the birth is given verbal form in the following manner. First, the preacher describes the birth in the Trinity thus:

Wan got gebirt sich ûz im selben in sich selben und gebirt sich wider in sich (Pr. 43; DW II, 320, 3–4).

For God gives birth to himself out of himself into himself and gives birth to himself back into himself.

God in his oneness is both the subject giving birth and the object being born. He is both that out of which the birth occurs and the "place" into which he gives birth and is born, a place identical with the subject giving birth. While this is certainly an eloquent description of the immanent workings of the Trinity, it functions here mainly to prepare the audience for a description of workings in the soul that are shocking in their similarity. Attributing the words to "a teacher," who is not otherwise identified and might be the preacher himself, he says some lines later:

Diu sêle gebirt sich selben in sich selben und gebirt sich ûz ir und gebirt sich wider in sich (Pr. 43; DW II, 328, 6–7).

The soul gives birth to itself into itself and gives birth to itself out of itself and gives birth to itself back into itself.

As Son and as intellect, the soul can be favored with the same description as God. The descriptions are in themselves linguistic tours de force. Their juxtaposition joins God and creature in an action that can only be thought of as divine.

Eckhart's play with *niht* (nothing) often achieves unusual effects. It has several meanings for him. So, for example, he is able to distinguish four meanings of the nothing which the stricken Saul (soon to become Paul) saw when he rose from the ground (Acts 9:8). First, he saw God, who is the nothing beyond being. Second, he saw nothing but God. Third, in all things he saw nothing but God, and fourth, when Saul saw God, he saw all things as nothing (Pr. 71; DW III, 211–231). As we have already noted, Eckhart states the paradox: "Whoever sees anything (*iht*) of God, sees nothing (*niht*) of God.[43] The most obvious meaning of this statement, and one that he certainly intended, is that the human intellect can never grasp the infinity of God's perfections, that our ignorance of God must always surpass our knowledge of him. However, the meaning of this paradox for the preacher does not stop there. It goes on to embrace the opposite, since as we have just seen, *niht* often signifies the fullness of God beyond our comprehension. Thus this paradox rests on a second paradox: The *iht gotes* that one sees is the *niht gotes* that surpasses the *iht*. And this is what one sees when one really sees *iht gotes*. That this second meaning is also actually intended by Eckhart is confirmed by the statement which follows shortly thereafter that the just man possesses God and "therefore he serves because of the *niht*" (*dar umbe endienet er umbe niht*; Pr. 62; DW III, 67, 1). Such a statement makes sense only if the *niht* for which the just man serves is not an ulterior motive, but rather the *niht* which is God.

Through the *vünkelîn*, man shares the nothingness beyond being which is God. It is the nothingness of the intellect, its basic difference from creatures which enables it to know.[44] It is with this ultimate *niht* beyond being that we must become one. Thus Eckhart can say: "A person who is resting on nowhere and is attached to nothing, if someone were to overturn heaven and earth, the person would be attached to nothing and nothing would be attached to him."[45] One can, of course, construe the words as a standard utterance on detachment. But because of the richness of Eckhart's notion of *niht*, it is clear that we are also being urged to attach ourselves to an absolutely firm foundation, to the *niht* of God beyond all human knowing.

Since *niht* is a word that very aptly describes God as something infinitely beyond any *iht* we might grasp, it is not surprising to find *niht* being used in conjunction with *unum*, the term that best points both to God's oneness with creatures and to his separateness from them. The soul must love God, we are told, apart from rationality (*geistekeit*) which, unlike *ein* or *niht*, tries to reduce God to the dimensions of intelligibility for the human mind. We must love God "as he is One not-God, One not-spirit, One not-person, One not-image, rather: as he is a pure clear One, apart from all duality, and in this one we shall eternally sink from nothing to nothing."[46]

If Eckhart often expresses a totality that is more than the sum of its parts, he is equally adept at positing parts, or things existing separately, which then surrender their stated separateness by being reduced to unity with something else, thereby losing their identity. This pattern can be found in one of his favorite texts: "In the beginning was the Word; the Word was with God and the Word was God" (John 1:1). In the sermons, however, it is not God and the Word but God and man that are first perceived as separate realities which then merge into one. Justice and the just man occur several times as the subject of this pattern. Thus, "Whoever loves justice, justice takes care of him and embraces him, and he is justice."[47] This passage shows a further linguistic refinement in that justice itself and man exchange the grammatical roles of subject and object before their identity is stated. The following similar formulation was noted by critics of Eckhart's orthodoxy: "and all his [the just man's] being, life, understanding, knowing, and loving is out of God and in God and [is] God."[48] But the preacher can be even more shockingly direct: "Whoever is in justice is in God, and is God."[49]

Eckhart's other favorite subject for this sentence pattern is the relationship between man and the Son. This can be stated as a moral or mystical imperative: "Now a person should so live that he is one with the only-begotten Son and that he is the only-begotten Son."[50] Or it can be stated as a fact resulting from man's ascetical efforts: "to the extent that the Son is born in us, we are also born in the Son and become one Son."[51] Once, in a single sermon, the preacher uses this pattern five times. The first time he wishes to clarify the difference between a spiritual vessel and a material vessel. In the case of a spiritual vessel, everything it receives is in the vessel, and the vessel is in it, and it is the vessel itself (Pr. 16b; DW I, 264, 8–9). He then twice employs the pattern to clarify the relationship of an image (*bilde*) to the object of which it is an image: The being (*wesen*) of the image is really the being of the object. The image has no other being (DW I, 269, 6–8; 270, 5–6). This leads us to the central point of the sermon, the union of the just man with the Son, where we find the pattern used twice more: "Such a person takes where the Son takes and is the Son himself" and "If you want to know God, you should not just be like the Son; rather you should be the Son himself."[52] Such a recurring pattern reveals well the mystical bent of the preacher. Things that are at first perceived as separate from God or the Son are then placed in their true perspective: as one with him who alone truly is.

The content of Eckhart's works ranges from ordinary pastoral concerns, through those of the professional theologian, to sublime heights of spirituality. To be sure, there are poetic elements scattered throughout, but it is especially when attempting to express his most exalted thoughts and most pressing concerns that, consciously or not, he most clearly displays his artistry with language. The loftiness of the subject matter calls forth the appropriate level of expression. At times a clearly poetic will to form predominates in him, displacing what one would expect to be his highest priority: the spiritual instruction of his audience. Forms of expression that most approximate the divine subject matter are then pursued at the expense of conceptual clarity or communication with a spiritually and intellectually less gifted audience. In such instances Eckhart makes no concessions to the audience other than, for example, in the case of his mind-staggering interpretation of poverty of spirit, to append the consoling comment: "Whoever does not understand these words should not be troubled in his heart about it" (Pr. 52; DW II, 506, 1). This existential need to give adequate form to his thought, inappropriate though this might be to the circumstances, might well provide the best context for understanding his often quoted assertion "Whoever has understood this sermon, I am happy for him. But if there had been no one here, I would still have had to preach it to the collection box."[53]

EPILOGUE
ECKHART'S MYSTICISM

Because of the various uses and misuses to which the term "mysticism" has been put, and because of the resulting variety of fantasies and expectations it can conjure up in the mind, one hesitates to introduce it into a discussion of Meister Eckhart. But introduce it one must, if for no other reason than that there is a long tradition which has labeled Eckhart a mystic, although there is not substantial agreement on what the term means when applied to him and some find its use inappropriate. In attempting to clarify the terms "scholasticism" and "mysticism" as they apply to Eckhart, the editor of his German works, Josef Quint, emphasized the latter term, declaring that the Dominican is a scholastic mystic rather than a mystical scholastic; that in the depths of his nature he possessed the mystical *intuitus*, but that he possessed it as knowledge rather than as feeling.[1] Another respected Eckhart scholar, Hermann Kunisch, attempted to show that everything in Eckhart's works stems from "the experienced reality of the ground of his own soul."[2] British scholar James Clark adds his weight to this point of view: "That Eckhart had profound mystical experiences cannot be doubted by the serious student of his works"; however, he then adds the disquieting disclaimer "but he never mentions them."[3] Undaunted at the prospect of never being admitted to the circle of serious Eckhart scholars, Heribert Fischer has challenged this dominant point of view, questioning whether one should talk of an *intuitus mysticus* in the case of Eckhart and suggesting that designating Eckhart a mystic comes from the murky waters of Germanistic and literary criticism and not from the crystalline springs of theological classification.[4] C. F. Kelley also rejects the title "mystic" for Eckhart, preferring to call him a pure metaphysician.[5] In the present study we have had recourse to the adjective "mystical" at times, but we have tried to use it sparingly.

185

Given the vagueness of the term, no purpose seems to be served by attempting to formulate a binding or essential definition. Nor shall we present in any detail all the applications of the word down through the centuries. It is sufficient to recall a few facts. Etymologically the word comes from the Greek verb *muein*, which means to shut or close, especially with regard to the lips or eyes. It also can refer to keeping one's eyes shut or to being lulled to rest and thus to cease activity. In medieval times, *mysticus* or *mystice* often referred to one of the nonliteral or nonhistorical senses according to which a Bible passage might be interpreted. "Mystic" and "mysticism," as the terms are generally understood today, were unknown to Eckhart and his contemporaries, and one searches in vain for an equivalent concept in Eckhart's works. The adjective *mysticus* appears occasionally in his Latin works, but not in any connection that would help us define "mystical" as it might apply to him. For example, Eckhart describes the conception of Christ's body as being the result not of male semen but of a mystical breath (*mystico spiramine; In Joh.* n. 349; LW III, 297), and he applies the word to the sacrament of the altar (*Serm.* V, 2, n. 48; LW IV, 46). In both cases he wishes to describe the mysterious, hidden, unfathomable nature of the object or event described. Without denying that such meanings touch the phenomenon mysticism as it is understood in more recent centuries, we must admit that it does not take us very far.

Two characteristics of a present-day understanding of the term "mysticism" which seem especially pertinent are, first, that mysticism is an experience and, second, that it is an experience of union with God as absolute being. The experience is generally said to surpass in intensity or clarity ordinary human experience. The divine being with whom the mystic is united is known, or its presence is felt, in ways that transcend both the normal faith experience of the believer and the professional knowledge of the theologian.

Mediating this experience of union, as soon as the mystic attempts to formulate or communicate it at least, is language. And some investigators too easily forget that whatever the mystic may experience is filtered through language. The experience can be passed on only to the extent that it is able to be fitted into what are largely already-formed concepts and modes of expression. The experience, at least to the extent that it is preverbal or inexpressible—and it is usually described as being essentially thus—is unreachable and incapable of being examined. The mystical experience as such cannot be judged. Only the mystic's skill in describing it can be evaluated. We cannot compare the description with the experience as we can when physical objects or events are being described. And though we can make some estimation of linguistic skill, we have no direct means of determining the accuracy of the description. The inaccessible nature of the experience, except through the *per definitionem* inadequate medium of language, needs to be emphasized to make clear how questionable the concept "experience" is. What can be examined is an effect of the experience, an effect whose similarity or correspondence to its cause escapes measurement. Since the notion of experience, and of experience differing markedly from ordinary human experience, seems essential to contemporaneous use of the term "mystic," one feels obliged to include it in any discussion of the topic; but one does well to be aware of the problems its introduction involves.

In the hope of avoiding many of the pitfalls encountered in such discussions, we shall reduce our inquiry to more definable areas. Three questions we might explore are: (1) In what sense or senses can Eckhart's thought be said to be mystical? (2) In what sense can one claim that his language is mystical? (3) Can we ascertain as the motivating or molding force for his thought and language something we can describe as a mystical experience?

Turning to the first point, one is justified in calling Eckhart's thought mystical because of certain aspects of his metaphysics, because of the goal his asceticism would have us attain, and because of his conception of human knowledge of the divinity. His metaphysical thought deserves to be characterized as mystical because of the overwhelming emphasis he puts on the union of God and creature—so much, in fact, that it appears to go beyond what orthodox Christian thought allows. When he uses *esse* in an all-encompassing sense—as when he states that *esse* is God, for example—creatures are said to be nothing in themselves and to have no real being that is not also the being of God. The only contribution they are able to make to their existence and the only thing distinguishing them from God is their nothingness. For Eckhart, being is God in a more exclusive sense than for most orthodox theologians. An important consequence of this position is that many of his statements sound traditional but really are not. For example, he writes: "Nothing is so close to a creature (*enti*), nothing is so intimate to it, as being (*esse*). But God is being, and from him all being (*esse*) comes directly." Traditionally this would mean that God alone can create and sustain the being possessed by a creature. But for Eckhart the being that comes from God directly is the divine being itself. It is this being that is united to creatures. This conviction certainly makes the thought which follows truly mystical, for he continues: "He [God] himself *alone* penetrates to the essences of things" (*In Joh.* n. 238; LW III, 199, 3–5).

The *magister*, therefore, does not view creatures as existing in any real sense separately or independently. Rather, they exist at the nondimensional intersection of nothingness and infinity. Or, to use Eckhart's own manner of speaking, to the extent that they are, are good, are just, and the like, there is no distinction between them and God. They are no more real, left to themselves, than the image of a real object is. Any reality they possess, like the image, is totally dependent on the object of which they are an image. Certainly the metaphysical union between God and creatures which this conception of the latter's nature entails, a union that so reduces the creature to the divinity that it has neither existence nor any positive quality of its own, merits the name mystical.

Similarly, Eckhart's view of the transcendental *unum* requires a connection between God and creature that declares them to be indistinct from each other. In other words, included in the definition of God's unity is his relationship to creatures. They are part of his oneness and cannot be separated from him. In considering these points about *esse* and *unum*, we must recall that we are not dealing with language that is describing thoughts or feelings of an undisciplined spiritual outlook. Rather, *esse* and *unum* are terms posited by a university professor in his professional writings, and they must be judged accordingly. Their relation to the personal experience of their author is unclear. What is clear from their context is that they were meant to be statements of a schoolman about the true nature of God and the world: Creatures are, according to their nature, really indistinguishable from God and have no being other than his.

While admitting the daring that these views manifest, we must recall that they do not represent Eckhart's total view. Certainly we must take their author at his word and not seek ways of excusing them. Eckhart considered them to be a true representation of reality. However, while it would be difficult to imagine formulations that stress the God-creature union more, we must bear in mind that the Dominican gave equal emphasis to declarations that are the very opposite. He considered nothing to be more distinct than God and creature. And what could be more opposed to or separate from the infinite being of God than the nothingness of creatures? His statements indicating division are as true for him as his statements claiming union. The fact that opposed affirmations are equally valid is simply a result of our insufficient capacity to deal adequately with God's being. Despite this necessary qualification, it remains true that, in its uncompromising insistence on the union of God and creature, Eckhart's metaphysical thought can justly be called mystical.

A similar judgment is appropriate regarding his preaching on the *vünkelîn*. Through the highest powers of his intellect, man is one with God in a manner that lower creatures do not share. Through the *vünkelîn*, man is united with God in nonbeing. He is not just a creature bound to God by dependence on the divine *esse*. As intellectual in nature, he shares with God the condition of existing and working in the nonbeing (*unwesen*) that the intellect necessarily is. It must be free of being in order to comprehend being. Since the purity of being that can rightfully be attributed to God is pure knowing, and since our intellect is the image of the divine *intelligere*, our knowing has the potential to be divine knowing: "The same knowledge in which God knows himself is the knowledge of every detached spirit. There is no difference" (Pr. 10; DW I, 162, 2–4).

Mystical too is Eckhart's ascetical thought. For it envisions as man's goal a union with God which transcends traditional ascetical notions. As the just man, it is not some quality faintly reflecting divine justice that one shares. Rather, insofar as one is just, one is informed by or filled with the divine justice which is God himself. In becoming the Son, the only-begotten Son, man becomes involved in the very life of the Trinity, begetting as the Father, being born as the Son, and becoming one with the fruit of this action: the Holy Spirit. Can a loftier goal for man be imagined, or a more intimate union with the divine, than to be part of the immanent action of the triune God? By the same token, *abegescheidenheit* or detachment is not merely "human" virtue, since it implies that we must change our nature and confront images (*bilde*) from a divine point of view. Similarly, the preacher's presentation of poverty of spirit surpasses more traditional exhortations to conform oneself to God. In Eckhart's view, there should remain in the poor man no self that wills, knows, or is. In the breakthrough one loses all creaturely distinctness to become in God what one always was, is, and will be.

The relationship between Eckhart's metaphysics and his ascetical thought can also be deemed mystical because these areas of reality, generally considered separate, merge in his thought. Although it would be going too far to state flatly that there is no difference for him between being and doing or between our being creatures and our becoming the Son, the role of ascetical practices in this latter process is a minor one indeed. As the Word had done while on earth, so Eckhart insists that any true conversion is essentially spiritual and thus interior. However, he emphasizes not so much a change of heart as that we realize what we are. Even though the preacher does not expect his listeners to understand everything about their true condition, he considers it his very serious task to present to them the facts concerning their marvelous opportunity to be transformed into the just man and the Son.

And yet, finally, this fact/event which seems to depend so much on our having insight into who we really are is also mystical in the sense that it is something essentially beyond our ability to comprehend. Eckhart's view of the capabilities of the human intellect as *human*, when confronted by a fact/event that is divine and thus infinitely beyond its grasp, is that ultimately it must remain shrouded in darkness. As creatures, even though creatures endowed with intellect, we are excluded from any adequate knowledge of what takes place in the *grunt* of the soul that is one with God's *grunt*. At best, we have only intimations, dimly perceived, of what we might call the birth or the breakthrough.

Turning now to the second area of inquiry, our examination of Eckhart's language allows us to conclude that it can often be called mystical. In so doing, however, we do not intend to establish mystical language in any formal sense as a category separate from philosophical-theological, rhetorical, and poetic language. In the sermons especially Eckhart employs all these categories, coordinating them in the service of the message to be preached. One point we have tried to make in various ways is that philosophical, rhetorical, and poetic language are all used to achieve mystical effects. The language of philosophy is employed in a twofold manner. On the one hand, it is used to describe a much closer union between God and the soul than the thought of the schools would generally allow. On the other hand, and ironically, it is used to demonstrate its own insufficiency: In attempting to give adequate expression to neat packages called concepts—themselves inadequate for any true understanding of an incomprehensible reality—philosophical terminology is ill-equipped for the task of depicting that same union. Since what is to be described is beyond the logic of conceptual thought, Eckhart frequently resorts to poetry and rhetoric. By these means, often in combination with the terms of philosophy , he describes the hidden godhead and our union with it in ways quite far removed from discursive exposition. Through paradox, for example, he tries to capture this union more completely by uniting contrary aspects of it. Through chiasmus he juxtaposes and intertwines God and the human person, achieving a union in words which imitates the reality in ways closed to philosophy. By means of negation (*un-, ab-, ent-, über-, -lôs, âne namen*, etc.) he is able, on one plane, to picture the soul divesting itself of the positive and thus limited characteristics which hinder union, and, on another plane, to free the divinity from being the "God" who could not satisfy a gnat.

Finally, we must return to our third question—that regarding mystical experience and its possible role as origin of the mystical aspects of Eckhart's thought and his mystical use of language. Was Meister Eckhart a mystic in the sense that he had mystical experiences? Are his works the product of a mind that has seen what is hidden from most of mankind, or was Eckhart simply a scholastic thinker more keenly aware than most of his contemporary colleagues of the limited results his profession could achieve, who then formulated his teaching and preaching accordingly?

Perhaps more troubling in this context than the word "mystical" is the word "experience." Eckhart, unlike many who have been labeled mystics, has left us no autobiographical writings. What we do have is impersonal in the sense that, aside from a rare peripheral reference, he tells us almost nothing about himself or the origins of his thought. Thus an approach like that of Carl Albrecht, which concentrates on the personal consciousness, is of little value here.[6] If mystical episodes did indeed play a part in the formulation of what Eckhart left us, certainly he never saw fit to confide such things to his audiences. Nor does the attainment of such states of consciousness, which are experienced as ecstatic and are clearly distinguishable from the consciousness of everyday existence, assume any importance for the spirituality he advocates for his listeners. Rather, as Richard Kieckhefer has convincingly shown, the goal Eckhart stresses is rather that his listeners become filled with the realization of their actual continuous state of union with God, a state they both strive for and possess.[7]

In view of the absence of any clear evidence of ecstatic consciousness in Eckhart's life, as well as its lack of importance for the spirituality he preached, what, if anything, can one say about the experience underlying his works? Certain characteristics of his thought and its expression allow us to draw limited conclusions about the experience from which they derived. Although they do not point clearly to a mystical experience in the sense of an ecstatic withdrawal from or heightening of normal states of consciousness, they do point to an experience which, in a broader sense, may be considered mystical.

First of all, Eckhart never tires of recalling to the minds of his audiences, both lay and professional, the truth and importance of the statement that God is closer to us than we are to ourselves. And we have noted also that, due to his understanding of this truth, it assumed greater importance in his teachings and sermons than it had in the works of most other scholastic thinkers. A vivid awareness of this divine presence permeates his works. Second, his description of the path to union does at times seem to be colored by the psychological or experiential. Thus he says, for example, "When the soul enters into the pure light [of the divinity], it falls into its utter nothingness, so far from its created somethingness in its utter nothingness that it cannot return of its own power to its created somethingness. And God supports its nothingness with his uncreatedness and holds it in his pure somethingness. The soul dared to become nothing and cannot on its own return to itself; so far did it go out of itself before God supported it."[8] Such passages at least hint at the dimensions of the consciousness that formulated them, a consciousness that may aptly be called mystical. Yet most of what Eckhart preached and wrote resembles, as much if not more, a phenomenon much more central to the best in human existence than the unusual and peripheral phenomenon of mysticism understood as ecstatic consciousness. His works are more clearly the products of that level of insight achieved by intellectual and artistic geniuses who have explored the uncharted worlds of the spirit and brought forth that which is best in our culture. The insight he experienced was that of our oneness with God, hence it is mystical. The intensity of expression, the various images, and the rich artistry he places in its service bear convincing witness to the intensity and clarity with which he experienced that insight.

His grasp of the truth of his message is too immediate and too secure to allow for doubt. The themes of the just man and the Son are clearly more than professional speculation. Truth is not just an idea. It is real and divine. We must become truth to escape our nothingness, and the human intellect must conform to truth to understand truth. The human person must simply become Truth: "For I say to you in everlasting Truth that if you are unlike this Truth of which we want to speak, you cannot understand me."[9] It is not the preacher's perception of the truth which guarantees the validity of his words. It is rather his realization that he speaks "in everlasting Truth." Eckhart will similarly vindicate his thoughts on the *vünkelîn*, namely, that it gives birth to the Son and is born the only-begotten Son; that in the clarity of this light the *vünkelîn*, our spirit, is simply Truth. What allows him to make such claims? He seeks no other authority for them than himself: "If you could perceive things with my heart, you would well understand what I say; for it is true and Truth itself speaks it."[10]

NOTES

Chapter 1: Background

1. For biographical data I am most indebted to Josef Koch, "Kritische Studien zum Leben Meister Eckharts," *Archivum Fratrum Praedicatorum* 29 (1959), 1–51 and 30 (1960), 1–52. Quotations here are from its reprinted version in Koch, *Kleine Schriften* (Rome, 1973), I, 247–347. This remains the most trustworthy and thorough treatment to date. Till Beckmann's more recent *Daten und Anmerkungen zur Biographie Meister Eckharts und zum Verlauf des gegen ihn angestrengten Inquisitionsprozesses* (Frankfurt, 1978) is a useful summary that depends almost exclusively on Koch for biographical details and concentrates heavily on the legal proceedings in Cologne and Avignon. Beckmann often diverges from Koch in judging the same facts. In English, see Jeanne Ancelet-Hustache, *Master Eckhart and the Rhineland Mystics* (New York, 1957), esp. pp. 23–51; and James M. Clark, *Meister Eckhart: An Introduction to the Study of His Works* (Edinburgh, 1957), esp. pp. 11–25. These authors present very readable and informative treatments. However, since they precede Koch's investigations, they are dated. For more recent remarks, see Colledge, "Historical Data," pp. 5–23. See also Matthew Fox, *Breakthrough: Meister Eckhart's Creation Spirituality in New Translation* (Garden City, N.Y., 1980), pp. 1–53. Though not without insight, Fox's remarks contain several factual errors about Eckhart's life and circumstances as well as many questionable judgments.

2. Koch, "Kritische Studien," pp. 248–251.

3. Ibid., pp. 252–254.

4. "Et contra ipsum sanctum Thomam frequenter a multis scriptum est, dictum et publice predicatum quod errores et hereses scripserit et docuerit. Sed favente domino tam Parisius quam per ipsum summum pontificem et romanam curiam ipsius vita et doctrina pariter sunt approbata." *RS*, Théry, p. 185. "Many have often written, declared and even publicly preached that Saint Thomas wrote and taught errors and heresies, but with God's aid his life and teaching alike have been given approval, both at Paris and also by the Supreme Pontiff and the Roman curia." McGinn, p. 72.

5. Koch has included a commentary on the *Sentences* in Volume V of Eckhart's Latin works, which he attributes to Eckhart. Not everyone, however, is convinced that Eckhart was its author. See Koch, "Kritische Studien," pp. 255–257.

6. "Et Albertus saepe dicebat: Hoc scio sicut scimus, nam omnes parum scimus." *Osterpredigt*, 1294. Quoted from ibid., p. 252.

7. Ibid., pp. 268–269.

8. Ibid., pp. 271–273, 281.

9. In addition to Koch, I have relied extensively for this section on Bernard McGinn, "Eckhart's Condemnation Reconsidered," *The Thomist* 44 (1980), 390–414.

10. Colledge, p. 270. *RdU*; DW V, 261,4–262,5.

11. Laurent, pp. 341–344.

12. Koch, "Kritische Studien," p. 319.

13. For his trouble, Nicholas was called before the archbishop's inquisitorial court on charges of obstructing justice. Laurent, pp. 333–341.

14. *RS*, Théry, pp. 185–186.

15. Laurent, pp. 341–344.

16. Ibid., pp. 344–346.

17. Ibid., pp. 346–348.

18. See Koch, "Kritische Studien," p. 310, for references to Ockham's remarks.

19. Pelster, *Gutachten*, pp. 1099–1124.

20. Eckhart may have gone in person before his judges, since the Avignon document, in referring to his arguments, frequently uses *ut dicit* (as he says).

21. For a text of the bull, see Laurent, pp. 435–444. For a translation, see McGinn, pp. 77–81.

22. Laurent, pp. 444–445.

23. Koch, "Kritische Studien," p. 322, note 198.

24. McGinn, "Eckhart's Condemnation," p. 397.

25. That Eckhart denied having said this puzzled his Avignon judges because it is found in several places in his works: "Qui[a] quid tamen negat, in pluribus locis reperitur et probatur hoc dixisse." Pelster, *Gutachten*, p. 1111. For references to a discussion of the problem in secondary literature, see McGinn, "Eckhart's Condemnation," p. 401 and notes 43 and 53.

26. Koch, "Kritische Studien," p. 339.

27. Ibid., pp. 336–339.

28. McGinn, "Eckhart's Condemnation," p. 411.

29. Laurent, p. 444. This is Colledge's very plausible explanation of the phrase *quoad illum sensum*. See Colledge, "Historical Data," pp. 14–15. Beckmann (*Daten und Anmerkungen*, p. 67) interprets this section of the bull in a similar, though less clear, fashion.

30. See the treatments of Ingeborg Degenhardt, *Studien zum Wandel des Eckhartbildes* (Leiden, 1967); Josef Koch, "Meister Eckharts Weiterwirken im Deutschen-Niederländischen Raum im 14. und 15. Jahrhundert," *La mystique rhénane* (Paris, 1963), pp. 133–156; Toni Schaller, "Die Meister Eckhart-Forschung von der Jahrhundertwende bis zur Gegenwart," *Freiburger Zeitschrift für Philosophie und Theologie* 15 (1968), 262–316, 403–426; Toni Schaller, "Zur Eckhart-Deutung der letzten 30 Jahre," *Freiburger Zeitschrift für Philosophie und Theologie* 16 (1969), 22–39; and Wolfram Malte Fues, *Mystik als Erkenntnis? Kritische Studien zur Meister-Eckhart-Forschung* (Bonn, 1981). In English, see Ancelet-Hustache, *Master Eckhart*, pp. 139–178; Clark, *Meister Eckhart: An Introduction*, pp. 113–124; James M. Clark and John V. Skinner, *Meister Eckhart: Selected Treatises and Sermons* (London, 1958), pp. 13–49; and more recently, Colledge and McGinn in *Meister Eckhart: The Essential Sermons, Commen-*

taries, Treatises and Defense, trans. and introduction by Edmund Colledge and Bernard McGinn (New York: Paulist Press, 1981), pp. 15–23, 62–68.

31. *In Joh.* n. 289; LW III, 241, and *In Joh.* n. 349; LW III, 297.

32. For praise of order as good in itself, see *Serm.* XXIV, 1, n. 226; LW IV, 211–212.

33. Fox (*Breakthrough,* pp. 21, 35–38) uses the term "feminist" vaguely and offers little evidence for the claim that Beguines greatly influenced Eckhart.

34. *BgT;* DW V, 60,28–61,3. Translation by Colledge, p. 239.

35. For woman as the sensitive part of the soul, see *In Exod.* n. 207; LW II, 174–175. For woman as matter: "Matter is for the sake of form, not vice versa, just as woman is for the sake of man and not vice versa" (*Materia est propter formam, non e converso, sicut mulier propter virum, non e converso; In Gen.* I, n. 55; LW I, 224).

36. One of the side effects of the critical edition was a rehabilitation of Pfeiffer's work. Judged against similar editions of the period and in view of limitations over which he had no control, his edition now seems admirable.

37. Seppänen, *Studien zur Terminologie des Paradisus anime intelligentis* (Helsinki, 1964), pp. 19–20, 262–268.

38. *RS,* Théry, II (11), p. 217; II (14), p. 219; II (15B), p. 220; and II (38), p. 242.

39. Those who have treated Eckhart's interpretation of scripture are Josef Koch, "Sinn und Struktur der Schriftauslegung," in *Meister Eckhart der Prediger,* ed. U. Nix and R. Ochslin (Freiburg, Ger., 1960), pp. 73–103, reprinted in Koch, *Kleine Schriften,* I, 399–428; Konrad Weiss, "Meister Eckharts biblische Hermeneutik," in *La mystique rhénane* (Paris, 1963), pp. 95–108; E. Winkler, *Exegetische Methoden bei Meister Eckhart* (Tübingen, 1965), the only lengthy study, which unfortunately does not yield very much; and McGinn, "Theological Summary," pp. 26–29.

40. Colledge, p. 185. "Nû merket disen sin gar eben; aleine er grop lûte und gemeine, sô ist er doch gar merklich und gar guot." Pr. 6; DW I, 99, 2–4.

Chapter 2: God and Creatures

1. For example, "Being (*ens*) in the most proper sense is God" (*Ens propriissime deus est*). *Serm.* LV, 2, n. 540; LW IV, 453.

2. The most thorough study of the main issues in the *Parisian Questions* is that of R. Imbach, *Deus est intelligere. Das Verhältnis von Sein und Denken in seiner Bedeutung für das Gottesverständnis bei Thomas von Aquin und in den Pariser Quaestionen Meister Eckharts* (Freiburg, Switz., 1976). For a recent treatment of many aspects of Eckhart's *Parisian Questions,* see *Maître Eckhart à Paris. Une critique médiévale de l'ontothéologie. Les Questions parisiennes n. 1 et n. 2 d'Eckhart.* Etudes, textes et traductions par Emilie Zum Brunn, Zénon Kaluzia, Alain de Libera, Paul Vignaux, and Edouard Wéber (Paris, 1984).

3. *Liber de Causis,* prop. 4; ed. Bardenhewer (Freiburg, Switz., 1882), p. 166.

4. "Sicut quando quaeritur de nocte ab aliquo, qui vult latere et non nominare se: quis es tu? respondet: 'ego sum qui sum', ita dominus volens ostendere puritatem essendi esse in se dixit: 'ego sum qui sum'." *Q. Par.* I, n. 9; LW V, 45.

5. "Dico enim quod deus omnia praehabet in puritate, plentitudine, perfectione, amplius et latius, existens radix et causa omnium. Et hoc voluit dicere, cum dixit: 'ego sum qui sum'." *Q. Par.* I, n. 12; LW V, 48.

6. "Notandum primo quod in deo, principio omnium, est considerare duo, ut sic dicamus, puta quod ipse est esse verum, reale, primordiale. Adhuc autem est

ipsum considerare sub ratione qua intellectus est. Et huius rationis proprietas altior apparet ex hoc, quod omne ens reale in natura 'procedit ad certos fines' et 'per media determinata' tamquam rememoratum per causam altiorem, ut ait Themistius. Propter quod etiam 'opus naturae dicitur' et est 'opus intelligentiae'." *In Gen.* II, n. 214; LW I, 690.

7. "Ein ieglich dinc würket in wesene, kein dinc enmac würken über sîn wesen. Daz viur enmac niht würken dan in dem holze. Got würket über wesene in der wîte, dâ er sich geregen mac, er würket in unwesene; ê denne wesen waere, dô worhte got; er worhte wesen, dô niht wesen enwas. Grobe meister sprechent, got sî ein lûter wesen; er ist als hôch über wesene, als der oberste engel ist über einer mücken. Ich spraeche als unrehte, als ich got hieze ein wesen, als ob ich die sunnen hieze bleich oder swarz. . . . Und sprichet ein meister: swer dâ waenet, daz er got bekant habe, und bekante er iht, sô enbekante er got niht. Daz ich aber gesprochen hân, got ensî niht ein wesen und sî über wesene, hie mite enhân ich im niht wesen abegesprochen, mêr: ich hân ez in im gehoehet." Pr. 9; DW I, 145,4– 146,2 and 146, 3–6. These excerpts do not represent all the meanings of *wesen* or being in this sermon. Some uses must remain mysterious and seemingly contradictory at the present state of our investigation.

8. "Als wir got nemen in dem wesene, sô nemen wir in in sînem vorbürge, wan wesen ist sîn vorbürge, dâ er inne wonet. Wâ ist er denne in sînem tempel, dâ er heilic inne schînet? Vernünfticheit ist der tempel gotes. Niergen wonet got eigenlîcher dan in sînem tempel, in vernünfticheit." Pr. 9; DW I, 150, 1–4.

9. Pr. 8; DW I, 131, 4. *Wesen* in Middle High German is generally less precise and more inclusive than *esse* because of the less strictly philosophical context in which it occurs. But here, as often elsewhere in the sermons, precision is not the point. For more on *wesen*, see Benno Schmoldt, *Die deutsche Begriffssprache Meister Eckharts* (Heidelberg, 1954), pp. 98–111.

10. ". . . Quod extra deum, utpote extra esse, non est aliud nec aliquid. Quod enim extra esse est, nihil est nec est." *In Joh.* n. 215; LW III, 181.

11. ". . . Creatum omne ex se nihil est." *In Sap.* n. 34; LW II, 354.

12. "Alle crêatûren sint ein lûter niht. Ich spriche niht, daz sie kleine sîn oder iht sîn: sie sint ein lûter niht. Swaz niht wesens enhât, daz enist niht. Alle crêatûren hânt kein wesen." Pr. 4; DW I, 69,8–70,2 (note 1 on page 70 gives appropriate references to the trial documents).

13. ". . . Creatura foris est, deus autem intimus et in intimis est. Patet hoc in effectu deo proprio, qui est esse, intimus omnibus, in intimis omnium. Et hoc est quod deus solus dicitur illabi animae ab Augustino, . . ." *In Joh.* n. 304; LW III, 253. Similarly he says: "God, however, is being and from him all being comes immediately. Therefore, he alone plunges into the essences of things. Everything which is not being itself stands outside and is distinct from and foreign to the essence of each thing" (*Deus autem esse est, et ab ipso immediate omne esse. Propter quod ipse solus illabitur rerum essentiis. Omne quod non est ipsum esse, foris stat, alienum est et distinctum ab essentia uniuscuiusque; In Joh.* n. 238; LW III, 199).

14. See Schmoldt, *Die deutsche Begriffssprache*, esp. pp. 106–109.

15. "Daz edelste, daz got würket in allen crêatûren, daz ist wesen." Pr. 47; DW II, 401, 1.

16. "Man muoz got nemen wîse âne wîse und wesen âne wesen, wan er enhât keine wîse. Dâ von sprichet sant Bernhart: swer dich, got, bekennen sol, der muoz dich mâzen sunder mâze." Pr. 71; DW III, 231, 1–3.

17. Elsewhere he refers to this as the negation of negation. This will be treated in detail in Chapter 3.

18. ". . . Quia ea obiciunt tanquam heretica que manifeste ponit sanctus Thomas in solutionibus quorundam argumentorum quas ipsi non viderunt aut non meminerunt, sicut est de distinctione et natura vniuocorum et equiuocorum et analogorum et similia." *RS*, Théry, p. 206.

19. The most important studies on the question of analogy in Eckhart's thought are given here in chronological order: Hans Hof, *Scintilla animae. Eine Studie zu einem Grundbegriff in Meister Eckharts Philosophie* (Lund, 1952); Josef Koch, "Zur Analogielehre Meister Eckharts," *Mélanges offerts à Etienne Gilson* (Paris, 1959), pp. 327–350 (also in *Altdeutsche und altniederländische Mystik*, ed. Kurt Ruh [Darmstadt, 1964], pp. 275–308; and in Koch, *Kleine Schriften*, I, 367–398); Vladimir Lossky, *Théologie négative et connaissance de Dieu chez Maître Eckhart* (Paris, 1960); Fernand Brunner, "L'analogie chez Maître Eckhart," *Freiburger Zeitschrift für Philosophie und Theologie* 16 (1969), 333–349; Karl Albert, *Meister Eckharts These vom Sein. Untersuchungen zur Metaphysik des Opus tripartitum* (Saarbrücken, 1976); Alain de Libera, *Le problème de l'être chez Maître Eckhart: Logique et métaphysique de l'anologie* (Geneva, 1980); Alain de Libera, "A propos de quelques théories logiques de Maître Eckhart: Existe-t-il une tradition médiévale de la logique néo-platonicienne?" *Revue de Théologie et de Philosophie* 113 (1981), 1–24; Burkhard Mojsisch, *Meister Eckhart. Analogie, Univozität und Einheit* (Hamburg, 1983); and Zum Brunn and Alain de Libera, *Maître Eckhart. Métaphysique du Verbe et théologie négative* (Paris, 1984). These authors represent the best thinking on the subject as well as the divergence of opinion. All agree that Eckhart's concept of *esse*, as he applies it to God and creatures, is clearly different from that of Thomas, but they disagree concerning how great the distance that separates them is.

20. "Sanitas una eademque, quae est in animali, ipsa est, non alia, in diaeta et urina, ita quod sanitatis, ut sanitas, nihil prosus est in diaeta et urina, non plus quam in lapide, sed hoc solo dicitur urina sana, quia significat illam sanitatem eandem numero quae est in animali, sicut circulus vinum, qui nihil vini in se habet. Ens autem sive esse et omnis perfectio, maxime generalis, puta esse, unum, verum, bonum, lux, iustitia et huiusmodi, dicuntur de deo et creaturis analogice. Ex quo sequitur quod bonitas et justitia et similia bonitatem suam habent totaliter ab aliquo extra, ad quod analogantur, deus scilicet." *In Eccli.* n. 52; LW II, 280–281.

21. ". . . In his quae dicuntur secundum analogiam, quod est in uno analogatorum, formaliter non est in alio, ut sanitas solum est in animali formaliter, in diaeta autem et urina non est plus de sanitate quam in lapide. Cum igitur omnia causata sunt entia formaliter, deus formaliter non erit ens." *Q. Par.* I, n. 11; LW V, 46.

22. ". . . Analogata nihil in se habent positive radicatum formae secundum quam analogantur. . . . Igitur omne ens creatum habet a deo et in deo, non in se ipso ente creato, esse, vivere, sapere positive et radicaliter." *In Eccli.* n. 53; LW II, 282.

23. ". . . Deus veniens et eius presentia immediate et nullo cooperante operatur in omnibus entitatem, unitatem, veritatem, et bonitatem analogice quidem." *In Joh.* n. 97; LW III, 84.

24. "Nullum autem ex entibus est esse, nec in ipso est radix esse." *In Eccli.* n. 44; LW II, 273. ". . . Non habet ex se, sed ab alio superiori esse quod sitit, esurit

et appetit. Propter quod in ipso non figitur nec haeret nec inchoatur esse." *In Eccli.* n. 45; LW II, 274.

25. *In Joh.* nn. 70–72; LW III, 58–60. For an example of the preacher's use of both hungering and the sun's light to explain the action of *esse* in a single context, see *Serm.* XIX, n. 188; LW IV, 175–176.

26. "Bilde nimet aleine sîn wesen âne mittel an dem, des bilde ez ist, und hât éin wesen mit im und ist daz selbe wesen." Pr. 16b; DW I, 270, 5–6. The remark by the preacher immediately following this quotation, that this is more suitable for the pulpit than for an academic context, would seem not to be directed to the use of the *image* simile as such, since he considers it valuable enough to employ in the *Commentary on John*: "Imago enim, in quantum imago est, nihil sui accipit a subjecto in quo est, sed totum suum esse accipit ab obiecto, cuius est imago. Iterum secundo accipit esse suum a solo illo." N. 23; LW III, 19.

27. "Man vrâget, wâ daz wesen des bilde aller eigenlîchest sî: in dem spiegel oder in dem, von dem ez ûzgât? Ez ist eigenlîcher in dem, von dem ez ûzgât. Daz bilde ist in mir, von mir, zuo mir. Die wîle der spiegel glîch stât gegen mînem antlite, sô ist mîn bilde dar inne; viele der spiegel, sô vergienge daz bilde." Pr. 9; DW I, 154, 1–5.

28. "Virtutes enim, iustitia et huiusmodi, sunt potius quaedam actu configurationes quam quid figuratum immanens et habens fixionem et radicem in virtuoso et sunt in continuo fieri, sicut splendor in medio et imago in speculo." *In Sap.* n. 45; LW II, 368.

29. Colledge, p. 224. "Allez, daz guot ist und güete, daz hât im got gelihen und niht gegeben. Wan, swer bekennet wârheit, der weiz, daz got, der himelsche vater, dem sune und dem heiligen geiste gibet allez, daz guot ist; aber der crêatûre engibet er kein guot, sunder er verlîhet ez ir ze borge. Diu sunne gibet dem lufte hitze, aber lieht gibet si im ze borge; und dâr umbe, alzehant sô diu sunne undergât, sô verliuset der luft daz lieht, aber diu hitze blîbet im, wan diu ist dem lufte gegeben alsam ze eigene." DW V, 36, 14–20.

30. "Alle crêatûren hânt kein wesen, wan ir wesen swebet an der gegenwerticheit gotes. Kêrte sich got ab allen crêatûren einen ougenblik, sô würden sie ze nihte." Pr. 4; DW I, 70, 2–4.

31. ". . . Utpote in se nuda et potentia ad esse, quae potentia appetitus est et sitis ipsius esse." *In Eccli.* n. 45; LW II, 274.

32. ". . . Forma ignis totam essentiam materiae suae se tota sine medio totam simul investit et format penetrando non partem post partem, sed partes singulas per totum." *Prol. prop.* n. 14; LW I, 174.

33. ". . . Unum est indistinctum ab omnibus. Igitur in ipso ratione indistinctionis sive unitatis sunt omnia et plenitudo esse. *Serm.* XXIX, n. 298; LW IV, 265.

34. This type of argumentation is also applied by the preacher to explaining the unity of the Trinity: "The difference comes from the oneness, the difference in the threeness (trinity). The oneness is the difference and the difference is the oneness. The greater the difference is, the greater is the oneness. For this is difference without difference" (*Der underscheit kumet von der einicheit, der underscheit in der drîvalticheit. Diu einicheit ist der underscheit, und der underscheit ist diu einicheit. Ie der underscheit mêr ist, ie diu einicheit mêr ist, wan daz ist underscheit âne underscheit*; Pr. 10; DW I, 173, 2–5). It is difference without difference because the difference is the cause of or reason for the oneness. This kind of reasoning is also at the base of his "more subtle" explanation of why there is no

relation between God and creature (*In Exod.* n. 40; LW II, 45–46). As distinct from God, a creature is nothing. Hence there can be no relation. Implied, of course, is that considered as indistinct God and creature are one. Hence there can be no relation.

35. The most important studies on dialectic in Eckhart's thought are Lossky, *Théologie négative,* esp. pp. 254–265; M. de Gandillac, "La 'dialectique' de Maître Eckhart," in *La mystique rhénane* (Paris, 1963), pp. 59–94; and Bernard McGinn, "Meister Eckhart on God as Absolute Unity," in *Neoplatonism and Christian Thought,* ed. Dominic J. O'Meara (Albany, 1981), pp. 128–139.

36. "Ipsum esse causa omnium est quae sunt entia, sicut albedo ipsa causa est omnium quae sunt alba. Sed deus est esse ipsum, . . . erit causa omnium aliorum quae sunt entia." *In Exod.* n. 102; LW II, 104. Among the many instances where the comparison of whiteness and *esse* occurs, see *Prol. gener.* n. 12; LW I, 157, where whiteness and white are mentioned in connection with God's activity in creating, and *Prol. prop.* n. 9; LW I, 170–171.

37. Eckhart too occasionally employs the notion of participation. See, for example, *In Exod.* n. 101; LW II, 103. However, it is not made to carry much weight in the total framework of his thought.

38. "Nota quod omnis creatura duplex habet esse. Unum in causis suis originalibus, saltem in verbo dei; et hoc est esse firmum et stabile. Propter quod scientia corruptibilium est incorruptibilis, firma et stabilis; scitur enim res in suis causis. Aliud est esse rerum extra in rerum natura, quod habent res in forma propria. Primum est esse virtuale, secundum est esse formale, quod plerumque infirmum et variabile. *In Gen.* I, n. 77; LW I, 238. "Rursus notandum quod esse virtute sive virtuale est longe nobilius et praestantius quam rerum esse formale." *In Gen.* I, n. 82; LW I, 242.

39. The following summary is taken from *In Gen.* II, nn. 52–69; LW I, 520–536. Other important sections on this topic are *In Joh.* nn. 4–14; LW III, 5–12; and *In Joh.* nn. 40–54; LW III, 33–46.

40. "Est ergo ratio *lux in tenebris,* id est rebus creatis, non inclusa, non permixta, non comprehensa. Et hoc est quod hic, cum dixisset: *lux in tenebris lucet,* addit *et tenebrae eam non comprehenderunt.* Et hoc est quod in *De causis* dicitur: 'causa prima regit res omnes praeter quod commisceatur cum eis.' Causa prima omnis rei ratio est, logos est, *verbum in principio.*" *In Joh.* n. 12; LW III, 12.

41. McGinn, p. 126. "Plena omnium rationum viventium incommutabilium, et omnes unum in ea." *In Joh.* n. 13; LW III, 12.

42. The divine side of creatures and creation in Eckhart's thought, and the resulting necessity of considering creatures and creation in a real sense eternal, caused many of the difficulties the Dominican had with ecclesiastical authorities. The first three articles of the bull of condemnation all focused on the problem of time and eternity. These articles condemned the view that God created the world "as soon as God existed" (*quamcito Deus fuit,* article 1); that one can admit that the world existed "from eternity" (*ab eterno,* article 2); and that God's begetting the Son and his creating the world happened "at one and the same time" (*simul et semel,* article 3). Laurent, pp. 436–437.

Chapter 3: The Nature of Language

1. "Und sprichet ein meister: swer dâ waenet, daz er got bekant hân, und bekante er iht, sô enbekante er got niht." Pr. 9; DW I, 146, 3–4.

2. Colledge, p. 204. "Swer iht bekennet in gote und im deheinen namen anekleibet, daz enist got niht. God ist über namen und über natûre." Pr. 53; DW II, 533, 5–6.

3. This inquiry, which we shall draw upon in detail, is contained in *In Exod.* nn. 34–78 and 143–184; LW II, 40–82 and 130–158. The texts treated are "Omnipotens nomen eius (Almighty is his name; 15:3) and "Non assumes nomen dei tui in vanum" (You shall not take the name of your God in vain; 20:7). For another detailed analysis of these sections of Eckhart's *Commentary on Exodus* and for a slightly different point of view, the reader is encouraged to consult Bernard McGinn, "Meister Eckhart on Speaking About God." This analysis makes up the second part of the introduction to the forthcoming volume of translations from Eckhart's Latin and German works, entitled *Meister Eckhart: Teacher and Preacher* (New York: Paulist Press), scheduled for publication in Spring 1986. Professor McGinn's analysis was available to me and was of great assistance as I revised this chapter. Other recent and valuable studies treating or touching upon the problem of language in Meister Eckhart, in addition to those mentioned in Chapter 2, note 19, are Alois M. Haas, "Seinsspekulation und Geschöpflichkeit in der Mystik Meister Eckharts," in *Sein und Nichts in der abendländischen Mystik*, ed. Walter Strolz (Freiburg, Ger., 1984), pp. 33–58; Alois M. Haas, "Meister Eckhart und die Sprache. Sprachgeschichtliche und sprachtheologische Aspekte seiner Werke," in *Geistliches Mittelalter* (Freiburg, Switz., 1984), pp. 194–200; and Bernard McGinn, "The God Beyond God: Theology and Mysticism in the Thought of Meister Eckhart," *Journal of Religion* 61 (1981), 1–19.

4. The most pertinent studies are Josef Koch, "Meister Eckhart und die jüdische Religionsphilosophie des Mittelalters," *Jahres-Bericht der Schlesischen Gesellschaft für vaterländische Cultur* 101 (1928), 135–148, reprinted in Koch, *Kleine Schriften*, pp. 349–365; Hans Liebeschütz, "Meister Eckhart und Moses Maimonides," *Archiv für Kulturgeschichte* 54 (1972), 64–96; Lossky, *Théologie négative*, esp. pp. 13–96; and Bardo Weiss, "'Gott ist anders' nach Meister Eckhart," *Theologie und Philosophie* 46 (1971), 387–396.

5. See Thomas Aquinas, *Sent.* I, d. 2 q. 1 a. 3, and *De Potentia Dei*, q. 7 a. 6.

6. "Qui enim duo vel distinctionem videt, deum non videt." N. 58, p. 65.

7. Article 23, Laurent, p. 441.

8. "Adhuc autem quarto, distinctio omnis infinito repugnat. Deus autem infinitus est. Nec tamen propter hoc vanae sunt aut falsae huiusmodi attributiones distinctae, eo quod ipsis aliquid vere et reale in deo respondet." N. 61, p. 66.

9. "Quod autem Dionysius dicit 2 c. Caelestis hierarchiae, quod 'negationes de deo sunt verae, affirmationes vero incompactae', non obstat. Hoc enim verum est quantum ad modum significandi in talibus. Intellectus enim noster perfectiones, quae ad esse pertinent, apprehendit ex creaturis, ubi huiusmodi perfectiones imperfectae sunt et divisae sparsim, et secundum illum modum significat. In his enim propositionibus est duo considerare, scilicet ipsas perfectiones significatas, puta bonitatem, veritatem, vitam, intelligere et huiusmodi; et sic sunt compactae et verae. Est etiam considerare in talibus modum significandi; et sic incompactae sint, quod ait Dionysius." N. 78, p. 81.

10. LW II, 81, note 3.

11. See Chapter 2, "Analogy."

12. See note 8 for this chapter.

13. For example, "Solus deus proprie est ens, unum, verum et bonum." *Prol. prop.* n. 4; LW I, 167.

14. "Patet igitur ex praemissis omnibus quod unitas sive unum propriissime deo convenit, magis etiam quam li verum et li bonum." *In Sap.* n. 149; LW II, 486.

15. "Nulla ergo negatio, nihil negativum deo competit, nisi negatio negationis, quam significat unum negative dictum: 'deus unus est,' Deut. 6; Gal. 3. Negatio vero negationis purissima et plenissima est affirmatio: 'ego sum qui sum'." *In Exod.* n. 74; LW II, 77.

16. This corresponds to the Hebrew name usually rendered in English as *Yahweh*.

17. "Nomen autem tetragrammaton, id est quattuor litterarum, quodcumque sit illud et quae sint illae quattuor litterae, a quibus nomen habet, absconditum est et secretum et ipsum est nomen domini ineffabile. Li enim tetragrammaton non est ipsum nomen, de quo nunc agitur, sed est circumlocutio cuiusdam nominis habentis quattuor litteras, quod est sanctum secretum. Propterquod nusquam invenitur apud nos expressum, sed est inexpressibile ex sui natura et puritate sicut et substantia dei quam significat." N. 146, p. 131.

18. "Et fortassis posset videri alicui quod esse esset ipsum nomen quattuor litterarum. Ad litteram enim li esse habet quattuor litteras, multas proprietates et perfectiones latentes. Ipsum etiam non videtur 'sumptum ab opere nec dictum a participatione.' Sed haec hactenus." N. 164, p. 144.

19. See *Q. Par.* I, nn. 9 and 12; LW V, 45 and 48, and the discussion of this in Chapter 2, "God as Intellect, as Nonbeing."

20. "Nû nement sie güete und legent sie ûf wesen: daz bedecket wesen und machet im eine hût, wan ez zuogeleget ist. Sô nement sie in, als er wârheit ist. Ist wesen wârheit? Jâ, wan wârheit bestât an wesene, wan er sprach ze Moyse: 'der dâ ist, der hât mich gesant.' Sant Augustinus sprichet: diu wârheit ist der sun in dem vater, wan wârheit bestât an wesene. —Ist wesen wârheit? Der des manigen meister vrâgete, er spraeche: 'Jâ!' Der mich selber gevrâget haete, ich haete gesprochen: 'Jâ!' Aber nû spriche ich 'Nein!' wan wârheit ist ouch zuogeleget. Nû nement sie in als er ein ist, wan ein daz ist eigenlîcher ein, dan daz dâ geeinet ist. Swaz ein ist, dâ ist al ander abegeleget; mêr doch daz selbe, daz dâ abegeleget ist, daz selbe daz ist zuogeleget, in dem daz ez andert.

"Und enist er noch güete noch wesen noch wârheit noch ein, waz ist er denne? Er ist nihtes niht, er enist weder diz noch daz. Gedenkest dû noch ihtes, daz er sî, des enist er niht." Pr. 23; DW I, 400,3–402,3.

21. "Ein meister sprichet: ein ist ein versagen des versagennes. Spriche ich, got ist guot, daz leget etwaz zuo. Ein ist ein versagen des versagennes und ein verlougen des verlougennes. Waz meinet ein? Daz meinet ein, dem niht zuogeleget enist. Diu sêle nimet die gotheit, als si in ir geliutert ist, dâ niht zuogeleget enist, dâ niht bedâht enist. Ein ist ein versagen des versagennes. Alle crêatûren hânt ein versagen, an in selben; einiu versaget, daz sie diu ander niht ensî. Ein engel versaget, daz er ein ander niht ensî. Aber got hât ein versagen des versagennes; er ist ein und versaget alle ander, wan niht ûzer gote enist. Alle crêatûren sint in gote und sint sîn selbes gotheit und meinet ein vüllede, als ich ê sprach. Er ist ein vater aller gotheit. Ich spriche dar umbe ein gotheit, dâ noch niht ûzvliezende enist und niendert enrüeret noch bedâht enwirt. In dem daz ich gote versage etwaz—versage ich gote güete, ich enmac gote niht versagen—in dem daz ich gote versage, dâ begrîfe ich etwaz von im, daz er niht enist; daz selbe muoz abe. God ist ein, er ist ein versagen des versagennes." Pr. 21; DW I, 361,10–364,4.

22. "Vernünfticheit ziuhet gote daz vel der güete abe und nimet in blôz, dâ er entkleidet ist von güete und von wesene und von allen namen." DW I, 152, 6–8.

23. "Bekantnisse brichet durch wârheit und güete und vellet ûf lûter wesen und nimet got blôz, als er âne namen ist." DW I, 122, 6–8.

24. "Si gründet und suochet vort und nimet got in sîner einunge und in sîner einoede; si nimet got in sîner wüestunge und in sînem eigenen grunde." Pr. 10; DW I, 171, 13–15. Here again the preacher emphasizes the dynamism in the power of the soul which drives it to search beyond the limits of the negative way, for he continues: "Therefore it does not rest satisfied but seeks further what that might be that God is in his godhead and as he possesses himself in his own proper nature" (*Dar umbe enhât si ir niht genüegen, si suochet vürbaz, waz daz sî, daz got in sîner gotheit ist und in sînem eigentuome sîner eigenen natûre*; Pr. 10; DW I, 171,15–172,2).

25. This is not quite as radical a pronouncement as it sounds. If one looks at its context (*In Exod.* n. 44; LW II, 48–50) and the examples used to clarify it, it becomes clear that Eckhart does not mean that "evil" and "false" are just as suitable terms for God as "good" and "true." "Evil" and "false" are negations of positive attributes, and he consistently denies that there are any negations in God except the negation of negation. Rather, he is thinking that God can be called, for example, both angry and merciful. Or he points out that avarice in man is a fault, whereas in ants it is a virtue because their "inordinate" gathering of food in the autumn allows them to survive the winter. The point is the utter relativity of positive terms when applied to God.

26. "In summa nota quod omne quod de trinitate beata scribitur aut dicitur, nequaquam sic se habet aut verum est. Primo ex natura condivisionis, quae potissime est inter distinctum et indistinctum, inter res temporis et aeternitatis, inter caelum sensibile et intellectuale, inter corpus materiale et corpus spirituale. Secundo, quia, cum deus sit in sui et ex sui natura indicibilis, utique quod dicitur esse, non est in ipso. Unde Psalmus: 'omnis homo mendax'. Verum quidem est quod est aliquid in deo respondens trinitati quam dicimus et ceteris similibus." *Serm.* IV, 2, n. 30; LW IV, 31.

27. Colledge, p. 204. "Got ist ein wort, ein ungesprochen wort. "Augustînus sprichet: 'alliu diu schrift ist îtel. Sprichet man, daz got ein wort sî, sô ist er gesprochen; sprichet man, daz got ungesprochen sî, sô ist er unsprechelich.' Sô ist er aber etwaz; wer kan diz wort gesprechen? Daz entuot nieman, dan der diz wort ist. Got ist ein wort, daz sich selben sprichet. . . . Alle crêatûren wellent got sprechen in allen irn werken; sie sprechent alle, sô sie nâhest mügen, sie enmügen in doch niht gesprechen. Sie wellen oder enwellen, ez sî in liep oder leit: sie wellent alle got sprechen, und er blîbet doch ungesprochen." Pr. 53; DW II, 529, 2–6, and 531, 1–4.

28. See the related conclusions of Lauri Seppänen, *Studien zur Terminologie des Paradisus Anime Ingelligentis* (Helsinki, 1964), esp. pp. 265–268.

Chapter 4: Characteristic Themes

1. "Swer underscheit verstât von gerehticheit und von gerehtem, der verstât allez, daz ich sage." Pr. 6; DW I, 105, 2–3.

2. See Pr. 6; DW I, 99, 5–6: "Ein geschrift sprichet: 'der ist gereht, der einem ieglîchen gibet, daz sîn ist.'" See note 2 on page 99 for further references and their source in Justinian's *Institutiones*.

3. ". . . Und in einem andern sinne sô sint die gereht, die alliu dinc glîch enpfâhent von gote, swaz ez joch sî, ez sî grôz oder klein, liep oder leit, und al glîch, noch minner noch mêr, einz als daz ander." Pr. 6; DW I, 102, 1–4.

4. See, for example, *BgT*, DW V, 9–13, quoted in part below.

5. We have discussed Eckhart's use of *in quantum* previously in relation to *esse*. See Chapter 2, "Further Clarification of *Esse*."

6. Colledge, pp. 209–210. "Von dem êrsten sol man wizzen, daz der wîse und wîsheit, wâre und wârheit, gerehte und gerehticheit, guote und güete sich einander ansehent und alsô ze einander haltent: diu güete enist noch geschaffen noch gemachet noch geborn; mêr si ist gebernde und gebirt den guoten, und der guote, als verre sô er guot ist, ist ungemachet und ungeschaffen und doch geborn kint und sun der güete. Diu güete gebirt sich und allez, daz si ist, in dem guoten. . . ." DW V, 9, 4–9.

7. From this line of argumentation we can see that Eckhart is much more concerned with the area of *formal* causality than with efficient causality. As already noted, this "Platonic" line of thought is repeatedly evident in his works where causality is discussed.

8. "Iustus enim . . . secundum se, secundum id quod est in se ipso lux non est. Unde de ipso Johanne baptista iusto sequitur: 'non erat ille lux'. Et hoc est quartum decimum quod iustus sive iustum, in se ipso tenebrosum, non lucet; in ipsa vero iustitia, suo principio, lucet, et ipsa iustitia in iusto lucet, sed iustus ipsam non comprehendit, utpote inferius." *In Joh.* n. 22; LW III, 18. Even when discussing the just man *in quantum iustus*, the *magister* will not always completely identify the just man with justice. In commenting on John the Baptist's being sent by God to give testimony to the light (John 1:6–7), he states that the just man as such is not justice but is sent or born from justice (*sed ipse non est iustitia, sed missus et genitus ab ipsa*). Yet the duality posited here is only that between Father and Son in the Trinity, for no one except the Son knows the Father (Matt. 11:27), and the relationship is based on birth (*genitus*) and not on creation (*In Joh.* n. 85; LW III, 73). Usually, however, the use of *in quantum* underlines oneness between the principle and the creature sharing the quality springing from the principle.

9. "Got minnet niht wan sich selben und als vil er sîn glîch vindet in mir und mich in im." Pr. 41; DW II, 285, 10.

10. "Er ensprichet niht 'der gerehte mensche' noch, 'der gerehte engel', er spricht aleine: 'der gerehte'." Pr. 39; DW II, 258, 1–2.

11. For a similar example, see *BgT*; DW V, 12, 7–9.

12. ". . . Und got und gerehticheit al ein ist." *BgT*; DW V, 12, 13–14.

13. "Und dar umbe sô nemet die gerehticheit nâch dem, und sî gerehticheit ist, wan alsô nemet ir sie nâch dem, und sie got ist." Pr. 46; DW II, 385, 3–4.

14. Pr. 39; DW II, 254, 1. This seems clearly to be a rendering of the Latin *informari* and *transformari*. Interpreting *în-* and *überbilden* thus is consonant with the preeminence of formal cause in Eckhart's thought, a line of thought for which the preacher finds backing in scripture since Paul uses *transformare* to explain how one becomes Christ (2 Cor. 3:18). We shall meet this passage from Corinthians again. See also Pr. 16b; DW I, 273, 1–3.

15. ". . . Hat daz selbe eine wesen, daz diu gerehticheit hât und ist, und tritet in alle die eigenschaft der gerehticheit und der wârheit." *BgT*; DW V, 11, 17–19.

16. "Got gibet dem gerehten menschen ein götlich wesen und nennet in mit dem selben namen, der sînem wesen eigen ist." Pr. 45; DW II, 371,9–372,2.

17. "Alsô sol diu gerehte sêle glîch bî gote sîn und bî neben gote, rehte glîch, noch unden noch oben." Pr. 6; DW I, 107, 3–4.

18. "Der gerehte mensche der ist ein mit gote. Glîcheit wirt geminnet. Minne minnet alwege glîch; dar umbe sô minnet got den gerehten menschen im selber glîch." Pr. 10; DW I, 174, 3–5.

19. "Er [Johannes] sprichet 'bî,' und dar umbe ist der gerehte glîch gote, wan

got ist diu gerehticheit. Und dar umbe: swer in der gerehticheit ist, der ist in gote und ist got." Pr. 39; DW II, 257, 4–6.

20. "Swer dâ minnet die gerehticheit, des underwindet sich diu gerehticheit und wirt begriffen von der gerehticheit, und er ist diu gerehticheit." Pr. 28; DW II, 62, 1–3. For a similar formulation, see Pr. 29; DW II, 82, 3–4.

21. "Der gerehte mensche endienet weder gote noch den crêatûren, wan er ist vrî; und ie er der gerehticheit naeher ist, ie mê er diu vrîheit selber ist und ie mê er diu vrîheit selber ist. Allez daz, daz geschaffen ist, daz enist niht vrî." Pr. 28; DW II, 62, 3–6. Translation: "The just man serves neither God nor creatures, for he is free; and the closer he is to justice the more he is freedom *itself* and the *more* he is freedom. Everything created is not free."

22. Especially in his *Commentary on John.* See, aside from other shorter mentionings, *In Joh.* nn. 106–123; LW III, 90–107.

23. See Hugo Rahner, "Die Gottesgeburt. Die Lehre der Kirchenväter von der Geburt Christi aus dem Herzen der Kirche und der Gläubigen," *Zeitschrift für katholische Theologie* 59 (1933), 333–418. Reprinted in *Symbole der Kirche* (Salzburg, 1964), pp. 13–87.

24. Colledge, pp. 187–188. "Der vater gebirt sînen sun in der êwicheit im selber glîch. 'Daz wort was bî gote, und got was daz wort': ez was daz selbe in der selben natûre. Noch spriche ich mêr: er hât in geborn in mîner sêle. Niht aleine ist si bî im noch er bî ir glîch, sunder er ist in ir, und gebirt der vater sînen sun in der sêle in der selben wîse, als er in in der êwicheit gebirt, und niht anders. Er muoz ez tuon, ez sî im liep oder leit. Der vater gebirt sînen sun âne underlâz, und ich spriche mêr: er gebirt mich sînen sun und den selben sun. Ich spriche mêr: er gebirt mich niht aleine sînen sun, mêr: er gebirt mich sich und sich mich und mich sîn wesen und sîn natûre. In dem innersten quelle dâ quille ich ûz in dem heiligen geiste, dâ ist éin leben und éin wesen und éin werk.

"Allez, waz got würket, daz ist ein; dar umbe gebirt er mich sînen sun âne allen underscheit. Mîn lîplîcher vater ist niht eigenlîche mîn vater sunder an einem kleinen stückelîn sîner natûre, und ich bin gescheiden von im; er mac tôt sîn und ich leben. Dar umbe ist der himelische vater waerlîche mîn vater, wan ich sîn sun bin und allez daz von im hân, daz ich hân, und ich der selbe sun bin und niht ein ander. Wan der vater ein werk würket, dar umbe würket er mich sînen eingebornen sun âne allen underscheit.

"'Wir werden alzemâle transformieret in got und verwandelt.' Merke ein glîchnisse. Ze glîcher wîse, als an dem sacramente verwandelt wirt brôt in unsers herren lîchamen, swie vil der brôte waere, sô wirt doch éin lîchame. Ze glîcher wîse, waeren alliu diu brôt verwandelt in mînen vinger, sô waere doch niht mêr dan éin vinger. Mêr: würde mîn vinger verwandelt in daz brôt, sô waere diz als vil als jenez waere. Waz in daz ander verwandelt wirt, daz wirt ein mit im. Alsô wirde ich gewandelt in in, daz er würket mich sîn wesen ein unglîch: bî dem lebenden got sô ist daz wâr, daz kein underscheit enist." Pr. 6; DW I, 109,2–111,7.

25. "Simili modo sicut in sacramento panis convertitur in corpus Christi, sic ego convertor in eum quod ipse operatur me suum esse unum, non simile." Pelster, *Gutachten,* p. 1118. See also *In agro dominico,* article 10; Laurent, p. 438.

26. McGinn, "Theological Summary," p. 31.

27. Josef Quint, *Meister Eckehart. Deutsche Predikten und Traktate* (Munich, 1963), "Einleitung," pp. 20–21.

28. "Der vater gebirt sînen sun den gerehten und den gerehten sînen sun." Pr. 39; DW II, 258, 2–3.

29. "Non enim est imaginandum falso quasi alio filio sive imagine Christus sit filius dei, et alio quodam homo iustus et deiformis sit filius dei." *In Joh.* n. 119; LW III, 104.

30. "Daz diu wârheit selber ist, des ensîn wir niht, mêr: wir sîn wol wâr, dâ bî ist etwaz unwâr. Alsô enist ez in gote niht." Pr. 19; DW I, 316, 9–10.

31. "Jâ, bî guoter wârheit: waere mîn sêle als bereit als diu sêle unsers herren Jêsû Kristî, sô würkte der vater in mir als lûterlîche als in sînem eingebornen sune und niht minner; wan er minnet mich mit der selben minne, dâ er sich selben mite minnet." DW II, 306, 10–13.

32. ". . . Nâch dem, daz sie minner oder mê lûterlîche von gote aleine geborn sint. . . ." *BgT*; DW V, 41, 13–14.

33. The complete sentence is: "Und daz ein machet uns saelic und ie wir dem einen verrer sîn, ie minner wir süne und sun sîn und der heilige geist minner volkommenlîche in uns entspringet und von uns vluizet; und dar nâch wir naeher sîn dem einen, dar nâch sîn wir waerlîcher gotes süne und sun und ouch vliuzet von uns got-der-heilige-geist." *BgT*; DW V, 41,21–42,4.

34. "*Fieri*, ait, *filios dei*; fieri imperfectum est, moveri est; *filios* perfectum est. In nomine ergo filii credit qui fidem habet, qui iam fit, sed nondum est filius, Marc. 9: 'omnia possibilia sunt credenti.'" *In Joh.* n. 159; LW III, 131.

35. See McGinn, "Theological Summary," p. 51.

36. "Dar umbe sîn wir hie in disem sun und sîn der selbe sun." Pr. 4; DW I, 73, 5.

37. ". . . Sô muoz er [der mensche] ein einiger sun sîn mit Kristo des vaters; . . . sô müezet ir éin sun sîn, niht vil süne, mêr: éin sun." Pr. 46; DW II, 378, 7–9.

38. ". . . Daz wir sîn ein einiger sun, den der vater êwichlîche geborn hat. . . . Und [ich] bleip doch inne in dem vater." Pr. 22; DW I, 376, 6–8.

39. ". . . Deus etiam in hoc mundo concessit nobis 'potestatem filios dei fieri,' etiam unigenitos sive potius unigenitum, sic ut vivamus per eum." *Serm.* VI, 2, n. 58; LW IV, 58.

40. ". . . Daz er ein sî mit dem eingebornen sune und daz der der eingeborne sun sî. Zwischen dem eingebornen sune und der sêle enist kein underscheit." Pr. 10; DW I, 169, 2–4.

41. "Dar umbe sage ich, daz ich niht sîn enmac der sun gotes, niuwan ich enhabe daz selbe wesen, daz dâ hât der sun gotes, und von habunge des selben wesens werden wir im glîch, und wir sehen in, als er got ist. . . . Dar umbe sage ich, daz in disem sinne kein glîch enist noch kein underscheit, mêr: âne allen underscheit werden wir daz selbe wesen und substancie und natûre, diu er selber ist." Pr. 76; DW III, 320, 1–6.

42. "Und waz hülfe mich, daz der vater sînen sun gebaere, ich engebaere in denne ouch? Dar umbe gebirt got sînen sun in einer volkomenen sêle und liget alsô kindes inne, ûf daz si in vort ûzgebaere in allen irn werken." Pr. 75; DW III, 301, 1–3. One should note that the Middle High German verb *gebern*, which Eckhart uses for the birth action, is much broader in application than modern counterparts. It can mean simply "to bring" or "to produce." More often it does refer to birth, but in such contexts it can refer as readily to the masculine act of *begetting* as it can to the feminine *bearing* or *giving birth to*. Generally birth was considered to be due to the action of the male semen. The mother's contribution was limited to providing with her womb a suitable environment in which the semen might develop. See G. Prerodovic, "Uberlegungen zu *Geburt* und *generatio* bei Meister Eckhart," *Récherches Gérmanique* 5 (1975), 3–11.

43. "Dâ bin ich ein mit im, er enmac mich ûzgesliezen niht, und in dem werke dâ enpfaehet der heilige geist sîn wesen und werden von mir als von gote." Pr. 25; DW II, 11, 3–4.

44. ". . . Jâ, ûz dem selben grunde, dâ der vater ûz gebernde ist sîn êwic wort, dar ûz wirt si vruhtbaere mitgebernde. . . . dirre Jêsus ist mit ir vereinet und si mit im, und si liuhtet und schînet mit im als ein einic ein und als ein lûter klâr lieht in dem veterlîchen herzen." Pr. 2; DW I, 31, 2–8.

45. Colledge, p. 194. "'In principio.' Hie ist uns ze verstânne geben, daz wir ein einiger sun sîn, den der vater êwiclîche geborn hât ûz dem verborgenen vinsternisse der êwigen verborgenheit, inneblîbende in dem êrsten beginne der êrsten lûterkeit, diu dâ ist ein vülle aller lûterkeit. Hie hân ich êwiclîche geruowet und geslâfen in der verborgenen bekantnisse des êwigen vaters, inneblîbende ungesprochen. Ûz der lûterkeit hat er mich êwiclîche geborn sînen eingebornen sun in daz selbe bilde sîner êwigen vaterschaft, daz ich vater sî und geber den, von dem ich geborn bin." Pr. 22; DW I, 382,3–383,1.

46. ". . . Des vaters wesen ist, daz er den sun geber, und des sunes wesen ist, daz ich in im und nâch im geborn werde; des heiligen geistes wesen ist, daz ich in im verbrant werde und in im zemâle versmolzen werde und zemâle minne werde." Pr. 39; DW II, 264, 3–6.

47. "Ein meister sprichet: diu sêle gebirt sich selben in sich selben und gebirt sich ûz ir und gebirt sich wider in sich." Pr. 43; DW II, 328, 6–7.

48. "Dâ ist gotes tac, dâ diu sêle stât in dem tage der êwicheit in einem weselîchen nû, und dâ gebirt der vater sînen eingebornen sun in einem gegenwertigen nû und wirt diu sêle wider in got geborn. Als dicke sô diu geburt geschihet, als dicke gebirt si den eingebornen sun." DW I, 166, 8–12.

49. Colledge, p. 194. "In dem selben, daz er gebirt sînen eingebornen sun in mich, sô gebir ich in wider in den vater." Pr. 22; DW I, 383, 7–8.

50. "Swenne der wille alsô vereinet wirt, daz ez wirt ein einic ein, sô gebirt der vater von himelrîche sînen eingebornen sun in sich in mich. War umbe in sich in mich? Dâ bin ich ein mit im. . . ." Pr. 25; DW II, 11, 1–3.

51. See, for example, Sermon 6; DW I, 109, 4–7, quoted earlier.

52. "Der vater sprichet vernünfticlîche in vruhtbaerkeit sîne eigene natûre alzemâle in sînem êwigen worte. Niht von willen sprichet er daz wort als ein getât des willen, als sô swaz dâ wirt gesprochen oder getan von gewalt des willen, in der selben gewalt mac er ez ouch wol lâzen, ob er will. Alsô enist ez niht umbe den vater und umbe sîn êwic wort; mêr: er welle oder enwelle, er muoz diz wort sprechen und gebern âne underlâz; . . . In disem worte sprichet der vater mînen geist und dînen geist und eines ieglîchen menschen geist glîch dem selben worte. In dem selben sprechenne bist dû und ich ein natiurlich sun gotes als daz selbe wort." DW II, 434,4–435,5 and 435,8–10.

53. "Der mich vrâgete: war umbe beten wir, war umbe vasten wir, war umbe tuon wir alliu unseriu werk, war umbe sîn wir getoufet, war umbe ist got mensche worden, daz daz hoehste was? —ich spraeche: dar umbe, daz got geborn werde in der sêle und diu sêle in gote geborn werde. Dar umbe ist alliu diu schrift geschriben, dar umbe hât got die werlt geschaffen und all engelische natûre, daz got geborn werde in der sêle und diu sêle in got geborn werde." Pr. 38; DW II, 227,6–228,3.

54. "War umbe ist got mensche worden? Dar umbe, daz ich got geborn würde der selbe." Pr. 29; DW II, 84, 1–2.

55. McGinn, p. 170. "Ipse unigenitus, a solo patre scilicet, nos geniti quidem, sed non ab uno patre. Ipse ergo per generationem, quae est ad esse, ad speciem et naturam et propter hoc est filius naturalis, nos vero per regenerationem, quae est ad conformitatem naturae." *In Joh.* n. 123; LW III, 107.

56. *In Joh.* n. 106; LW III, 90. See also n. 117; LW III, 102–103, where the idea that we become co-heirs (*coheredes*) is added to that of adoption.

57. "Und alsô als der sun ein ist mit dem vater nâch wesene und nâch natûre, alsô bist dû ein mit im nâch wesene und nâch natûre." Pr. 46; DW II, 383, 6–7.

58. "Âne allen underscheit werden wir daz selbe wesen und substancie und natûre, diu er selber ist." Pr. 76; DW III, 320, 5–6.

59. "Daz êwige wort ennam niht an sich dísen menschen noch dén menschen, sunder ez nam an sich eine vrîe, ungeteilte menschlîche natûre, diu dâ blôz was sunder bilde; wan diu einvaltige forme der menscheit diu ist sunder bilde. Und dar umbe, [wan] in der annemunge diu menschlîche natûre von dem êwigen worte einvalticlîche sunder bilde angenomen wart, sô ward daz bilde des vaters, daz der êwige sun ist, bilde der menschlîchen natûre. Wan als daz wâr ist, daz got mensche worden ist, als wâr ist daz, daz der mensche got worden ist. Und alsô ist diu menschlîche natûre überbildet in dem, daz si worden ist daz götlîche bilde, daz dâ bilde ist des vaters. Und alsô, sult ir ein sun sîn, sô müezet ir abescheiden und abegân alles des, daz underscheit an iu machende ist. Wan der mensche ist ein zuoval der natûre, und nemet iuch nâch der vrîen, ungeteilten menschlîchen natûre. Und wan denne diu selbe natûre, nâch der ir iuch nemende sît, sun des êwigen vaters worden ist von der annemunge des êwigen wortes, alsô werdet ir sun des êwigen vaters mit Kristô von dem, daz ir iuch nâch der selben natûre nemende sît, diu dâ got worden ist." Pr. 46; DW II, 379,6–382,3.

60. "Swenne der mensche entbloezet und entdecket daz götlîche bilde, daz got in im natiurlich geschaffen hât, sô wirt gotes bilde in im offenbaere." Pr. 40; DW II, 275,4–276,1.

61. "Quarto: alternatio afficit passum tantum secundum accidentia et accidentibus, generatio vero afficit passum forma substantiali." *In Joh.* n. 146; LW III, 122.

62. ". . . [Anima] transformatur siquidem in illud esse divinum, quo utique esse divino deus est et vivit. Sic enim dicimus animal cibo vivere et ignem suo modo vivere lignis transformatis in esse ignis." *Serm.* LV, 4, n. 556; LW IV, 465.

63. "Nota: cibus convertitur in naturam cibati. Sic anima in deum [et eo magis], quo ista sunt spiritualiora." *Serm.* LIV, n. 527; LW IV, 444. Eckhart's responses to the objections of the commission in Avignon (Pelster, *Gutachten*, p. 1118) to this line of thought do little to clarify the issue. The fact remains that several times in his works the idea of substantial union between God and creature-become-Son is stated.

64. A few examples of Eckhart's justification of his conception of union on the basis of such scripture texts are:

1. *Serm.* LV, 4 n. 556; LW IV, 465: "'. . . vivit in me Christus'" (Gal. 2:20), where he maintains that the soul is transformed into the *esse divinum* by which God is and lives.

2. Pr. 24; DW I, 414–423, a sermon in which he discusses union with Christ and takes as his text "intuot iu, einiget iu Kristum" (Put on the Lord, Jesus Christ; Rom. 13:14).

3. References to our being transformed into the same image. A few examples:

Pr. 6; DW I, 110, 8. Pr. 23; DW I, 397, 3–5, and 398, 4. Pr. 41; DW II, 296, 4–5. *In Joh.* nn. 106, 119; LW III, 90 and 104. *Serm.* XXXI, n. 326; LW IV, 285.

65. Some authors assuming a traditional view of grace and using it to free the controversial Dominican from the taint of heterodoxy are Wilhelm Bange, *Meister Eckharts Lehre vom göttlichen und geschöpflichen Sein, dargestellt mit besonderer Rücksicht auf die lateinischen Schriften* (Limburg, 1937), esp. p. 169; James M. Clark, *Meister Eckhart: An Introduction to the Study of His Works* (Edinburgh, 1957), pp. 54–57; Otto Karrer, *Das Göttliche in der Seele bei Meister Eckhart* (Würzburg, 1928), pp. 34–41; and Herma Piesch, *Meister Eckharts Ethik* (Lucerne, 1935), pp. 27ff. In defense of Karrer and Piesch, it must be remarked that they were countering such wild claims about Eckhart and the nature of his teachings that the overall effect of their work was nonetheless to push research efforts in some right directions.

Some authors approaching the issue of grace with sophistication are: Lossky, *Théologie négative*, esp. pp. 182–192; Josef Zapf, *Die Funktion der Paradoxie im Denken und sprachlichen Ausdruck bei Meister Eckart* (Cologne, 1966), pp. 168–201; John Caputo, "Fundamental Themes in Eckhart's Mysticism," *The Thomist* 42 (1978), 218–222; and Konrad Weiss, "Meister Eckhart der Mystiker," in *Freiheit und Gelassenheit. Meister Eckhart heute*, ed. Udo Kern (Munich, 1980), pp. 113–114.

66. Pr. 43; DW II, 326, 1–3. It is texts such as this that justify Richard Kieckhefer's ("Meister Eckhart's Conception of Union with God," *Harvard Theological Review*, LXXI [1978], 210) bringing up the notion of "uncreated grace," i.e., that God dwells within the soul, even though there seems to be no clear reference to this doctrine in Eckhart's works. After all, because of Eckhart's conception of the accident of place when dealing with union, there is really no difference in saying God dwells within the soul or in saying the soul dwells in God. However, in order to achieve a better understanding of the meaning of a traditional concept like uncreated grace for Eckhart, we must see how it fits into his more specific statements on the nature of creator and creature and their mutual relationships. Otherwise, it remains only very loosely connected to Eckhart's thought and of limited value in understanding it.

67. *Serm.* XXV, 1, nn. 258–259; LW IV, 235–237. This conception of grace seems parallel with or identical to the flowing out of creatures from, and their return to, God in Pr. 52 (*Beati pauperes spiritu*); DW II, 486–506.

68. For example, *In Joh.* n. 106, LW III, 90, and n. 184, LW III, 154. Similarly, in a vernacular sermon, when a man has become completely free of self and lives only for God, "he is truly the same by grace that God is by nature" (*sô ist er waerlîche daz selbe von gnâden, daz got ist von natûre. . .* ; Pr. 66; DW III, 109, 7–10).

69. "Unser herre lêret uns in disen worten, wie edel der mensche geschaffen ist in sîner natûre und wie götlich daz ist, dâ er zuo komen mac von gnâden." *VeM*; DW V, 109, 2–4. "Gratia enim inspirat et allevat naturam." *In Exod.* n. 13; LW II, 19. "Ouch diu gnâde enzerstoeret die natûre niht, si volbringet sie." *RdU*; DW V, 288, 12.

70. "Suln wir dar în komen, sô müezen wir klimmen von natiurlîchem liehte in daz lieht der gnâde und dar inne wahsen in daz lieht, daz der sun selber ist." Pr. 75; DW III, 299,9–300,2.

71. "Daz lieht der gnâde, swie grôz ez ist, ez ist doch kleine wider dem götlîchen liehte. . . . Die wîle man zuonimet in der gnâde, sô ist ez gnâde und ist

kleine, dar inne man got bekennet von verre. Wenne aber diu gnâde wirt volbrâht
ûf daz hoehste, sô enist ez niht gnâde; ez ist ein götlich lieht, dar inne man got
sihet." Pr. 70; DW III, 196, 4–10. In a Latin sermon (XLIX, 1, n. 507; LW IV,
422–423) Eckhart says something similar, using Thomistic terms for the stages of
the soul's progress: (1) the *lumen naturale* or natural light, (2) the *lumen gratiae* or
light of grace, and (3) the *lumen gloriae* or light of glory, which is synonymous
with the soul's life in heaven. But use of these terms does not allow us to assume
complete conformity between the two thinkers on this point. Their differing view
on *esse* as it applies to God and creature results in a divergence on the question of
grace. The ensuing treatment of Eckhart's statements on the role of grace in bringing about union should clarify this.

72. Part of the mystery of these passages is bound up with Eckhart's difficult
teaching on the "spark of the soul." We will attempt some clarification of this
teaching later.

73. ". . . Gnâde enwürket kein werk, wan alle gezierde giuzet si zemâle in die
sêle; daz ist ein vüllede in dem rîche der sêle. Ich spriche: gnâde eneiniget niht die
sêle mit gote, si ist ein volbringen; daz ist ihr werk, daz si die sêle wider ze gote
bringet. Dâ wirt ir diu vruht von dem bluomen." Pr. 21; DW I, 367, 1–5. Just previous to this passage, Eckhart had used the blossom-fruit image to explain the relationship of grace on earth to eternal happiness, but it does not seem that this
quotation covers exactly the same ground. Given his view of man's "simultane-
ous" existence in time and eternity and the sense of these lines, grace is a preparation and the goal is beyond grace. For another example of grace as a means to
becoming divine (*götlich*), see Pr. 82; DW III, 428,9–430,4.

74. "Dâ gnâde inne ist in der sêle, daz ist sô lûter und ist gote sô glîch und sô
sippe, und gnâde ist âne werk, als in der geburt, dâ ich vor von gesprochen hân,
kein werk enist. Gnâde enwürket kein werk. Sant Johannes engetete nie kein
zeichen." Pr. 38; DW II, 242, 3–6. See also on page 242, in note 3, the reference to
In Joh. n. 521: "Adhuc autem tertio potest dici: . . . —secundum doctores me-
liores—non operatur proprie nec immediate per se miracula vel opera exteriora,
sed per se dat esse divinum, secundum illud Cor.: 'gratia dei sum id quod sum.'"
Notice that in the Middle High German quotation grace is taken to be something
analogous or parallel to the birth of the Son. This indicates that they are not identical. The birth seems to be one formulation of man's goal, while the function of
grace is to prepare the way for it. The Pauline *gratia dei* . . . will be discussed below. Eckhart also discusses grace in connection with the birth of John the Baptist
in Pr. 11; DW I, 177, 1–9.

75. ". . . Et quia vivere viventibus est esse, ideo Cor. 15 dicitur 'gratia dei sum
id quod sum'. Ubi notandum quod li 'quod' prae 'sum' potest accipi pro [pro]-
nomine vel pro coniunctione, et utroque modo convenienter exponitur in propo-
sito. Sed subtilius et melius est quod accipiatur pro coniunctione. Dat enim gratia
homini abnegare se ipsum et tollere crucem suam et sequi deum, vivere deo, non
sibi, Cor. 5c: 'qui vivunt, iam non sibi vivant'; Gal. 5d 'vivo ego iam non ego.'
Iustus siquidem soli iustitiae vivit." *Serm.* II, 2 n. 16; LW IV, 17. Note the parallel
to the just man's relation to justice.

76. "Ez ist sant Pauli wort, der sprichet: 'allez, daz ich bin, daz bin ich von der
gnâde gotes.' Nû schînet disiu rede ob gnâde und ob wesene und obe verstantnisse
und obe willen und ob aller begirde—wie mac denne sant Pauli wort wâr sîn? Hie
zuo antwürtet man alsô, daz sant Pauli wort wâr sîn: daz diu gnâde gotes in im
was, des was nôt; wan diu gnâde gotes diu worhte in im, daz diu zuovellicheit vol-

brâhte daz wesen. Dô diu gnâde endete und ir werk volbrâhte, dô bleip Paulus, daz er was. Pr. 52; DW II, 501,6–502,3. In view of Eckhart's professed preference for *quod* as a conjunction, and in light of what makes best sense in this context, I have translated the last phrase "that he was" in opposition to Colledge's (p. 202) "Paul remained what he was."

77. Eckhart's conception of grace seems to have many affinities with that of the Eastern church. See, for example, Vladimir Lossky, *The Mystical Theology of the Eastern Church* (Crestwood, N.Y., 1976), pp. 100–102. These affinities deserve a detailed investigation.

78. "Homo enim sanctus sive bonus quicunque non fit ipse Christus. . . . Sic mens nostra per gratiam adoptionis et nos unimur vero filio dei, membra unius capitis ecclesie qui est Christus." *RS*, Théry, p. 199. Karl Kertz's "Eckhart on the Birth of the Divine Word in the Soul," *Traditio* 15 (1959), 327–363, which makes extensive use of Eckhart's *Defense*, is a good example of how a serious study carried out with a high degree of competence can achieve results of only limited validity because, first of all, a concept in Eckhart (here, grace) is assumed to have a completely traditional sense, and second, because the wish to establish the Dominican's orthodoxy takes precedence over and colors the attempt to discover what Eckhart really thought. However, coming as it did before the best work on Eckhart's conceptions of *esse* and analogy was available, the article deserves our respect.

79. "Gratia est ipsa gloria subtracta sola nostra imperfectione." *Serm.* IX, n. 100; LW IV, 95.

80. ". . . Quantum bonum [est] ibi vivere, immo in *ipso deo omnis gratiae* ubi iam gratia non gratia formaliter, sed virtualiter sicut calor in caelo, ubi iam nec bonum nec suave nec esse, sed supra 'in regione et regno dissimilitudinis' infinitae." *Serm.* IX, n. 102; LW IV, 96–97.

81. "Deus assumpsit vestem nostram, ut vere, proprie et per substantiam sit homo et homo deus in Christo. Natura autem assumpta communis est omni homini sine magis et minus. Ergo datum est omni homini filium dei fieri, per substantiam quid[em] in ipso, in se autem adoptive per gratiam." *Serm.* LII, n. 523; LW IV, 437. The occasion for these remarks is Paul's "Put on the Lord Jesus Christ" (Rom. 13:14). Another aspect of these claims of identity in substance worth mentioning is that, for a thinker with Neoplatonic leanings like Eckhart, the term "substance" may well have different implications from those it would have for a strict Aristotelian.

82. "Sumlîche lêraere wellent, daz der geist neme sîne saelicheit in der minne; etlîche wellent, daz er sie neme in dem anesehenne gotes. Aber ich spriche: er ennimet sie noch in minne noch in bekennenne noch in anesehenne. Nû möhte man sprechen: enhât der geist kein anesehen in dem êwigen lebene an got? Jâ und nein. Dâ er geborn ist, dâ enhât er kein ûfsehen noch kein anesehen an got. Aber dâ er geborn wirt, dâ hât er anesehen gotes. Dar umbe ist des geistes saelicheit, dâ er geborn ist, und niht, dâ er geborn wirt, wan er lebet, dâ der vater lebet, daz ist: in einvalticheit und in blôzheit des wesens." Pr. 39; DW II, 265,1–266,2

83. See McGinn, "Theological Summary," p. 51.

84. I gladly leave a discussion of the orthodoxy of this teaching to others.

85. Pr. 86; DW III, 481–492. For a detailed and valuable analysis of this sermon, see Dietmar Mieth, *Die Einheit von vita activa und vita contemplativa in*

*den deutschen Predigten und Traktaten Meister Eckharts und bei Johannes Tau-
ler* (Regensburg, 1969), pp. 186–233.

86. "Swer sînen willen genzlîche gibet gote, der vaehet got und bindet got,
daz got niht enmac, dan daz der mensche wil. Swer gote sînen willen genzlîche
gibet, dem gibet got sînen willen wider als genzlîche und als eigenlîche, daz gotes
wille des menschen eigen wirt . . . , wan got enwirt niemans eigen, er ensî ze dem
êrsten sîn eigen worden." DW II, 8,9–9,2.

87. See esp. Schmoldt, *Die deutsche Begriffssprache*, pp. 27–33.

88. Alois Haas, "Meister Eckharts mystische Bildlehre," in *Der Begriff der
Repraesentatio im Mittelalter. Stellvertretung, Symbol, Zeichen, Bild*, ed. Albert
Zimmermann (Berlin, 1971), pp. 113–138, gives a good analysis of the use of *bilde*
by Eckhart as a term with positive value.

89. See Chapter 3, "Consequences."

90. From Sermon 5b; Colledge, p. 184. The insertions are mine. "Dâ diu crêatûre endet, dâ beginnet got ze sînne. Nû begehrt got niht mê von dir, wan daz dû
dîn selbes ûzgangest in crêatiurlîcher wîse und lâzest got got in dir sîn. Daz min-
neste crêatiurlîche bilde, daz sich iemer in dir erbildet, daz ist als grôz als got grôz
ist. War umbe? Dâ hindert ez dich eins ganzen gotes. Rehte dâ daz bilde îngât, dâ
muoz got wîchen und alliu sîn gotheit. Aber dâ daz bilde ûzgât, dâ gât got în. Got
begert des alsô sêre, daz dû dîn selbes ûzgangest in crêatiurlîcher wîse, als ob alliu
sîn saelicheit dar an lige." Pr. 5b; DW I, 92,7–93,5.

91. "Sehet, nû möhte man vrâgen, wie der mensche, der geborn ist und vor ge-
gangen ist in vernünftic leben, wie er alsô ledic müge sîn aller bilde, als dô er niht
enwas, und er weiz doch vil, daz sint allez bilde; wie mac er denne ledic sîn? Nû
merket daz underscheit, daz wil ich iu bewîsen. Waere ich alsô vernünftic, daz alliu bilde vernünfticlîche in mir stüenden, diu alle menschen ie enpfiengen und diu
in gote selber sint, waere ich der âne eigenschaft, daz ich enkeinez mit eigenschaft
haete begriffen in tuonne noch in lâzenne, mit vor noch mit nâch, mêr: daz ich in
disem gegenwertigen nû vrî und ledic stüende nâch dem liebsten willen gotes und
den zu tuonne âne underlâz, in der wârheit sô waere ich juncvrouwe âne hinder-
nisse aller bilde als gewaerlîche, als ich was, dô ich niht enwas." Pr. 2; DW I,
25,2–26,3.

92. One cannot help but notice how these demands parallel those urging us to
become the Son. It would seem that only as the Son can we really see things and
their dematerialized *bilde* as God sees them. If one asks how a man endowed with
a limited human intellect can possibly see things from the divine point of view,
one is asking about Eckhart's doctrine of the *scintilla animae* (*vünkelîn*), which
we shall try to illumine below.

The most thorough study of Eckhart's thought, taking as its point of departure Eckhart's demand that reality be seen from God's point of view, is C. F. Kelley's
Meister Eckhart on Divine Knowledge (New Haven, 1977). In this book Kelley
attempts to show how central this change to a divine point of view is for understanding the Dominican's thought. Though at times confusing and needlessly polemical, the volume casts light on what is clearly an issue important for an
understanding of Eckhart.

93. "Swer diu dinc laezet, als sie zuoval sint, der besitzet sie, dâ sie ein lûter
wesen sint und êwic sint. Pr. 16b; DW I, 264, 2–3.

94. Some pertinent secondary sources are Reiner Schürmann, *Meister Eckhart: Mystic and Philosopher* (London and Bloomington, 1977), pp. 63–64, 111–

114; and McGinn, "Theological Summary," pp. 59–60. For a broader framework, see John Caputo, *The Mystical Element in Heidegger's Thought* (Athens, Ohio, 1978), III: "The Rose Is Without Why: Meister Eckhart's Mysticism."

95. See Chapter 2, "God as Being: *Esse est Deus*," for these phrases as expressions of kinds of causality in God.

96. "Secundo, nota quod non ait nec addit: 'propter ipsum' *sunt omnia*: primo, quia deus, et per consequens homo divinus, non agit propter cur aut quare. Secundo, quia omnia operantur ex deo, per deum, quod in deo, sed et ipse deus omnia operatur in se ipso. *In ipso* autem non est propter." *Serm.* IV, 1, n. 21; LW IV, 22–23.

97. "Puta, iustus ex iustitia, non habet principium nec finem extra se, sed in se et ex se." *In Joh.* n. 341; LW III, 290.

98. "Ûzer disem innersten grunde solt dû würken alliu diniu werk sunder warumbe. Ich spriche waerlîche: al die wîle dû diniu werk würkest umbe himelrîche oder umbe got oder umbe dîn êwige saelicheit von ûzen zuo, sô ist dir waerlîche unreht. Man mac dich aber wol lîden, doch ist ez daz beste niht. Wan waerlîche, swer gotes mê waenet bekomen in innerkeit, in andâht, in süezicheit und in sunderlîcher zuovüegunge dan bî dem viure oder in dem stalle, sô tuost dû niht anders dan ob dû got naemest und wündest im einen mantel umbe daz houbet und stiezest in under einen bank. Wan swer got suochet in wîse, der nimet die wîse und lât got, der in der wîse verborgen ist. Aber swer got suochet âne wîse, der nimet in, als er in im selber ist; und der mensche lebet mit dem sune, und er ist daz leben selbe. Swer daz leben vrâgete tûsent jâr: war umbe lebest dû? solte ez antwürten, ez spraeche niht anders wan: ich lebe dar umbe daz ich lebe. Daz ist dâ von, wan leben lebet ûzer sînem eigenen grunde und quillet ûzer sînem eigen; dar umbe lebet ez âne warumbe in dem, daz ez sich selber lebet. Swer nû vraget einen wârhaften menschen, der dâ würket ûz eigenem grunde: war umbe würkest dû dîniu werk? solte er rehte antwürten, er spraeche niht anders dan: ich würke dar umbe daz ich würke." Pr. 5b; DW I, 90,11–92,6. Another interesting passage on this theme is Pr. 26; DW II, 26,3–27,10.

99. [*Unus*] nota[tur] primo, quia negatione scitur deus; est enim incomprehensibilis. Secundo, quia est indistinctus. Per quod patet ipsius sublimitas sive nobilitas, et notatur dei bonitas et amor ad nos. Separari non vult, non potest. . . . Et notatur etiam in hoc creaturae nihileitas, Joh. 1: 'sine ipso factum est nihil.' Tertio, quia in ipso omnia sunt unum, et sic beatificat. Quarto, quia volens deo uniri, ipsum invenire, debet esse unus, divisus ab omnibus, in se indivisus abnegatione sui." *Serm.* XXXVII, n. 375; LW IV, 320–321.

100. "Bekante der geist sîne blôze abegescheidenheit, er enmöhte sich ûf kein dinc geneigen, er enmüeste blîben ûf sîner blôzen abegescheidenheit." Pr. 10; DW I, 170, 8–9. Notice the use of the unreal subjunctive. Our success in becoming *abegescheiden* is not total, but it is not the less real or radical for that.

101. This analysis of the spark of the soul is based on the following passages: In DW I: Pr. 2; 32,1–45,3. Pr. 9; 150,1–154,6. Pr. 10; 161,1–163,5 and 171,12–173,9. Pr. 11; 182,7–184,8. Pr. 12; 196,6–198,5 (see also note 1, p. 198). Pr. 13; 220,4–222,2. Pr. 17; 283,4–284,6. Pr. 20a; 332,2–334,4. Pr. 22; 380,5–381,2. Pr. 24; 415,2–418,9.

In DW II: Pr. 26; 31,1–32,3. Pr. 27; 52,4–53,3. Pr. 28; 66, 1–11. Pr. 29; 88, 3–10. Pr. 30; 94,9–97,3. Pr. 37; 211,1–223,5. Pr. 40; 279,4–281,2. Pr. 42; 308,2–309,5. Pr. 46; 382, 5–10. Pr. 48; 416,1–421,3. Pr. 59; 624, 7–10.

In DW III: Pr. 69; 169,1–180,2. Pr. 76; 315,6–317,2.

In LW I: *In Gen.* I, n. 168; 313–314. *In Gen.* II, n. 113; 579–580, and nn. 138–153; 604–624.

In LW II: *In Sap.* n. 21; 342, and n. 24; 343–344.

In LW III: *In Joh.* n. 38; 32. N. 84; 72. Nn. 119–120; 103–105. N. 123; 107. N. 318; 265–266.

In LW IV: *Serm.* XI, 1, nn. 112–115; 105–109. *Serm.* XXIV, 2, n. 248; 227. *Serm.* XXIX, nn. 301–304; 267–270.

In LW V: *Q. Par.* I, II, and III; 37–71.

102. Some helpful secondary literature: J. Caputo, "The Nothingness of the Intellect in Meister Eckhart's 'Parisian Questions,'" *The Thomist* 39 (1975), 85–115. J. M. Clark, *Meister Eckhart: An Introduction to the Study of His Works* (Edinburgh, 1957), pp. 60–61, 87–90. A. M. Haas, "Zur Frage der Selbsterkenntnis bei Meister Eckhart," *Freiburger Zeitschrift für Philosophie und Theologie* 15 (1968), 190–261. R. Imbach, *Deus est Intelligere. Das Verhältnis von Sein und Denken in seiner Bedeutung für das Gottesverständnis bei Thomas von Aquin und in den Pariser Quaestionen Meister Eckharts* (Freiburg, 1976). Lossky, *Théologie négative*, passim; refer to the "Index des Themes," esp. under "Intellect," pp. 439–440. McGinn, "Theological Summary," pp. 42–43. J. Quint, "Mystik und Sprache," *Deutsche Vierteljahresschrift für Literaturwissenschaft und Geistesgeschichte* 27 (1953), 65–67, reprinted in *Altdeutsche und Altniederländische Mystik*, ed. K. Ruh (Darmstadt, 1964), pp. 136–139. Schmoldt, *Die deutsche Begriffssprache*, esp. pp. 15–27, 30, 74–98. Bernard Welte, "Meister Eckhart als Aristoteliker," *Philosophisches Jahrbuch der Görres Gesellschaft* 69 (1961), 64–74.

103. For *ad imaginem* see, for example, *In Gen.* II, nn. 138, 143, 154; LW I, 604–605, 612, 624–625; and *In Joh.* n. 123; LW III, 107. For *imago* see, for example, *In Gen.* II, nn. 139–140; LW I, 605–608; and *In Joh.* n. 84; LW III, 72. Eckhart also seems to feel justified in using *imago* when the *in quantum* principle is being applied to man. See, for example, *In Joh.* nn. 119–120; LW III, 103–105.

104. "Notandum quod homo id quod est per intellectum est." *In Gen.* II, n. 113; LW I, 579.

105. "Et quod aliquid sit in anima, si ipsa tota esset talis, ipsa esset increata, intellexi verum esse et etiam secundum doctores meos collegas, si anima esset intellectus essentialiter. Nec etiam umquam dixi, nec sensui, quod [aliquid] sit in anima, quod sit aliquid anime, quod sit increatum et increabile, quia tunc esset pecia[ta] ex [c]reato et [increato], cuius oppositum scripsi et docui, nisi quis vellet dicere: increatum vel non creatum [id est] non per se creatum sed concreatum." Laurent, p. 345.

106. Some of the more interesting passages on uncreatedness are: Pr. 10; DW I, 172, 6–8. Pr. 12; DW I, 197,8–198,5. Pr. 13; DW I, 220, 4–8. Pr. 22; DW I, 380,5–381,2. Pr. 48; DW II, 418, 1–11. On the other hand, Pr. 20a; DW I, 332, 2–3, speaks of the *vünkelîn der sêle* as created. Here its function is also different from usual in that it seeks what is good.

107. See Chapter 2, "God as Intellect, as Nonbeing."

108. "Et hoc est quod . . . nos docere voluit quod deus sit intellectus purus, cuius esse totale est ipsum intelligere." *In Gen.* I, n. 168; LW I, 314.

109. ". . . Ipsum principium semper est intellectus purus, in quo non sit aliud esse quam intelligere, nihilo nihil habens commune." *In Joh.* n. 38; LW III, 32.

110. "Sicut enim dicit Aristoteles, quod oportet visum esse abscolorem, ut

omnem colorem videat, et intellectum non esse formarum naturalium, ut omnes intelligat." *Q. Par.* I, n. 12; LW V, 47–48. Eckhart uses this example frequently in both the Latin works and the German works.

111. ". . . Intellectus, in quantum intellectus, nihil est eorum quae intelligit, sed oportet quod sit 'inmixtus', 'nulli nihil habens commune', ut omnia intelligat. . . . Si igitur intellectus, in quantum intellectus, nihil est, et per consequens nec intelligere est aliquod esse." *Q. Par.* II, n. 2; LW V, 50.

112. "Ens ergo in anima, ut in anima, non habet rationem entis et ut sic vadit ad oppositum ipsius esse. Sicut etiam imago in quantum huiusmodi est non ens, quia quanto magis consideras entitatem suam, tanto magis abducit a cognitione rei cuius est imago." *Q. Par.* I, n. 7; LW V, 43–44.

113. "Item: universale non est ens. Universale autem fit per intelligere. Ergo nec intelligere, per quod fit universale, erit ens. Item: ens est aliquid determinatum. . . . Sed intellectus et intelligere est aliquid indeterminatum. Ideo non est ens." *Q. Par.* II, n. 9; LW V, 53.

114. See Chapter 2, "Analogy."

115. It is this unreal subjunctive "were" that we see more than once in the sermons. See, for example, Pr. 2; DW I, 34, 2–3. Pr. 12; DW I, 198, 1–4. Pr. 13; DW I, 220, 4–5.

116. "Rursus sexto notandum quod ratio creabilitatis est esse, secundum illud: 'prima rerum creatarum est esse.' Unde res producta a deo, quam sit ens, vivens, et intelligens, ratione tamen solius esse est creabilis. Unde si quid esset vivens aut intelligens, non habens esse aliquod praeter et extra vivere et intelligere, ipsum esset ut sic increabile." *In Sap.* n. 24; LW II, 344.

117. See Chapter 2, "*Esse Formale* and *Esse Virtuale*."

118. ". . . Wan in die kraft enkumet niht anders wan got, und diu kraft ist alle zît in gote. Und alsô: sölte der mensche alliu dinc nemen in der kraft, sô naeme er sie niht, daz sie dinc sint, sunder er nimet sie nâch dem, daz sie in gote sint." Pr. 40; DW II, 280, 2–4.

119. "In dem innigestem und in dem hoehsten der sêle, dâ meine ich sie beide in einem. Dâ nie zît în enkam, dâ nie bilde îngeliuhtete, in dem innigestem und in dem hoehsten der sêle schepfet got alle dise werlt. Allez, daz got noch geschaffen sol über tûsent jâr, ob diu werlt sô lange bestât, daz schepfet got in dem innigesten und in dem hoehsten der sêle. Allez, daz vergangen ist, und allez, daz gegenwertic ist, und allez, daz künftic ist, daz schepfet got in dem innigestem der sêle." Pr. 30; DW II, 95,4–96,7.

120. "Dô got geschuof alle crêatûren, und haete dô got niht vor geborn etwaz, daz ungeschaffen waere, daz in im getragen haete bilde aller crêatûren: daz ist der vunke— . . . —diz vünkelîn ist gote alsô sippe, daz ez ist ein einic ein ungescheiden und daz bilde in sich treget aller crêatûren, bilde sunder bilde und bilde über bilde." Pr. 22; DW I, 380,5–381,2.

121. For more on *grunt*, see Schmoldt, *Die deutsche Begriffssprache*, pp. 49–62.

122. "Als waerlîche der vater in sîner einvaltigen natûre gebirt sînen sun natiurlîche, als gewaerlîche gebirt er in in des geistes innigestez, und diz ist diu inner werlt. Hie ist gotes grunt mîn grunt und mîn grunt gotes grunt. Hie lebe ich ûzer mînem eigen, als got lebet ûzer sînem eigen." Pr. 5b; DW I, 90, 6–9.

123. ". . . In substantia animae habitat proprie deus. Haec autem altior est intellectu." *Serm.* XXIV, 2, n. 248; LW IV, 227.

124. "Ez ist ein kraft in der sêle, und niht aleine ein kraft, mêr: wesen, und niht aleine wesen, mêr: ez loeset wesen." Pr. 42; DW II, 308, 2–3. How the *kraft* "dissolves" *esse* will be discussed below.

125. "Nota: revelatio proprie est apud intellectum vel potius in essentia animae quae proprie esse respicit. Esse autem deus esse nudum sine velamine est. Vel dic utrumque: in essentia ut intellectiva, sic copulatur sui supremo deo, secundum Rabbi Moysen, sic est 'genus dei.'" *Serm.* XI, 1, n. 115; LW IV, 108–109. Note the play with *revelatio* and *velamen*.

126. "In dem, daz disiu kraft nihte glîch ist, sô ist si gote glîch. Rehte, als got niht glîch enist, als enist disiu kraft nihte glîch." Pr. 69; DW III, 171, 1–2.

127. "Daz selbe bekantnisse, dâ sich got selben inne bekennet, daz ist eines ieglîchen abegescheidenen geistes bekantnisse und kein anderz." Pr. 10; DW I, 162, 2–4.

128. See Chapter 2, "Images of *Esse*."

129. "Und wan denne sîn bekennen mîn ist und wan sîn substancie sîn bekennen ist und sîn natûre und sîn wesen, dar nâch volget, daz sîn wesen und sîn substancie und natûre mîn ist. Und wan denne sîn substancie, sîn wesen und sî natûre mîn ist, sô bin ich der sun gotes." Pr. 76; DW III, 321, 1–4.

130. Colledge, pp. 197–198. "Dô ich hiute her gienc, dô gedâhte ich, wie ich iu alsô vernünfticlîche gepredigete, daz ir mich wol verstüendet. Dô gedâhte ich ein glîchnisse, und kündet ir daz wol verstân, sô verstüendet ir mînen sin und den grunt aller mîner meinunge, den ich ie gepredigete, und was daz glîchnisse von mînen ougen und von dem holze: wirt mîn ouge ûfgetan, sô ist ez ein ouge; ist ez zuo, sô ist ez daz selbe ouge, und durch der gesiht willen sô engât dem holze weder abe noch zuo. Nû merket mich vil rehte! Geschihet aber daz, daz mîn ouge ein und einvaltic ist in im selben und ûfgetan wirt und ûf daz holz geworfen wirt mit einer angesiht, sô blîbet ein ieglîchez, daz ez ist, und werdent doch in der würklicheit der angesiht als ein, daz man mac gesprechen in der wârheit: ougeholz, und daz holz ist mîn ouge. Waere aber daz holze âne mâterie und ez zemâle geistlich waere als diu gesiht mînes ougen, sô möhte man sprechen in der wârheit, daz in der würklicheit der gesiht daz holz und mîn ouge bestüenden in éinem wesene. Ist diz wâr von lîplîchen dingen, vil mê ist ez wâr von geistlîchen dingen. Ir sult daz wizzen, daz mîn ouge vil mê einicheit hât mit eines schâfes ougen, daz jensît mers ist und daz ich nie gesach, dan mîn ouge habe einicheit mit mînen ôren, mit den ez doch ein ist in dem wesene; und daz ist dâ von, wan des schâfes ouge hât die selben würklicheit, die ouch mîn ouge hât; und dâ von gibe ich in mê einicheit in dem werke dan ich tuon mînen ougen und mînen ôren, wan diu sint gesundert an den werken." DW II, 416,1–417,6.

131. ". . . Und diz selbe lieht nimet got sunder mittel und sunder decke und blôz, als er in im selben ist; daz ist ze nemene in der würklicheit der îngeberunge." DW II, 418, 3–4. Notice the added emphasis on act or operation achieved here by the use of *îngeberunge* instead of the usual *geburt*. In Sermon 76 (DW III, 320,9–321,1) the preacher again stresses the unity achieved in operation: ". . . his [God's] causing me to know and my knowing are the same thing." To clarify he then adds the common example: "And therefore his knowing is mine, just as what the teacher teaches and what the pupil is taught are one" (*Und ez ist daz selbe, daz er mich machet bekennende und daz ich bekenne. Und dar umbe ist sîn bekennen mîn, als in dem meister ein ist, daz er lêret, und in dem jünger, daz er gelêret wird*). In this example, two types of unity are implied: the unity of two

knowers who know the same thing (the unity being spoken of here) and the unity of two intellects engaged in the same act of knowing (which is taken up in the following paragraph of text).

132. Bernhard Welte, "Meister Eckhart als Aristoteliker," *Philosophisches Jahrbuch der Görres Gesellschaft* 69 (1961), 64–74; and Reiner Schürmann, *Meister Eckhart: Mystic and Philosopher* (London and Bloomington, 1978), esp. pp. 104–109 both rightfully give great importance to this identity in knowing, which is quite different from substantial unity. However, a question and a comment seem appropriate. Does this unity *in actu* have the same meaning for Eckhart, whose basic orientation is Platonic, as it did for its originator, Aristotle? The comment: In view of what has been said about the relationship of God and creatures in Chapter 2 and in the present chapter, unity *in würklicheit* should not be viewed as the only way Eckhart chooses to express the oneness of God and creature. There is just too much evidence to the contrary. One should not overemphasize the claims made for unity in knowing by the preacher when he introduces the idea. Eckhart frequently makes similar claims about other teachings. Rather, unity *in würklicheit* seems to be one way among several of stating unity. We have seen him stress other approaches in other contexts, and each way is basically inadequate.

133. See Chapter 3, "*Unum* and *Esse.*"

134. ". . . In sînem kleithûse, blôz, als er ist ein âne underscheit." Pr. 37; DW II, 217, 4–5.

135. See Chapter 3, "*Unum* and *Esse.*"

136. "Ez ist ein elende und ist ein wüestunge und ist mê ungenennet, dan ez namen habe, und ist mê unbekant, dan ez bekant sî." Pr. 28; DW II, 66, 6–7.

137. See Schmoldt, *Die deutsche Begriffssprache*, pp. 85–86.

138. The preacher tells us in connection with the birth, for example, that even if we do not hear and understand what the Father says, it is understood *in der kraft.* Pr. 27; DW II, 52,8–53,3.

139. God's presence in the soul, closer as he is to it than the soul is to itself, is not directly experienced. Otherwise, the preacher would have no need to explain this to his audience: "Diu sêle nimet ihr wesen âne mitel von gote; dar umbe ist got der sêle naeher, dan si ir selber sî; dar umbe ist got in dem grunde der sêle mit aller sîner gotheit." Pr. 10; DW I, 162, 4–6. Indeed, it is the soul's contact with sense objects which, as Eckhart admits with Aristotle, is the beginning of all human knowledge that rules out the divine light's presence not only in the essence of the soul but also in its powers: "Götlich lieht daz ist ze edel darzuo, daz ez den kreften niht gemeinschaft enmac tuon; wan allez, daz dâ berüeret und berüeret wirt, dem ist got verre und vremde. Und dar umbe wan die krefte berüeret werdent und berüerent, sô verliesent sie irn magetuom." Yet this does not seem to be an absolute condition. It appears that one can, through *abegescheidenheit*, learn to know *âne eigenschaft*, thus changing the state of things. For the preacher continues: "Götlich lieht enmac niht in sie [die krefte] geliuhten; aber mit üebunge und mit abelegunge mügen sie enpfenclich werden." Pr. 10; DW I, 162, 9–14. This close relationship between theory of knowledge, which medieval scholastics would consider part of psychology (the study of the soul), and the ascetical-mystical concern for emptying the soul that it may receive God is very Eckhartian.

140. "Jâ, got der rouwet selbe niht dâ, dâ er ist der êrste begin; er ruowet dâ, dâ er ist ein ende und ein rast alles wesens, niht daz diz wesen ze nihte werde, mêr: ez wirt dâ vor volbrâht in sînem lesten ende nâch sîner hoehsten volkomenheit. Waz

ist daz leste ende? Ez ist diu verborgen vinsternisse der êwigen gotheit und ist unbekant und wart nie bekant und enwirt niemer bekant." Pr. 22; DW I, 389, 3–8.

141. Colledge, p. 200. "Als lange als der mensche daz hât, daz daz sîn wille ist, daz er will ervüllen den allerliebsten willen gotes, der mensche enhât niht armuot, von der wir sprechen wellen; wan dirre mensche hât einen willen, mit dem er genuoc wil sîn dem willen gotes, und daz enist niht rehtiu armuot." DW II, 491, 4–7.

142. See Chapter 2, "*Esse Formale* and *Esse Virtuale*," and note 38 of this chapter.

143. Colledge, p. 200. The enclosure in brackets is mine. "Dô ich stuont in mîner êrsten sache, dô enhâte ich keinen got, und dô was ich sache mîn selbes; dô enwolte ich niht, noch enbegerte ich niht, wan ich was ein ledic sîn und ein bekennaere mîn selbes nâch gebrûchlîcher wârheit. Dô wolte ich mich selben und enwolte kein ander dinc; daz ich wolte, daz was ich, und daz ich was, daz wolte ich, und hie stuont ich ledic gotes und aller dinge. Aber dô ich ûzgienc von mînem vrîen willen und ich empfienc mîn geschaffen wesen, dô hâte ich einen got; wan ê die crêatûren waren, dô enwas got niht 'got', mêr: er was, daz er was. Aber dô die crêatûren gewurden und sie enpfiengen ir geschaffen wesen, dô enwas got niht 'got' in im selben, mêr: er was 'got' in den crêatûren." DW II, 492,3–493,2.

144. Colledge, p. 202. "Wan mîn wesenlich wesen ist obe gote, alsô als wir got nemen begin der crêatûren; wan in dem selben wesene gotes, dâ got ist obe wesene und ob underscheide, dâ was ich selbe." DW II, 502, 6–8.

145. Colledge, p. 201. "Mêr: er sol alsô ledic sîn alles wizzennes, daz er niht enwizze noch enbekenne noch enbevinde, daz got in im lebe." DW II, 494,8–495,1.

146. Colledge, p. 202. "Er alsô ledic stâ gotes und aller sîner werke, welle got würken in der sêle, daz er selbe sî diu stat, dar inne er würken wil." ". . . Daz êwic wesen, daz er ist gewesen und daz er nû ist and daz er iemer blîben sol." DW II, 500,8–501,1, and 501,4–5.

147. Colledge, p. 203. "Mêr: ich bin, daz ich was und daz ich blîben sol nû und iemermê." DW II, 504,8–505,1.

148. Colledge, p. 203. "Wan ich enpfâhe in disem durchbrechen, daz ich und got einz sîn. Dâ bin ich, daz ich was, und dâ nime ich weder abe noch zuo, wan ich bin dâ ein unbewegelîchiu sache, diu alliu dinc beweget." DW II, 505, 4–6. In saying that the soul, in breaking through to the *esse virtuale*, neither diminishes nor increases, Eckhart implies that the soul has gone beyond the state of John the Baptist (John 3:30: "He must grow greater, I must grow smaller") and has achieved oneness with God.

149. Colledge, p. 203. "Wer dise rede niht enverstât, der enbekümber sîn herze niht dâ mite. Wan als lange der mensche niht glîch enist dirre wârheit, als lange ensol er dise rede niht verstân; wan diz ist ein unbedahtiu wârheit, diu dâ komen ist ûz dem herzen gotes âne mittel." DW II, 506, 1–3.

150. See Chapter 2, "*Verbum in Principio*: The Word in Its Principle."

151. We have seen Eckhart admit in the case of the birth of the Son that all duality between God and creature is not overcome in heaven.

Chapter 5: Master of Language

1. Some representative studies on Eckhart's language are R. Fahrner, *Wortsinn und Wortschöpfung bei Meister Eckhart* (Marburg, 1929); H. Kunisch, *Das Wort "Grund" in der deutschen Mystik* (Osnabrück, 1929); J. Quint, "Die Sprache

Meister Eckharts als Ausdruck seiner mystischen Geisteswelt," *Deutsche Vierteljahresschrift für Literaturwissenschaft und Geistesgeschichte* 6 (1927), 671–701; J. Quint, "Mystik und Sprache," *DVJS* 27 (1953), 48–76; J. Margetts, *Die Satzstruktur bei Meister Eckhart* (Stuttgart, 1969); G. Stölzel, "Zum Nominalstil Meister Eckharts. Die syntaktischen Funktionen grammatischer Verbalabstrakte," *Wirkendes Wort* 16 (1966), 289–309; and G. von Siegroth-Nellessen, *Versuch einer exakten Stiluntersuchung für Meister Eckhart, Johannes Tauler und Heinrich Seuse* (Munich, 1979).

2. Although they contain some interesting insights, the studies by Margetts and Siegroth-Nellessen mentioned in the previous note suffer from the problems incurred when scholars try to reach significant conclusions about Eckhart's linguistic creativity from the starting point of the basic structure of Middle High German. One must honestly conclude that Eckhart's structure does not differ markedly from the general norms.

3. The very valuable insights provided by Quint in "Mystik und Sprache" (see note 1, above) seem to be only very loosely connected to the linguistic underpinnings from the work of Porzig, Weisgerber, and others, which Quint presents in the first part of his article.

4. James M. Clark, *Meister Eckhart: An Introduction to the Study of His Works* (Edinburgh, 1957), p. 108.

5. *RS*, Théry, II (11), p. 217; II (14), p. 219; II (15b), p. 220; and II (38), p. 242.

6. As Clark does in *Meister Eckhart: An Introduction*, p. 111.

7. "Nû sint alliu dinc glîch in gote und sint got selber. Hie ist gote als lustlich in dirre glîcheit, daz er sîne natûre und sîn wesen alzemâle durchgiuzet in der glîcheit in im selber. Daz ist im lustlich; ze glîcher wîse, als der ein ros lât loufen ûf einer grüenen heide, diu zemâle eben und glîch waere, des rosses natûre waere, daz ez sich zemâle ûzgüzze mit aller sîner kraft mit springenne ûf der heide, daz waere im lustlich und waere sîn natûre." Pr. 12; DW I, 199, 6–11.

8. "Ze glîcher wîs, als ob einer stüende vor einem hôhen berge und ruofte: 'bistû dâ?' der gal und der hal ruofte wider; 'bistû dâ?' Spraeche er: 'kum her ûz!' der gal spraeche ouch: 'kum her ûz!'" Pr. 22; DW I, 383, 1–3.

9. See Pr. 4; DW I, 69, 1–4 and also the rebuke in Pr. 5b; DW I, 91, 3–7 that such people wrap God's head in a cloak and throw it under a bench.

10. Especially worthy of mention are Josef Koch, "Zur Analogielehre Meister Eckharts," *Mélanges offerts a Etienne Gilson* (Toronto and Paris, 1959), pp. 327–350; and Lossky, *Théologie négative*, esp. pp. 286–298.

11. These images have been treated at some length in Chapter 2.

12. *Middle High German Translation of the Summa Theologica by Thomas Aquinas*, ed. B. Q. Morgan and F. W. Strothmann (Stanford, 1950).

13. See Chapter 4, "*Abegescheidenheit.*"

14. The accidental properties determining a substance (e.g., man) are quantity (six feet tall), quality (white), relation (father), action (singing), passion (being rained upon), time (on Tuesday), place (in the garden), position (standing), and dress (in a raincoat).

15. This is probably an allusion to Christ's speaking to the multitudes only in parables, while revealing the mysteries of the kingdom of heaven only to the disciples (Matt. 13 : 10–17, Mark 4 : 10–12, Luke 8 : 9–10).

16. For a third extended example, one might consider the context that Eckhart structures for *wesen* in the first half of Sermon 9 (DW I, 141–150) in preparation for presenting the *vünkelîn* idea.

17. "Nû, daz ist daz allerminste von der zît; ez enist noch ein stücke der zît noch ein teil der zît: ez ist wol ein smak der zît und ein spitze der zît und ein ende der zît. Nochdenne, swie kleine ez sî, ez muoz abe." Pr. 69; DW III, 170, 2–4. Augustine's famous deliberations about time are in the *Confessions* XI, 14.17–30.40.

18. "Ich hân underwîlen gesprochen, ez sî ein kraft in dem geiste, diu sî aleine vrî. Underwîlen hân ich gesprochen, ez sî ein huote des geistes; underwîlen hân ich gesprochen, ez sî ein lieht des geistes; underwîlen hân ich gesprochen ez sî ein vünkelîn. Ich spriche aber nû: ez enist weder diz noch daz." Pr. 2; DW I, 39, 1–4. Colledge, p. 180.

19. "Ich enmac niht sehen, daz ein ist. Er sach niht, daz was got. Got ist ein niht, und got ist ein iht. Swaz got ist, daz ist er alzemâle." Pr. 71; DW III, 222,11–223,2.

20. "Mit guoter wârheit, der alsô getriuwe waere, got der haete in im als unsprechelîche grôze vröude, der im die vröude benaeme, der benaeme im sîn leben und sîn wesen und sîne gotheit." Pr. 66; DW III, 113, 5–7.

21. "Der himel ist sô grôz und sô wît, und sagete ich ez iu, ir engloubet sîn niht. Der eine nâdel naeme und den himel rüerte mit dem spitze, daz der spitze der nâdel begriffe des himels, daz waere groezer gegen dem himel und aller dirre werlt, dan der himel und diu werlt gegen gote sî." Pr. 69; DW III, 161,5–162,3.

22. See Chapter 1: "Eckhart as Interpreter of Scripture."

23. See Chapter 4: "Poverty of Spirit."

24. "Augustinus sprichet: 'alliu diu schrift ist îtel. Sprichet man, daz got ein wort sî, sô ist er gesprochen; sprichet man, daz got ungesprochen sî, sô ist er unsprechelich.' Sô ist er aber etwaz; wer kan diz wort gesprechen? Daz entuot nieman, dan der diz wort ist. Got ist ein wort, daz sich selben sprichet. Swâ got ist, dâ sprichet er diz wort; swâ er niht enist, dâ ensprichet er niht. Got ist gesprochen und ist ungesprochen." Pr. 53; DW II, 529, 3–7.

25. See DW III, 160,4–163,5. The *modicum* of the Gospels is here equated with *paululum* in the Song of Songs (3:4): "Paululum cum pertransissem eos, inveni quem diligit anima mea." One has to pass through or spring over (*überhüpfen*) the *modicum* or *paululum* which all creatures are.

26. "Daz êwic wort ist daz mittel und daz bilde selbe, daz dâ ist âne mittel und âne bilde, ûf daz diu sêle in dem êwigen worte got begrîfet und bekennet âne mittel und âne bilde." DW III, 168, 8–10.

27. "Bilde und bilde ist sô gar ein und mit einander, daz man keinen underscheit dâ verstân enmac." DW III, 176,4–177,1.

28. "Swer iht sihet an gote, der ensihet gotes niht." Pr. 62; DW III, 66, 4.

29. See, for example, Pr. 30; DW II, 94, 1–4, and Pr. 24; DW I, 415, 8–17.

30. "Wan waere ez begrîfelich und waere ez glouplich, sô enwaere ez niht reht." Pr. 30; DW II, 94, 4–5.

31. "Got ist in allen dingen. Ie mê er ist in den dingen, ie mê er ist ûz den dingen: ie mê inne, ie mê ûze, ie mê ûze, ie mê inne." Pr. 30; DW II, 94, 6–7.

32. "Und als got in die sêle vliuzet, alsô vliuzet si wider in got." Pr. 84; DW III, 463, 5.

33. "Ein vberwesende wesen." Pr. 83; DW III, 438, 1. The translation, "a being above being," does not do justice to the original, especially to the dynamic nature of the participial *vberwesende* (being over).

34. See note 31 above. The repetition of *ie* shows how chiasmus can be combined with its opposite: parallelism.

35. The Son-creature relationship, which is here described as that of a word

and its echo, or as that of a word and a response that is identical, is also aptly put by the preacher when he describes the activity of the resurrected son of the widow of Nain who "sat up and began to talk" (Luke 7:15) by creating the verb *worten* (Pr. 18; DW I, 296, 6). The activity of the creature-become-Son is simply to "word."

36. Pr. 6; DW I, 109, 8–10. "He gives me birth, me, his Son and the same Son. I say more: He gives birth not only to me, his Son, but he gives birth to me as himself and himself as me and to me as his being and nature." Colledge, p. 187.

37. Students of Middle High German literature will be reminded of the close of the prologue in Gottfried's *Tristan*, where the poet uses this device for uniting the lovers: "ein man ein wip, ein wip ein man, / Tristan Isolt, Isolt Tristan" (ll. 129–130, ed. F. Ranke [Zurich, 1967]).

38. See Chapter 3, "Naming God."

39. "Diz wörtelîn 'et' bediutet in latîne eine einunge und ein zuobinden und ein însliezen. Swaz alzemâle zesamengebunden und îngeslozzen ist, daz meinet einunge. Hie meine ich, daz der mensche zesamengebunden und îngeslozzen und geeiniget ze gote sî." Pr. 44; DW II, 337,7–338,2.

40. *In Joh.* n. 8; LW III, 9. A similar treatment of *erat* occurs in Pr. 44; DW II, 347,6–350,9. In that sermon, however, it is the *erat* of Luke 2:25, which has Simeon as its subject.

41. This is in Pr. 39; DW II, 257,1–260,6. See Chapter 4, "The Just Man," for a more detailed explanation.

42. "Quia deus est nobis innominabilis propter infinitatem omnis esse in ipso. Omnis autem noster conceptus et nomen aliquid designatum importat." *Serm.* VIII, n. 84; LW IV, 80. The same point is made concerning the same parable in two German sermons: Pr. 20a; DW I, 328, 14, and Pr. 20b; DW I, 346, 1–3, and 352, 5–6.

43. See note 28 for this chapter.

44. See Chapter 4, "The Spark of the Soul."

45. "Der mensche, der niergen ûf gebûwet enwaere noch an nihte enhaftete, der danne umbekêrte himel und erde, er blibe unbeweget, wan er enhaftete an nihte, noch niht enhaftete an im." Pr. 69; DW III, 174, 2–4.

46. "Dv solt in minnen, als er ist Ein nit-got, Ein nit-geist, Ein nit-persone, Ein nit-bilde, Mer: als er ein luter pur clar Ein ist, gesvndert von aller zweiheite, vnd in dem einen svlen wir ewiklich versinken von [n]ite zv nvte." Pr. 83; DW III, 448, 7–9.

47. "Swer dâ minnet die gerehticheit, des underwindet sich diu gerehticheit und wirt begriffen von der gerehticheit, und er ist diu gerehticheit." Pr. 28; DW II, 62, 1–3.

48. "Und allez sîn [the just man's] wesen, leben, bekennen, wizzen und minnen ist ûz gote und in gote und got." *BgT*; DW V, 13, 3–4.

49. "Swer in der gerehticheit ist, der ist in gote und ist got." Pr. 39; DW II, 257, 5–6.

50. "Nû sol der mensche alsô leben, daz er ein sî mit dem eingebornen sune und daz er der eingeborne sun sî." Pr. 10; DW I, 169, 2–3.

51. "Als vil wirt der sun in uns geborn, und wir werden geborn in dem sune und werden éin sun." Pr. 41; DW II, 293, 9–10.

52. "Der [such a] mensche nimet, dâ der sun nimet und ist der sun selber. . . . wellet ir got bekennen, sô sult ir niht aleine glîch sîn dem sune, sunder ir sult der sun selber sîn." Pr. 16b; DW I, 273, 3–6.

53. "Swer dise predie hât verstanden, dem gan ichz wol. Wêre hie nieman gewesen, ich müeste sie disem stocke geprediet hân." Franz Pfeiffer, *Meister Eckhart*, 4th ed. (Göttingen, 1924), Sermon 56, p. 181.

Epilogue: Eckhart's Mysticism

1. Josef Quint, "Die Sprache Meister Eckharts als Ausdruck seiner mystischen Geisteswelt," *Deutsche Vierteljahresschrift für Literaturwissenschaft und Geistesgeschichte* 6 (1927), 674.
2. Hermann Kunisch, *Meister Eckhart. Offenbarung und Gehorsam* (Munich, 1962), esp. p. 33.
3. James Clark, *Meister Eckhart: An Introduction to the Study of His Works* (Edinburgh, 1957), p. 92.
4. Heribert Fischer, "Grundgedanken der deutschen Predigten," in *Meister Eckhart der Prediger*, ed. U. Nix and R. Oechslin (Freiburg, Ger. 1960), pp. 58–59.
5. C. F. Kelley, *Meister Eckhart on Divine Knowledge* (New Haven, 1977), pp. 106–110.
6. Carl Albrecht, *Psychologie des mystischen Bewusstseins* (Bremen, 1951; reprint, Mainz, 1976).
7. Richard Kieckhefer, "Meister Eckhart's Conception of Union with God," *Harvard Theological Review* 71 (1978), 203–225.
8. "Swenne diu sêle kumet in daz ungemischte lieht, sô sleht si in ir nihtes niht sô verre von dem geschaffenen ihte in dem nihtes nihte, daz si mit nihte enmac wider komen von ir kraft in ir geschaffen iht. Und got der understât mit sîner ungeschaffenheit ir nihtes niht und enthelet die sêle in sînem ihtes ihte. Diu sêle hât gewâget ze nihte ze werdenne und enkan ouch von ir selber ze ir selber niht gelangen, sô verre ist si sich entgangen, und ê daz si got hât understanden." Pr. 1; DW I, 14, 2–8.
9. Colledge, p. 199. I have taken the liberty of capitalizing Truth. "Wan ich sage iu in der êwigen wârheit: ir ensît denne glîch dirre wârheit, von der wir nû sprechen wellen, sô enmuget ir mich niht verstân." Pr. 52; DW II, 487, 5–7.
10. "Und der geist gebirt mit dem vater den selben eingebornen sun und sich selber den selben sun und ist der selbe sun in disem liehte und ist diu wârheit. Möhtet ir gemerken mit mînem herzen, ir verstüendet wol, waz ich spriche, wan ez ist wâr und diu wârheit sprichet ez selbe." Pr. 2; DW I, 41, 3–7.

BIBLIOGRAPHY

The most useful bibliography on Meister Eckhart is the one that appeared in *The Thomist* 42 (1978), 313–336. Though not complete, it contains most of the important material. The following selective list confines itself to major contributions with emphasis on more recent work.

Editions of Eckhart's Works

All serious work on Eckhart is now based on the Kohlhammer edition described in detail in the Abbreviations. There one will also find listed all documents pertaining to his trials in Cologne and Avignon. Since the Kohlhammer edition is not yet complete, one might wish to consult, for additional, possibly genuine German works of Eckhart, the edition of Franz Pfeiffer, *Meister Eckhart. Predigten und Traktate.* (Leipzig, 1857; Aalen, 1962).

English Translations of Eckhart's Works

Meister Eckhart: The Essential Sermons, Commentaries, Treatises and Defense. Edited and translated by Edmund Colledge and Bernard McGinn. New York, 1981.
Meister Eckhart: Teacher and Preacher. Translation and Introduction by Bernard McGinn with the collaboration of Frank Tobin and Elvira Borgstädt. Scheduled for publication in Spring 1986.

    The above two volumes furnish enough material from both the Latin and German works to provide a basis for the serious student who is unfamiliar with these two languages.
Meister Eckhart: German Sermons and Treatises. Translated by M. O'C. Walshe. London and Dulverton, 1979 and 1981. These two volumes contain good translations of all the sermons contained in DW I–III and also some contained only in Pfeiffer's edition. Translations of the treatises have not yet been published.
Breakthrough: Meister Eckhart's Creation Spirituality in New Translation. Edited by Matthew Fox. Garden City, N.Y., 1980. Contains generally reliable translations of several German sermons.

223

Master Eckhart: Parisian Questions and Prologues. Translated with an introduction by Armand Maurer. Toronto, 1974. Contains material from the Latin works not in the McGinn translations.

Meister Eckhart: An Introduction to the Study of His Works with an Anthology of His Sermons. James M. Clark. Edinburgh, 1957.

Treatises and Sermons of Meister Eckhart. Translated by James M. Clark and John V. Skinner. New York, 1958.

The last two volumes were for many years the only reliable translations available. They have since been superseded both in accuracy and in the amount of material they provide.

The translations of Raymond Blakney (*Meister Eckhart: A Modern Translation* [New York and London, 1941] and C. de B. Evans (*Meister Eckhart* [London, 1924 and 1931]), which are not based on the critical edition and contain numerous errors, should be avoided by the serious student.

Lengthy Studies

Albert, Karl. *Meister Eckharts These vom Sein. Untersuchungen zur Metaphysik des Opus tripartitum*. Saarbrücken, 1976.

Altdeutsche und altniederländische Mystik. Edited by Kurt Ruh. Darmstadt, 1964.

Ancelet-Hustache, J. *Meister Eckhart and the Rhineland Mystics*. New York, 1957.

Beckmann, Till. *Daten und Anmerkungen zur Biographie Meister Eckharts und zum Verlauf des gegen ihn angestrengten Inquisitionsprozesses*. Frankurt, 1978.

Caputo, John. *The Mystical Element in Heidegger's Thought*. Athens, Ohio, 1978.

Degenhardt, Ingeborg. *Studien zum Wandel des Eckhartbildes*. Leiden, 1967.

Fues, Wolfram Malte. *Mystik als Erkenntnis? Kritische Studien zur Meister-Eckhart-Forschung*. Bonn, 1981.

Haas, Alois M. *Sermo mysticus. Studien zu Theologie und Sprache der deutschen Mystik*. Freiburg, Switz., 1979.

Hof, Hans. *Scintilla animae. Eine Studie zu einem Grundbegriff in Meister Eckharts Philosophie*. Lund, 1952.

Imbach, Ruedi. *Deus est Intelligere. Das Verhältnis von Sein und Denken in seiner Bedeutung für das Gottesverständnis bei Thomas von Aquin und in den Pariser Quaestionen Meister Eckharts*. Freiburg, Switz., 1976.

Kelley, C. F. *Meister Eckhart on Divine Knowledge*. New Haven and London, 1977.

Kunisch, H. *Meister Eckhart. Offenbarung und Gehorsam*. Munich, 1962.

———. *Das Wort "Grund" in der deutschen Mystik*. Osnabrück, 1929.

de Libera, Alain. *Le problème de l'être chez Maître Eckhart: Logique et métaphysique de l'anologie*. Geneva, 1980.

Lossky, Vladimir. *Théologie négative et connaissance de Dieu chez Maître Eckhart*. Paris, 1960.

Maître Eckhart a Paris. Une critique médiévale de l'ontothéologie. Les Questions parisiennes n. 1 et n. 2 d'Eckhart. Études, textes et traductions par Emilie Zum Brunn, Zénon Kaluzia, Alain de Libera, Paul Vignaux, Edouard Wéber. Paris, 1984.

Margetts, J. *Die Satzstruktur bei Meister Eckhart.* Stuttgart, 1969.

Meister Eckhart der Prediger. Festschrift zum Eckhart-Gedenkjahr. Edited by Udo Nix and Raphael Öchslin. Freiburg, Ger., 1960.

Mieth, D. *Die Einheit von vita activa und vita contemplativa in den deutschen Predigten und Traktaten Meister Eckharts und bei Johannes Tauler.* Regensburg, 1969.

Mojsisch, Burkhard. *Meister Eckhart. Analogie, Univozität und Einheit.* Hamburg, 1983.

Schmoldt, Benno. *Die deutsche Begriffssprache Meister Eckharts.* Heidelberg, 1954.

Schürmann, Reiner. *Meister Eckhart: Mystic and Philosopher.* London and Bloomington, 1978.

Seppänen, Lauri. *Studien zur Terminologie des Paradisus anime intelligentis.* Helsinki, 1964.

Soudek, E. *Meister Eckhart.* Stuttgart, 1973.

Welte, Bernhard. *Meister Eckhart. Gedanken zu seinen Gedanken.* Freiburg, Ger., 1979.

Zapf, J. *Die Funktion der Paradoxie im Denken und sprachlichen Ausdruck bei Meister Eckhart.* Cologne, 1966.

Zum Brunn and de Libera. *Maître Eckhart. Métaphysique du Verbe et théologie négative.* Paris, 1984.

Articles

Brunner, Fernand. "L'analogie chez Maître Eckhart." *Freiburger Zeitschrift für Philosophie und Theologie* 16 (1969), 333–349.

Caputo, John. "Fundamental Themes in Meister Eckhart's Mysticism." *The Thomist* 42 (1978), 197–225.

———. "The Nothingness of the Intellect in Meister Eckhart's 'Parisian Questions.'" *The Thomist* 39 (1975), 85–115.

Duclow, Donald. "Hermeneutics and Meister Eckhart." *Philosophy Today* 28 (1984), 36–43.

———. "My Suffering Is God": Meister Eckhart's *Book of Divine Consolation.*" *Theological Studies* 44 (1983), 570–586.

Gandillac, M. de. "La 'dialectique' de Maître Eckhart." In *La mystique rhénane. Colloque de Strasbourg 1961.* Paris, 1963. Pp. 59–94.

Haas, Alois. "Meister Eckharts mystische Bildlehre." In *Der Begriff der Repraesentatio im Mittelalter. Stellvertretung, Symbol, Zeichen, Bild.* Edited by Albert Zimmermann. Berlin, 1971. Pp. 113–138.

———. "Meister Eckhart und die Sprache. Sprachgeschichtliche und sprachtheologische Aspekte seiner Werke." In *Geistliches Mittelalter.* Freiburg, Switz., 1984.

———. "Seinsspekulation und Geschöpflichkeit in der Mystik Meister Eckharts." In *Sein und Nichts in der abendländischen Mystik.* Edited by Walter Strolz. Freiburg, Ger., 1984. Pp. 33–58.

Kertz, Karl G. "Meister Eckhart's Teaching on the Birth of the Divine Word in the Soul." *Traditio* 15 (1959), 327–363.

Kieckhefer, Richard. "Meister Eckhart's Conception of Union with God." *Harvard Theological Review* 71 (1978), 203–225.

Koch, Josef. "Kritische Studien zum Leben Meister Eckharts." *Archivum*

Fratrum Praedicatorum 29 (1959), 1–51; 30 (1960), 1–52. Reprinted in his *Kleine Schriften* (Rome, 1973), I, 247–347.

———. "Meister Eckharts Weiterwirken im Deutschen-Niederländischen Raum im 14. und 15. Jahrhundert." In *La mystique rhénane*. Paris, 1963. Pp. 133–156.

———. "Meister Eckhart und die jüdische Religionsphilosophie des Mittelalters." *Jahresbericht der Schlesischen Gesellschaft für vaterländische Cultur 1928* 101 (1929), 134–148. Reprinted in his *Kleine Schriften* (Rome, 1973), I, 349–365.

———. "Sinn und Struktur der Schriftauslegung." In *Meister Eckhart der Prediger. Festschrift zum Eckhart-Gedenkjahr*. Edited by Udo Nix and Raphael Öchslin. Freiburg, Ger., 1960. Pp. 73–103.

———. "Zur Analogielehre Meister Eckharts," *Mélanges offerts a Etienne Gilson*. Paris, 1959. Pp. 327–350. Reprinted in his *Kleine Schriften* (Rome, 1973), I, 367–398.

de Libera, Alain. "A propos de quelques théories logiques de Maître Eckhart: existe-t-il une tradition médiévale de la logique néoplatonicienne?" *Revue de Théologie et de Philosophie* 113 (1981), 1–24.

McGinn, Bernard. "Eckhart's Condemnation Reconsidered." *The Thomist* 44 (1980), 390–414.

———. "The God Beyond God: Theology and Mysticism in the Thought of Meister Eckhart." *Journal of Religion* 61 (1981), 1–19.

———. "Meister Eckhart: An Introduction." *An Introduction to the Medieval Mystics of Europe*. Edited by Paul Szarmach. Albany, N.Y., 1984. Pp. 237–257.

———. "Meister Eckhart on God as Absolute Unity." *Neo-Platonism and Christian Thought*. Edited by Dominic O'Meara. Albany, N.Y., 1982. Pp. 128–139.

Quint, Josef. "Einleitung." *Meister Eckehart. Deutsche Predigten und Traktate*. Edited by Josef Quint. Munich, 1959. Pp. 9–50.

———. "Mystik und Sprache." *Deutsche Vierteljahresschrift für Literaturwissenschaft und Geistesgeschichte* 27 (1953), 48–76. Reprinted in *Altdeutsche und altniederländische Mystik*. Edited by Kurt Ruh. Darmstadt, 1964. Pp. 113–151.

———. "Die Sprache Meister Eckharts als Ausdruck seiner mystischen Geisteswelt." *Deutsche Vierteljahresschrift* 6 (1927), 671–701.

Schaller, Toni. "Die Meister-Eckhart Forschung von der Jahrhundertwende bis zur Gegenwart." *Freiburger Zeitschrift für Philosophie und Theologie* 15 (1968), 262–316, 403–426.

———. "Zur Eckhart-Deutung der letzten 30 Jahre." *Freiburger Zeitschrift* 16 (1969), 22–39.

Stölzel, G. "Zum Nominalstil Meister Eckharts. Die syntaktischen Funktionen grammatischer Verbalabstrakta." *Wirkendes Wort* 16 (1966), 289–309.

Welte, Bernhard. "Meister Eckhart als Aristoteliker." *Philosophisches Jahrbuch der Görres Gesellschaft* 69 (1961), 64–74.

INDEX OF NAMES AND TERMS

INDEX OF CITATIONS

This index includes passages from Eckhart's works cited in the text or notes. The German and Latin works are listed according to the volumes in which they appear. References or quotations occurring only in the body of the book are listed according to the page or pages on which they occur. If a citation includes a reference to a note, the page on which the note appears and the number of the note are given in parentheses, e.g.,

In Joh. nn.40–54, 33–46: 60–62(199n.39)

THE MIDDLE AGES

Edward Peters, General Editor

Christian Society and the Crusades, 1198–1229. Sources in Translation, including The Capture of Damietta by Oliver of Paderborn. Edited by Edward Peters

The First Crusade: The Chronicle of Fulcher of Chartres and Other Source Materials. Edited by Edward Peters

Love in Twelfth-Century France. John C. Moore

The Burgundian Code: The Book of Constitutions or Law of Gundobad and Additional Enactments. Translated by Katherine Fischer Drew

The Lombard Laws. Translated, with an Introduction, by Katherine Fischer Drew

From St. Francis to Dante: Translations from the Chronicle of the Franciscan Salimbene (1221–1288). G. G. Coulton

The Duel and the Oath. Parts I and II of Superstition and Force. Henry Charles Lea. Introduction by Edward Peters

The Ordeal. Part III of Superstition and Force. Henry Charles Lea

Torture. Part IV of Superstition and Force. Henry Charles Lea

Witchcraft in Europe, 1110–1700: A Documentary History. Edited by Alan C. Kors and Edward Peters

The Scientific Achievement of the Middle Ages. Richard C. Dales

History of the Lombards. Paul the Deacon. Translated by William Dudley Foulke

Monks, Bishops, and Pagans: Christian Culture in Gaul and Italy, 500–700. Edited, with an Introduction, by Edward Peters

The World of Piers Plowman. Edited and translated by Jeanne Krochalis and Edward Peters

Felony and Misdemeanor: A Study in the History of Criminal Law. Julius Goebel, Jr.

Women in Medieval Society. Edited by Susan Mosher Stuard

The Expansion of Europe: The First Phase. Edited by James Muldoon

From Servitude to Freedom: Manumission in the Sénonais in the Thirteenth Century. William Chester Jordan

Ransoming Captives in Crusader Spain: The Order of Merced on the Christian-Islamic Frontier. James William Brodman

Aristocracy in Provence: The Rhône Basin at the Dawn of the Carolingian Age. Patrick J. Geary

Meister Eckhart: Thought and Language. Frank Tobin